Bizarre-Privileged Items

in the Universe

Bizarre-Privileged Items in the Universe

The Logic of Likeness

Paul North

ZONE BOOKS · NEW YORK

2021

© 2021 Paul North

ZONE BOOKS

633 Vanderbilt Street

Brooklyn, NY 11218

Printed in the United States of America.

Distributed by Princeton University Press,
Princeton, New Jersey, and Woodstock, United Kingdom

Library of Congress Cataloging-in-Publication Data
Names: North, Paul, 1971– author.
Title: Bizarre-privileged items in the universe : the logic of likeness /
    Paul North.
Description: New York : Zone Books, 2021. | Includes bibliographical
    references and index. | Summary: "This book affirms the
    experience of likeness at the heart of many, if not all, disciplines
    of knowledge and seeks to formalize that basic experience into
    a science of its own, 'homeotics.'" —Provided by publisher.
Identifiers: LCCN 2020021855 (print) | LCCN 2020021856 (ebook) |
    ISBN 9781942130468 (hardback) | ISBN 9781942130499 (ebook)
Subjects: lcsh: Representation (Philosophy)
Classification: LCC B105.R4 N67 2020 (print) | LCC B105.R4 (ebook) |
    DDC 110 —dc23
LC record available at https://lccn.loc.gov/2020021855
LC ebook record available at https://lccn.loc.gov/2020021856

To
Theo & Callie

... to establish the existence of bizarre-privileged items
in the universe, which served as objective guarantors
for lyrical emotion and the poetic image at the same time.

— *Roger Caillois*

Contents

Preamble

The sentences that follow move through seven major premises that lay out something like a logic of likeness. Through their stepwise progression and in their accumulated intentions, the premises reflect two separate aspirations. First, they are meant to bring a reader from a naïve and defensive position toward likeness to a discerning and receptive position toward it. At least, that is the wish. A receptive position is approached through a modification of the initial naïve premise, "Everything is like everything in some respect," a mainstay of empiricism since Hume. Further premises travel away from the initial naïve premise. Each subsequent premise follows from the previous, as premises are supposed to do, but also modifies it. As they are modified, the premises converge on a topic, homeosis, homeosis being a name for the happening of likeness. A "subsequent" is a better premise, that is to say a more homeotic premise, than an "antecedent" premise. Second, while departing from a naïve position and transiting toward a reflective position, the premises also conjure up a complex cosmos in which homeosis is the basic element. For example, Premise 4 says "World is an asymmetrical array."

To move from a naïve view of a trivial phenomenon toward a reflective encounter with a new whole that acts by and large according to likeness's eccentric habits — this is the book's wager. The stakes are high. If likeness is the basic element of this cosmos, then there are no beings and no being. Instead, there is an arraying display of inertial pairs with overlapping traits. In place of individual objects in motion, this cosmos displays pairs in inertia with respect to one another. In place of independent entities, this cosmos arrays nodes or points of qualitative overlap. These pairs with overlaps were best described by Roger Caillois when he proposed "to establish the existence of bizarre-privileged items [*éléments insolites-privilégiés*] in the universe" ("The Natural Fantastic," in *The Edge of Surrealism*, p. 350, note 1; "Le fantastique naturel," in *Cases d'un échiquier*, p. 62, note 1).

Caillois's most provocative example of a bizarre-privileged item is the praying mantis. As he sees it, the mantis overlaps with a human fear and a human desire, the fear of death and the desire for sex, turning the figure that results into a "bizarre" amalgam of human and animal, nature and psyche and culture, will and being, an eccentric conjunction among the most disparate regions. The mantis is one example of such an item. As it turns out, a community of bizarre-privileged items exists, cosmic points at which likenesses, which cut across modes of existence, overlap. Overlapping is homeosis's mode of existence. The presentation that follows collects a menagerie of bizarre overlaps. Along the way, the presentation also collects a vocabulary for talking about a likeness cosmos. As the premises proceed, terms are gathered from historical sources that depended on likeness, even if those sources only ever partially theorized it.

"Likeness" or figures like it have played decisive roles in a variety of discourses over the history of Europe and its satellites. Aristotle makes homeosis, at one point in the *Poetics*, the operative force within mimesis. Plotinus makes homeosis the glue holding the ladder of emanations together and to the One. Much later in chronological history, Darwin, following a long lineage of taxonomists, makes "resemblance" the highest principle in nature, while at the same time altering the meaning and scope of the term. Before him, Hume makes it the highest principle of mind. None of these thinkers, except for Plotinus, and then only in a roundabout way, tells you where exactly likeness fits among the other basic principles. Here, the individual sources for a likeness lexicon have been chosen for their conceptual daring and terminological precision, and they are arranged by their best placement in a theory of likeness under construction, rather than according to their chronological place in a history.

"History," in the European sense, has never got past likeness. When it comes to likeness, modernity and antiquity are not really distinct. Foucault's version of things simply cannot be right. The argument in *The Order of Things* hinges in part on the presupposition that likeness was once a basic principle, and "modernity" abandoned it or relegated it to a trivial position. Modernity is on the whole and in its essence anhomeotic, or so goes the thesis. From the perspective of likeness, the modern world never happened. This is not all that tragic, since the classical world never ended, either, or to use a more apt term, the archaic — the archaic does not release its grip on mind and nature, then and now. A scene that repeats across this swampy nonhistory is one in which a thinker compares likeness unfavorably with being and then surreptitiously explains being by means of likeness. In the garden of ontology, the alien seed likeness sprouts everywhere, and discourses committed to a cosmos full of entities struggle to contain its weedy growth. The philosophical purpose of this book is to challenge ontology with an alternative discipline that can be called homeotics. Homeotics would make the third in a triptych of fundamental explanatory schemata whose inner relations still need to be understood: ontology — semiotics — homeotics.

1. *Everything is like everything in some respect.*

This may not be the first thing you think of when you think of likeness, but it is usually the second. First there is an immediate spark, "this — like — that." Likeness strikes and wakes you, if only for a moment, from your ontological slumber. The strike expresses itself in an awkward syntagm: "This here like that there." Suddenly and without warning, a far thing comes close. The world gets edited, a gap gets spliced out, one character shimmies up to another. A thing, distant in space from another thing, overlaps with the other thing in one or more of its qualities. After the first impact of a likeness, though, whenever you should consider the matter further, if you take even one further step toward the phenomenon, thinking through its ramifications or its potential origins, you arrive at a realization. Everything is like everything in some respect. Upon arriving at this premise, it becomes much easier to dismiss likeness as a principle. The premise is much too general to be useful — it seems to say "It's all about the same." "Nothing stands out." As if to confirm this, when I want to say that something is totally unique, I say, "the likes of which I never saw," which means, conversely, everything else would be the likes of which I have seen, many times over.

Where you can go from this most general premise is unclear, if already at the very beginning of an inquiry into likeness you are stuck in the perspective of everything. What can be learned from such a position, which is all positions and no position at all? "Everything" says a lot, and saying so much, it says very little. The premise that everything is like everything in some respect seems empty or nearly empty, since on first hearing, it sounds like a merely descriptive statement. It sounds like: given time enough and energy enough, if you sorted painstakingly through everything there is, you would find that each thing in the universe is like every other thing in at least one way, and often probably more. And the more likenesses you catalog, the harder it becomes to distinguish anything from anything. An experiment in indistinction — nothing escapes the leveling, dulling gauze of similarity.

The expanded premise, everything is like everything, is not only a reference to a set of things, however; it also carries a specific sense. A difficulty lies in the semantics of the premise; an opaque spot makes it hard to connect its sense to the idea it is supposed to give sense to. "Is like" is never really said of everything altogether in its generality; it is said of something specific in its specificity. Likeness characterizes the detail — concrete, empirical, particular — and since no detail is specified in the general premise, therefore no trait is concretized, perceived, or singularized in the phrase "Everything is like everything in some respect." Insofar as it refers to any and all details, the phrase refers to none in particular and thus does not correspond to the sense of likeness.

This dilemma is worth unfolding. A single detail blocks out the All, but the All blocks out every single detail. Because it addresses "everything," the premise denies that there are details, whose existence as details, that is, as not general, is what allows likenesses to form in the first place. Another way to say this is that a likeness world cannot be described with the word "everything." Even if it were demonstrably true, even if you had time enough, if somehow you could show that the proposition "Everything is like everything in some respect" held, a description this general would fail its object, which is unfailingly specific, concrete, empirical, and temporally limited each time it happens. Further, if you did go one by one through all the phenomena, you would also find, beyond the incommensurability of the detail with the All, a huge, if not infinite set of unexpected juxtapositions. Likenesses need not be restricted to categories familiar to us. If everything is like everything, given that this phrase makes any sense at all, one butterfly is like another butterfly, no doubt, and it is also true that an elephant is like an atom bomb, a praying mantis like a lover, a word like an object — strangeness blooms in likeness's garden. And yet the strange is soon pruned. Where it describes a potential infinity of peculiar partners, the premise, everything is like everything in some respect, comes to look banal. Where the likeness of an elephant to an atom bomb can be counted as one among a pleroma of likenesses, strangeness gets flattened into normalcy, irregularity into regularity. In turns, then, banal, absolutely detailed, and indeterminate, the premise is also often, under a slightly different perspective, self-evident. It makes immediate intuitive sense that everything should be like everything in some respect, and like other immediate intuitions, it offers little information. It tells you what you already know.

You are like your parents — hardly worth the breath to say it, a self-evident truth and a piece of cultural knowledge no one would think to question — with an even more peculiar and less remarked upon addendum that your parents are like their parents, and so on. In truth, there are as many instances of this self-evident fact as there are new generations; each level adds little information to the initial flat truth. Right there where it is like its progenitor, the new generation is not new. Likeness is the not new in the new, which is to say again, it is a phenomenon of little information. Now more than ever, this type of low-information phenomenon needs to be studied.

Another example lies even closer to home and more deeply embedded in our cultural understanding. A butterfly is like a butterfly — this may be the definition of self-evidence, a tautology or a mere identification. The definition has its complexities — this kind of sentence may serve two distinct semantic functions. As Gertrude Stein's favorite sentence does — "A rose is a rose is a rose" — it may indicate a vivid, singular experience, not comparable with any other, the most incomparable phenomenon that can only be named, never explained. A rose is unlike anything other than itself, and refuses paraphrase. Or it may serve just as easily to indicate a complete mundanity and total uniformity. A rose is not in any way unlike itself, a rose uniformly rose — nothing new in it and never will be. Further, every rose is uniformly rose.

How to reconcile these two meanings, the most singular singularity and the most general generality? Like any being, a butterfly is totally unique and purely general at the same time, a paradox that philosophical millennia have yet to dissolve. It is butterfly, nothing but butterfly, all butterfly and purely butterfly — absolutely like itself, and in being absolutely like itself, there is nothing else that it is like. If something else were this much like it, it would be subsumed into the butterflies and lose its distinction. It would lose its distinction and become a butterfly, which, it is understood, is indistinct with respect to itself.

It hardly counts as knowledge to say that a butterfly is like itself, and no more so to say this butterfly is like that butterfly. Knowledge is when we say: this butterfly is a nymphalid whose habitat stretches from Japan to India. Knowledge is when we use Latin, *Kallima inachus*, when we move the locus of distinction to the genus. Knowledge is when we add a description that holds in all cases: in the dry season, *Kallima* behaves in the following way. It flutters, appearing to fall onto a tree branch, where, when its wings are closed showing their brown undersides, it is the spitting image of a dead leaf. When you want knowledge, avoid the obvious, the banal, the detail poor, and the indistinct — and that also means avoid what is too much like what you already know, both what is too like itself or too like every other. Old knowledge is already no longer knowledge. At just this point, at the point of deep habituation or almost perfect likeness of one moment or one entity to the next, the nearest, oddities begin to emerge. Within banal, almost uniform, old, obvious knowledge, blossoms the bizarre.

So it is with *Kallima*: a butterfly may be like itself and also like a leaf.[1] This would be a category error if we didn't first tame the suggestion by giving it an official name, "mimicry," a purpose, "anti-predator adaptation," and an etiology, natural selection — all of which purportedly belong to the butterfly and not to the leaf, making the likeness into a semblance and thereby changing the category from a homeotic to an ontological one. A mimic is a semblance of another being, not its sibling or clone or child. Suspend for a moment, however, the will to being, cause, purpose, and name. Take the statement on its face. This is often the best way to find/make likenesses, to take statements on their face. Butterfly and leaf are alike; they enliken one another. From this position, other potential likenesses suggest themselves. Take a bumblebee, a school bus, and a journalist. They are alike in yellowness. Alike in carrying and transmitting important things. Alike in punishing you when you misbehave. In one light, the resemblance of the radically nonsimilar is encompassed by the premise, everything is like everything in some respect. At first dull, banal, and so on, the premise turns interesting again. Where is the limit to its extension? What phenomenon, real or imagined, ideal or material, will not be touched by it? The premise leads you down strange alleyways, to wild gardens of mismatched and antithetical things; and nevertheless, when you extend the strings of unexpected likenesses out to infinity, in order to encompass truly everything, no matter how strange they seem at first glance, heaped together in a virtually horizonless scape, again the world comes to seem flat, features vanish into indistinction, and the strange dissolves back into the ordinary.

Out of this effect you could formulate a rule, one that points to a contradiction to be analyzed more carefully later. The more striking a likeness, the farther it will spread out along its pathways, pulling more and more phenomena into its purview; the farther it spreads out, the closer it comes to generality; the closer to generality, the less striking any single likeness seems; the less striking any single likeness seems, the less like likeness the phenomenon becomes and the more like indeterminacy or even sameness. Likeness, from a far perspective, presents a self-diminishing tendency. From bumblebee, school bus, and journalist, we could, for instance, move to a string of all yellow things, including all things said to be yellow, like journalists but also like cowards, and then we could move further on to the string of all colored things, and then to the delirious series of all colored and uncolored things that are alike in being colorable, and so on — until in the end, once again, we have very little information.

Between a banality of sameness and a delirium of difference likeness likes to hide. This may well have been the problem it posed to theory all along, from the time of the earliest European ontologies up to empiricism and current scientism. When other fundamental phenomena are around, likeness hides. The basis for this is that you cannot tell whether it tends toward uniformity or toward difference. It is not different enough from uniformity to be picked up by epistemic frameworks. The question underlying the tension or confusion that likeness suffers, caught between difference, tending toward absolute difference, and uniformity, tending toward absolute uniformity, is this one, I believe: are likenesses all alike? This question is really asking whether there is one special quality called "likeness," that is shared out equally among like things or, on the other hand, whether you can identify anything unique about likeness at all. Is likeness a distinct mode, or does it name something that participates in all modes and in which all modes participate?

When you say everything is alike, you see the world as sunk into an undifferentiated, homogeneous gel. When you affirm "Everything is like everything," the premise may therefore repulse you, as though likeness were an invitation to indifference, an excuse for mysticism or depression unto death. With regard to difference and sameness, you can take the premise in two ways. That everything is like everything in some respect could mean all things are alike in a similar way. This picture is gray. Like a cloud on a cloudy day in a month of rain, it depresses our faculties. The premise, however, does not say "Everything is like everything in the very same respects." Nor does it say everything is alike in one single respect, as would be the case with substance ontology. Assume the respects in which everything is alike are multiple. Multiple respects, multiploid likenesses — one thing could then be like many others in various of its (and their) respects. This picture is motley. Like a shapely cloud among multiform clouds in a blue sky, it may invigorate us. How can the decision be made between the two pictures, gray and motley, depressing and invigorating? This may be the biggest problem for the initial stage under the force of the preliminary premise.

To see the conflict more vividly, take the case of what evolutionary biologists call "mimicry." A butterfly is like a leaf. It must be conceded that the leaf that the butterfly is like is also like another leaf. And so it must be asked: are the two likenesses, butterfly-leaf and leaf-leaf, alike? Yes and no. Are the respects in which butterfly is like leaf the same as those in which leaf is like leaf? Yes, and again, no. Things don't become less complicated here. Look at one aspect of the organism, the undersurface of *Kallima inachus*'s wings. In the dry season, the wing underside can be called "brown," as can the leaf; indeed all the leaves around it can be called "brown" as well (Figure 1). Are these browns the same brown? In part, no — because color in nature is not a pointlike datum, but a mottled, marbled, or streaked group of overlapping stains, as unlike as alike, spreading over an expanse, over wing, up and down leaf, through the patina of another leaf and another, such that the color name "brown" is first a nominal designation and second also a wish for uniformity in an object. "Brown" is an approximation for the purposes of classifying beings, a comparison to an ideal standard. Here is a good moment to note what will be emphasized again later — that a name and a phenomenon are not best described as matching, but rather as alike in some respect.

In the series leaf-leaf-lepidopter, you observe three motley, stained expanses. They do not match, and they don't have to match to be alike. Lay one over top of another, and some points roughly correspond. Others do not. Etiology has a role to play here — brown in the wing underside is an adaptive strategy, and so let's say that mutation, adaptation, and selection are the brushes that paint the wing to an extent that, from a certain distance, to a certain eye, it will not be perceived as unlike the leaf's brown. Likeness in this case is a bare minimum.

Figure 1. Kallima Butterfly. Plate II in *Animal Coloration* by Frank Evers Beddard. London, Swan Sonnenschein & co., 1892.

"The lowest possible likeness so as not to be perceived as very unlike by a hungry bird," you could say, for instance. In the leaves, in contrast, brown is more like a failure of adaptation—a nonadaptive, status-quo response to drought, a limited succumbing to the dearth of water in the dry season, a sacrifice of greenery while the tree conserves its life. The leaf brown may be more thorough, less artful, a maximal brown of death, as opposed to the minimal brown of the life adaptation of the butterfly, which is, you could say, an evolutionary decoration, as opposed to the leaf's loss of evolutionary color. To be sure, the mechanisms for producing color are also incompatible in leaf and wing.

All of this is apparent, and yet it shows, when you move further into these sorts of phenomena with an ear for likeness, that the objects, leaf, leaf, and lepidopter, are alike in similar respects and they are alike in unlike ways. From a certain distance, in a certain frame—later it will be given the name "atmosphere"—the three nominally separate items, nymphalid and two leaves, approach each other in color, where they are alike in like respects to a particular depth of analysis. From one distance, "brown" is a point at which the three distinct beings become indistinct. Yet within the colors—brown, brown, brown—there are also undoubtedly subtle and not so subtle unlikenesses across any fraction of any expanse that we call only for the sake of efficiency "brown."

I.I. *Some likenesses are alike in a like way, and some likenesses are alike in unlike ways.*

That is, the respect in which something is like is not the only determinant of likeness. Likeness also knows manners or ways. Leaves and butterflies are alike in respect of body and, in certain cases, in respect of color, and yet color likeness (respect: brown) and body likeness (respect: leafiness or wingyness or wingyleafiness) do not share a manner. Color, for example, is a likeness in the way it reflects light into the eye of a predator or a scientist. The paper-thinness and specific aerodynamism of wing and leaf are alike in the way they flutter, say, in a breeze. Another way to say this is that likeness in color respect is relative to predator sight, and likeness in aero shape is relative to physics, specifically, to movement in relation to air. Undoubtedly, you cannot collapse the two frames, being like in view of predator eye and being like in view of lift in air. There are established practices for grouping ways of likeness, such as coloration for predator evasion (the study of mimicry). Other ways are left floating, so to speak, without a science of their own, such as shape or density for physical existence in a gaseous milieu, which would unite leaves, butterflies, sails, flags, and maybe also Wi-Fi and other spirits.

Modifying the original premise in this way leads to another problem. Saying that the ways of likeness are alike and unlike, and sometimes alike in their unlikeness, verges on nonsense. Sense, at a minimum, requires what has sense to be clearly demarcated from other senses. An American philosopher attuned to nonsense, Donald Davidson, once called likeness without further qualifications not exactly nonsensical — or banal or indeterminate — but "trivial," "because everything is like everything, and in endless ways" ("What Metaphors Mean," p. 254). Davidson agrees that not only things, but also the ways of likeness may be alike. His adjective, "trivial," can be added to the others, put alongside "banal" and "nonsense" — even if these characterizations are in some way themselves banal.

Nonetheless, in the intellectual archive in which Davidson and some other philosophers dwell, "being like" has played a pivotal role. Locke and then Hume relied on "resemblance," a slightly different but related term, to explain connections between things previously explained by metaphysical principles. It is no secret that the premise on the likeness of everything is a founding gesture of empiricism. Hume remarks in a footnote to his *Treatise* that all things "admit of infinite resemblances upon the general appearance and comparison, without having any common circumstance the same" (*Treatise*, 1.1.7, note from the 1740 appendix, pp. 18–19). Alone and without the support of commonality or sameness, generalized likeness is a fundamental assumption for empiricist thinking, even if the premise comes into ill repute with later philosophers in that tradition. Davidson prima facie accepts the likeness foundation of everything and then, without further discussion, dismisses it as trivial. Hilary Putnam, importing reasoning from his teacher Quine, repeats the premise "everything is similar to everything else in infinitely many respects" and after a short discussion he labels it paradoxical and leaves it aside as too limited to explain anything ("Two Philosophical Perspectives," p. 64).

Likeness wants to be understood, if only because without it, the empirical basis of much of our current thinking would turn into a loose, unprincipled gathering of sensations without resemblances by which to assemble them. Hume needs likeness, and yet likeness, as a general principle, seems too vague, too unprincipled, to help very much. It is not like causality or substance, alternative generalities for governing the manifold. Likeness doesn't stick everything together with the same strength as cause or substance, probably because it doesn't structure the world into unambiguously independent individuals with modular parts.

One reason likeness seems almost useless as a principle is its closeness to infinity. In the basic intuition of likeness, your mind travels from one quality to another like quality, and you can discover no natural end to this process. It is a short step from infinity to generality and from there to banality, indifference, indeterminacy, triviality, paradox, and finally, perhaps, in some cases, to foolishness and the loss of reason—to nonsense. True, everything is not like everything in the same way—that would be metaphysics, a return to Parmenides. In Putnam's and Davidson's formulations, on the basis of Hume's intuition, because there is no absolute uniformity, or no access to such, the number of likenesses ratchets up to infinity, which leaves things alike in ways that cannot be easily limited and which at the same time and for the same reason leaves things both so unlike as not to be uniform and not unlike enough to be counted as distinct.

Standing close to uniformity on one side and to chaos on the other, the premise does not convince Davidson or Putnam of its usefulness for philosophizing, although both seem to recognize that an infinity one iota to the side of uniformity is a logical presupposition of empiricism. Henri Bergson recognizes something similar in 1896 in his critique of associationism: "as, after all, everything resembles everything else, it follows that anything can be associated with anything" (*Matter and Memory*, p. 168). Experience is radically motile for Bergson, and nonetheless, it has more structure and more delimitation than this trivial, general, indeterminate, banal, quasi-uniform or quasi-chaotic mere or bare fact that no one interested in experience, it seems, can accept. Neither can they deny it. As the fact that for Bergson fatally ruins Humean empiricism, and as the fact that after Hume everyone apparently has to confront and, at the same time as they confront it, also have to deny it importance (with a few exceptions), the principle of the likeness of everything has an unprecedented power — the power of total association — and this fact deserves long and deliberate thinking.

Philosophy does not hold the patent on likeness, however. Every mode of knowledge — it is safe to say, I think, every region of being — be it suit-and-tie philosophy or sleeves-rolled-up natural science, whether it happens in the library or the laboratory, or for that matter on the artist's palette or in the pollster's survey — every discourse that tells you what there is and how truth appears is forced to confront the nymph likeness, not just once, but over and over. There's one, a likeness, and one more, a likeness, as unlike as it is alike, as alike as it is unlike.[2] Whatever benefit the proposition "Everything is like everything" may ultimately provide, the intuition of a great proliferation of likenesses cannot easily be avoided. What there is and what we know, who we are and whom we meet, what used to happen and what is likely to, inventories of things and inventions of the future are so thoroughly pervaded by likenesses that questions what and who and why could without hesitation be subsumed under a different question: "What is it like?" and further: "What is it like to be like?"

What is it like to be like? The wager of these sentences is to respond to this nearly tautological, quasi-banal, trivial, and also inescapable question that is useful when it's needed and trivial when it isn't. Without knowing what it would mean to win the bet, I gamble on a broad redescription of everything in terms of likeness. It's a risk — who would deny it? At any moment, the argument can look nonsensical, skirting the edge of tautology and uselessness, not to mention flaunting its proximity to transcendence. There are reasons for taking the risk. Such a lacuna in our thinking could harm us and all of our knowledges. Indeed, the worry that goes along with like-ness is a very old one — "archaic," it might better be called, though it is still with us. What if what we know is only like what is or only like knowledge, merely like or sheerly like, in the sense of "not like," or for that matter "very like," but not "exactly like"?

I ask you to imagine: another layer, a separate plane, a fifth dimension, if you will, a "homeoplex." Believe for a moment that the separate plane, the place of pure likeness unimpeded by beings or causes, is a significant aspect of the real and no less of the imaginary. Concede, provisionally, that the homeotic layer does not just coexist with, but gives rise to the other dimensions — being, thought, image, language, history, sociality both human and animal. The wager is to take "likeness" as the fundamental element of everything, to reverse the conclusion that it is trivial and general and place it at the genera-tive core of not just world history, but cosmic history.

Philosophy, I say, is not the only place to look for fundamental likeness. Other discourses and other regions have better or at least different views on the matter. Poetry, for instance, has its *comme*, its *wie*, its "this is like that"; representational art has its likenesses, its mimetic "this is that"; these theoretical clichés are so familiar that the parameters of likeness can be quite hard to see in discourses in which they are actually essential. In the arts, modes of likeness are so familiar and theoretical chestnuts about them are so abundant that they can be virtually invisible, and further, they are often made to seem like technical problems specific to particular arts. Literary criticism worries over mimesis, art criticism worries over repre-sentation, film studies worries over verisimilitude, and so on. Each muse believes likeness is her own personal bane and boon, a technical problem for it alone. Mnemosyne knows it belongs to each of her children equally. For philosophy, that raises the general question of likeness — likeness appears as the thing that can't be generalized without becoming trivial or banal or empty. And so the one, philosophy, formulates it and loses it,[3] the other, the muses, don't formulate it and have it. If these discourses are invited to reveal their commonalities, the beautiful muses with haggard, ugly philosophy, the hope is that the question of the scope of likeness (of what is like what) and the question of generation (how this comes to be like that) can be addressed. As a preliminary step, look into three regions: what has been called "nature," what has been called "mind," and what stands outside both, a "surnature" that is neither the soul nor god.

One discourse on nature — evolution theory — bets big on likeness. The passage that opens chapter 8 of *On the Origin of Species*, "Mutual Affinities of Organic Beings," acknowledges as much. Darwin writes: "From the first dawn of life, all organic beings are found to resemble each other in descending degrees, so that they can be classed in groups under groups. This classification is evidently not arbitrary like the grouping of the stars in constellations" (p. 303).

The lineup of look-alikes and near look-alikes in evolution theory stretches into the deepest history, and yet, although resemblance marks every living organism, this quality or effect still retains enough specificity or structure so as not to become trivial, for Darwin — so as not to become arbitrary or produce regress.[4] Evolution theory, a playground for homeotics, has a tolerance for likeness as high as its tolerance for complexity. From its obscure origin, the history of life branches out into a tree, or better, a bush, or better, a thicket, whose vines exfoliate a vast forking resemblance system that evolutionists have come to believe also forks back into itself, forming significant tangles in some areas.[5] If evolution talk is something beyond the current hegemonic explanatory mechanism for everything, if the theory's aesthetic whisper can be heard, there comes an echo of its original intuition, one that animates all naturalism beyond mere astonishment at the panoply of nature, the intuition: "This is like that."

To the same degree as we use Darwin's theory in this way, we misuse it. We take an effect and make it a cause, we affirm the consequent, when, for the purposes of demonstration, we make resemblance the pivotal phenomenon. Neither evolution scientists nor philosophers of evolution would validate the theory as homeotic *in se*, but only *pro tanto*, as a means to a scientific end and a symptom of an underlying process. Similarity is considered evidence for a set of probabilistic operations whose result, or whose being, is life.[6] I am neither qualified nor interested to dispute this understanding. I can remark, however, that from an evolutionary point of view, as well as from a homeotic one, similarity may be evidence, but it is also a final cause of evolution processes, insofar as it can be said without reservation that if organisms did not end up similar to one another in multiple ways. there would be no life. There would be no life without final resemblance in two ways. Nothing would be recognizable as life, for evolution science, since species would never arise. And adaptation would be fleeting and, overall, maladaptive, if a niche did not support multiple organisms whose similarities were precisely their adaptive traits.

Is this sine qua non the same kind of condition as other sorts of necessary conditions for life? It may well be a different kind of condition, but it still carries a force that is more than heuristic. Even if a species is defined minimally as a population with gene flow,[7] similarity is more than merely evidence; one could argue that it is the essence of a "population." Take similarity, provisionally, as something more than a surface effect of organisms or species, more than just a "look" of things that opens onto deeper issues; take it as applicable to genetic as well as phenotypic characteristics, to environmental as well as behavioral conditions; let it stand closer to the very structural, operational, semiotic, genetic, environmental, habitual, instinctive operations that permit reproduction in the first place. If you do this, a circle emerges. When similarity is considered evidence, it is evidence for a generative mechanism that leads to similarities. Similarity as evidence leads to similarity as condition for life.

What, then, precedes what, among reproduction, selection, and similarity? In the case of evolutionary similarity, the proper response to the logical fallacy of affirming the consequent or the ontological error of taking effect as cause is to adjust the logic, and if it is tolerable, abandon, if for a moment, the ontological presuppositions of evolution theory. This Darwin already does in one sense in *On the Origin of Species*. He rejects the idea that a natural living entity, such as a species, has transcendent limits. And, the two chief innovations in the theory, the principle of natural selection and the image of a tree of life, have intimate, if not incestuous relations with the homeotic principle and the homeotic picture. Although he did not go so far as to adjust the logic, I can do that for him, with his help.

It is well known that Darwin deduced the idea of natural selection in part from the practice of artificial selection, the breeding of domesticated animals and cultivated plants, which he read about extensively and also observed in person. *On the Origin of Species* opens with a chapter on artificial selection in which Darwin presents a field of almost unlimited variation (breeds) within partial limits (a species), and a force, in this case, the hand of the breeder, of selection by which variations can be channeled toward this or that phenotype (p. 26). In pursuit of the facts of artificial selection, in late June and early July 1838, Darwin walked the Glen Roy River in Scotland and wrote in a special notebook during the trip, which, although less famous than his Beagle notebooks, is also remarkable. In a letter, he called the article that emerged from the notebook "one of the most difficult & instructive tasks I was ever employed on" (quoted in *Notebooks*, p. 141), though later he took back this sentiment (p. 142). Nonetheless, he carried forward observations from his Glen Roy travels into one of the early evolution notebooks, known now as Notebook D. There, Darwin copied over for a second time an encounter with a breeder. "A Sphepherd [*sic*] of Glen Turret. said he learnt to know lambs, because in their faces they were most like their mothers believes this resemblance general" (note 43, p. 345). The task on this part of the trip was to discover which parent, if any, 'impresses' (note 44, p. 345) the offspring the most in reproduction, the mother or the father.

The test case for this were crossbreeds. If a crossbreed could be shown to carry more traits from a mother or, conversely, more from a father, the causal route of the parents' relative "impressions" could be traced. On one level, Darwin's note records the shepherd's opinion that the mother impresses the offspring more deeply. A slightly later note records a different opinion from another breeder Darwin met along the way: "half breed liable to vary" (note 47e, p. 346). What interests me about the original testimony of the shepherd of Turret, however, is not his answer to the impression question, but rather the suggestion contained in the phrase "believes this resemblance general." This is a critical logical leap — believing the resemblance a general fact — that comes after the intuition "this is like that" in a naturalist's thinking.

1.2. *In natural resemblances, the general phenomenon lies within the specific phenomenon. Everything is in one thing.*

How the general lies within the specific makes the difference between a triviality and a critical principle. It also shows that everything, even if it is permeated by likenesses, has a minimum of order. The shepherd of Glen Turret knew there was a minimum of order among likenesses in the Everything, and this became a crucial thought tool for a new science. Darwin took it up in his notebook, but did not quite draw the conclusion that the shepherd drew, to wit: resemblance means seeing many in one — to a potentially infinite horizon.

Out of his day-to-day practice, the shepherd concluded that "this is like that" makes sense only within a manifold in which everything is like everything in some respect. Without this intuition, the likeness would have to have a ground outside itself, and you would not be able to "see" the mother in the lamb; then likeness would indeed be a minor, trivial, banal ancillary premise in a world operating according to other fundamental principles, such as causality or substance. On the banks of a river in the Scottish Highlands, resemblance was of the essence, and it was also in the essence. Mother, father — it didn't matter who impressed the most, who was the cause of most of the offspring's salient traits. From the shepherd's vantage point, any single sheep was transparent to its parent, its family, its herd, and ultimately to its kind. A parent is also a transparent. Used to seeing in herds, the shepherd understood how instances let on to other dimensions, how the world "shows through" a being.

1.2.1.   *A single resemblance draws you effortlessly to a milieu of resemblances, from an individual to a family, say, which lets onto a breed, which lets onto a species, which lets onto . . . X, making, formally speaking, anything a milieu that lets onto a milieu of milieus. A thing is an X of Xs.*

Everyday thinking reaches its limit here, where what seemed to be a triviality takes on the hue of a complex, world-and-discourse-altering truth. Everything reveals its deep strangeness. Not simply an aggregate of individuated things — it is as though the Everything had a twisted shape, as though its outside were inside it and, further, as though the relations among likeness fields, despite the chaos, were both regular and severely lopsided. To be sure, the way a sheep contains all previous sheep and ultimately much of prior organic life in its being is not the same way Mammalia, as a class, contains or subsumes that same sheep. How does the being-in of the generic relation, which implies one kind of regularity among things, relate to the being-in of likeness, which implies another?

Farther on in the same notebook, Darwin tries to come to terms with the shepherd of Glen Turret's theorem under a different rubric. The shepherd's intuition is a tool, but it is also an obstacle in the formal study of natural organisms. When attempting to sort their objects into genera, naturalists confront first and foremost likenesses' multiplicity. This and that, that and those, those and those, and before long, everything altogether can be called alike, in some respects, in some ways. The question that follows from this is: If everything is alike in a respect and a way, and in this manner a single organism opens up to many others that form its homeotic penumbra, what is the correct principle for selecting some of these likenesses and placing natural entities into groups?

This confusion soon takes a particular shape. It gets turned into a question of rank order. Which likenesses are higher, and which are lower — but this really means which are decisive for classification and which are, as the empiricists will continue to say, trivial? The turn from a confusion into a rank ordering of likenesses at one moment of evolution theory is a critical turning point. Suffice it to say that a major preoccupation for theorists, from here on, will be how to distinguish among the many ways of resemblance and how to apportion value among them.

One thing is clear. There is no room in this schema for degrees of similarity. Even though the opening paragraph of chapter 13 of *Origin* proclaims, "From the first dawn of life, all organic beings are found to resemble each other in descending degrees," this has to be a post-hoc construction, useful for classification, but not justified by natural beings themselves. In the notebook, Darwin argues against the idea that likeness comes in degrees — note 51 deals swiftly with the assumption (p. 348). In the note, Darwin is taking issue with the notion of a "natural arrangement" of animals, which he finds in one account of the fauna of South Africa.[8] He asks critically, what is a "natural arrangement"? The question within his question is, what accounts for the apparent order in nature, and can it be traced back to a real order? Allergic to orders imposed from the outside, Darwin glosses "natural arrangement" as "affinities" among particular organisms.[9] This is the first step toward a sophisticated understanding of likeness. Affinity he then tries to represent as a specific amount of resemblance, but he is forced to contradict this assumption: "affinities, what is that, amount of resemblance — how can we estimate this amount, when ‹value› no scale of value of difference is or can be settled — " (note 51, p. 348). The shepherd of Glen Turret's theorem is raised to a higher level of abstraction here, and the problems it makes for evolution science become sharper. The shepherd turned Darwin's

33

attention to the staged, multidimensional field of likenesses, turned outside-in in the lamb's face, and yet as Darwin pursues this reasoning further, it turns out that the field has no real distinctions, only, so to speak, real overlaps.

First, Darwin proposes that the order of nature does not lie in an imposed "arrangement," as other naturalists might think, as though nature were a diagram of itself or a big organism that contains all other organisms. The order of nature lies within nature, he insists; it emerges among natural beings, in their affinities with one another, though these affinities are not immediately quantifiable. When you go so far as to say that the naturalness of the field of natural organisms consists in its inner affinities, you are also saying that affinities operate by a different logic than the arrangement of parts in a whole or the synergy of organs within an organism. Nature, a loose, baggy concept, too big to contain anything at the best of times, is stitched together, as it were, through the affinities among creatures, and though the thread of those stitches may be genetic, the pattern of the stitches is resemblance, not causal-functional arrangement. The thought of a general milieu of resemblance internal to the organic field, but of a different order than it, was with Darwin from early on.

To be sure, the thought was with naturalists before him and especially with taxonomists. The most famous in the period before Darwin, Linnaeus, set down the principle that "like always gives birth to like" in the "observations" to the first published edition of *Systema Naturae* in 1735 (§ 4, p. 18). Following this, the basic question about life had these terms: Which comes first, likeness or birth? It isn't so easy to tell from this statement, but in his taxonomic ordering of creatures, one comes to understand that for Linnaeus, likeness is subordinate to the order of birth. This is an attempt to give likeness relations an external origin and structure, guaranteed by the physics and metaphysics of birth. Nevertheless, Linnaeus's phrase captures the centrality of likeness for taxonomy as well as the instinct to bind and tame it under an ontological category. The matter to decide then becomes which likenesses count as birth likenesses and which count as trivial, banal, tautological, and so forth. Does one investigate this question under the science of birth or the science of likeness, if there could be one? In his notes on artificial selection, Darwin confronts this same question, and he discovers a first element to an answer — that resemblance cannot be measured as if it were a quantity, and thus, if you ban an external schema, you cannot classify organisms by ranking likenesses.

1.3.   *Likeness is not a variable grade or value.*

Say "very like," "like enough," or "like as not." American English assumes likeness has degrees. Surely, the degree of your likeness to your mother is higher than the degree of your likeness to a stone! Then again, it should be admitted that the degree itself has to be relative. In this thought lies the dissolution of the idea that likeness comes in degrees. For the world as we usually think of it, both philosophically and in our normal dealings, that is, as a jumble of existing things belonging to different classes — here a stone, there a cow, here a corner store, there a god — in this abstract perspective, members of a single class appear to exhibit more likeness among themselves than they do to members of another class. Presumably, this is why it has been called a "class." Go back to the mode of likeness, in respect and in manner. The construct "class" is nothing other than a set of traits that have been selected, which we name "respects in which," and a frame or relative reference point, which we name "manner or mode." If the trait is a detail of a phenotype, leaf color, for instance, or height, or what have you, and the mode or manner is "appearance," appearance is relative either to the everyday jumble of things or to a specific other class, a counterclass, with which these certain traits do not find correlatives.

Likenesses are not themselves things, and this means they cannot have magnitude. They are not a material of which there could be less or more, a stuff with intensive or extensive magnitude. Rather, they are triangulations of traits that refer to a certain frame or set of frames, a double relation, in and through two things, a pair that is in and through a frame or reference point that lends stability to this or that pattern. Darwin's reasoning for this is as follows. It is useless to think of likenesses among organisms as having degrees, because the standard of difference between creatures is relative, given that differences are multiple. Because you cannot say immediately which of all the differences among organisms are the higher ones or the more important ones without imposing an external hierarchy, you also cannot say that one creature is more or less like another. Relative to what? How would you choose which "what" to refer to? To be useful for naturalism, likeness cannot be a magnitude, intensive or otherwise, because magnitudes are relative, and if you reject a theological frame of fixed forms, no relative will have been specified, and for this reason, let us assume that the only consideration possible with regard to resemblance, in a strictly immanent view of nature, is whether it is there or not, among traits, and in what way or relative to what standard.

1.3.1.   *Likeness knows no degrees. There cannot be more or less of it.*

Yes, everything is like everything in some respect and in some way, but that does not mean that this is only a little like that, while something else is a lot more like it. This is like that, or else it is like another.[10] Such positivity is a feature of likeness, even if Darwin does not develop this in his thought. Likeness rebuffs lack. Regarding the everyday intuition that likeness can be more and less, when we say, as we do, "She is not very like him," we mean by this that she is "like something else" in some respect, in some frame. Likeness is relative and not rankable. In saying "You are more like your mother," I am saying you are more like your mother than like a stone under specific circumstances, that is, I single out traits in reference to something, which in this case would be a habitual way of classifying some kind of thing, as in the case of mother and stone, in reference to "family." Incidentally, "family" is one frame among many. There are more modes of resemblance than family resemblances. For certainly you are exactly as much like your mother as like a stone. You need only change the atmosphere. In reference to "physicality," against a background of immaterial things, gods, or future states of affairs, you are like a stone, as is your mother. Stone resemblances, divine resemblances, material resemblances, all resemblances are relative to one situation or another.

Since it can't be measured in degrees, given that there is no absolute frame, the immense field of actual resemblances has to be narrowed down in some other way in order to be useful for evolution theory. In note 51, Darwin tries to work out how resemblance can account immanently for order in nature. At the same time, he avoids making likeness into a general claim or founding, instead of a science of nature, a science of likeness. This he avoids even more assiduously in *Origin*. Although there is no definition of resemblance in the book and no systematic exposition of its laws, the drive to make critical distinctions among kinds of likeness or saliences of traits is written all over the book and leads to endless assumptions without a general theory of how or when to make them. You could almost say that the whole apparatus of heredity, which to Darwin in 1859 remained largely a mystery, gets conjured up in order to avoid too general a field of resemblances and the need to look into it further and more conceptually. If we can't construct a genus on the amount of resemblance among its members, we have to do it on either the kind of resemblance or the importance of the traits. Thus, Darwin constructs a genus in this way: x is like y in t respect, while x is not like z in t respect; thus, we say that x and y compose a genus, and x and z do not. He does not forget that y and z are just as likely to be alike in multiple respects, and yet he somehow fixes the criteria for critical and trivial resemblances at t. He chooses, without looking further into it, a single frame of reference whose choice is undoubtedly motivated by older stories. Darwin's early renown may have rested on his scandalous "will to make similar" simians and humans. And yet it also rests on his will not to make similar other groups, as well as not to allow simians and humans to coincide in those salient respects that had to distinguish them, whatever they might have been. Everything depended on choosing the right characteristics and the right manner or frame and on ending up with the right kind of likenesses so as not to upend too drastically the order of nature as Darwin inherited it. The appropriate method of the science, the method before the method, was a set of rules about how to distinguish among likenesses. And before method per se, resemblance was elementary.

1.3.2. *What something is is how and in what respects it is like other things.*

Likeness to your mother and likeness to a stone are, under this experiment, what give meaning to being family and being matter. Give priority to the order of implication over any sort of deduction from first principles. An evolution scientist — perhaps any scientist — begins from likenesses and, through a convoluted process, which includes no small degree of ideology and self-deception, assimilates the likenesses to an ontological schema. In the process, the likenesses go from the absolute center of experience to the margins of a structure, or worse, to its ornaments; where once they lit up in an originary connection, now they serve as evidence for something that never lights up.

The fact that likenesses do not come in degrees makes them a fixed characteristic of beings, more fixed, perhaps, than whatever lies beyond them. Because likeness is not an intensive magnitude, like a quality, of which there can be more or less in an absolute and not relative sense, because it cannot be dialed up or down, it has to be taken as a fixed proportion, which is, in the end, what we mean by "what something is." What something is is the respects and ways in which it is like other things.

Likeness serves as evidence for order in living nature. Darwin makes ontology lean and list, removing several key supports. The scale of being and the identity of substance are no longer there. He sees that likenesses are different than the beings they are said of, different and constitutive. They are the outside inside, the world imported into the being, crossing it and crossing out its purported independence, emphasizing things' constitutive interrelations through traits and manners.

1.3.3.   *Likeness has no properties. It is properties' distribution mechanism.*

If, provisionally, it is better to continue speaking the language of properties, which belongs to the discourse on beings, it is just in order to be able to say that likeness describes how properties disperse across and through things and how properties and things mutually reflect one another such that they never fully individuate.

Darwinian evolution is the story of traits, perhaps more than the story of organisms or species. In Darwin's second epochal concept, the tree of life, the skin of species and the skeleton of organisms fall away, leaving arabesque trails of traits that have lives of their own, with prelives and afterlives. Under this half light, in which creatures live or die, thrive or waste away at the behest of their traits, the principle of individuation comes to seem like an epiphenomenon of likeness, as well as an unfortunate disavowal of it. A pattern of traits extending well beyond them in time, place, and thingness, individuals nonetheless insist on their individuality.

This is another way to present the wager of this experiment. If the shepherd of Glen Turret welcomes a sheep into his herd, it will not be because of that sheep's incomparable self or irreplaceable singularity or individuality or distinct being or essence. It will not be because a virtuality actualized out of a field of pure diversity. It will be because an individual through likeness of traits is already a herd. The herd is in the sheep before the sheep enters the herd.

Some ways to say "likeness" should be handled with caution. Though they are sometimes treated as synonyms, "likeness," "resemblance," and "similarity" often entail different presuppositions. "Similar" is often, though not always, an ontological matter. Similarity classically obtains between entities in virtue of a third substantial thing outside the relation, be it a gene, a historical antecedent, or a metaphysical substance.[11] I am similar to you in virtue of a reserve of humanity held in common by us both or preceding us in time or held above us as a higher instance. At the same time, "similar" emphasizes the space between things that separates and individuates them, which is what forces us to search above or behind them after the reason for their affinity. In contrast, "resemblance" is usually, though not exclusively, an aesthetic matter. A thing resembles what lends it a look, and the thing that resembles something is a semblance of that thing. This brings into the foreground whatever deficiencies there are in the representation, and in doing so, it, too, reinforces an ontology of individuals. Finally, "likeness" — not equivalent to "similarity" or "resemblance" — has no fixed place in ontology or aesthetics. In the framework of ontology, likeness would probably fall into the category of relation, a category beset by its own difficulties. And yet, as will be shown, likeness does not intervene "between" things, nor is it a special kind of thing that joins other things that are metaphysically or physically separate. Then it is also not a species of reference, as it would be under the aegis of semiotics. When we say A is "like" B, we are not saying A is "about" B, as we would if we were pointing out a signifier and a signified. There is something else in play here — a disjointed effect, spooky action at a distance, a noncausal, nonranked affair, one that cannot be measured — "how can we estimate this amount?" Darwin asks (you might think, somewhat desperately).

Likeness is sui generis among modes of existence. Following the shepherd of Glen Turret, I want to say something that appears contradictory at first. Likeness is unique and general at the same time. It is predicated of a lamb with its mother, and a mother with all its parents, and never of a single lamb alone.

1.4. ***Likeness is in and through at least two, and toward these two it holds a thoroughly equitable attitude. It prefers neither one nor the other.***

"In and through two" moves beyond the image of particular, independent, relational beings to the unique overlap that confuses them, where two things appear almost to fuse. The designation "in and through" should be contrasted with "between." Placing a thing beside another thing, predicating of each about the other a "difference from," as for example Hegel does in the *Phenomenology of Spirit* (*Phenomenology*, p. 75; *Phänomenologie*, p. 102), but there are many other examples, as many as there are philosophies — these images will need to be abandoned or at least darkened. A thing is not either "for itself" or "for another" (p. 76; p. 104). Where a thing gets thinghood from likenesses, it does not have the freedom qua thing to act on its own — likenesses act in and through it, fusing it into an indeterminacy with others. A further expression of this: just as you cannot affix an amount or a degree to a likeness, you also cannot say a lamb is like its mother without admitting also that the mother is like its lamb. Reciprocity is one of the main sources of likeness's apparent generality. In our everyday dealings with it, we confuse this reciprocity and this "in and through" others for generality, banality, triviality, or nonsense.

1.4.1. *When we say "This is like that," we mean as well "That is like this" in the relevant respect, though at times in varying ways.*

A likeness cannot travel in one direction without also traveling in the other; the content of the one likeness is the other likeness.[12] Or you can say the likeness is in and through both, and the two are in and through their likeness. Disentangling things from one another becomes complicated or even violating, as does the attribution of qualities, even secondary qualities such as color, so far as they occur in unique combinations and degrees of intensity, which would make a thing seem uniquely itself.

The intertwining of things through likeness presents itself to the naturalist. Darwin's notebooks hint that this is intensely true for the tradition of natural inquiry: the fearful combination of uniqueness and generality in experiences of likeness offers a promise and a limit to the study of life. The promise of a "natural" connectedness of things and its limit in the confusing nature of that connectedness comes up at two distant ends of the tradition of natural inquiry. Both ends of the tradition, Aristotle in the fourth century BCE and Darwin in the nineteenth century CE, see a potential infinitude of similar points as necessary for science and integral to the whole of living nature, but also at the same time intolerable for science and contradictory among the parts of living nature.

From which perspective on ensouled beings should a study of their anatomy begin? Should it start from individuals, from species, or from the commonalities among species? Until this question is answered, Aristotle's science cannot even get started, since the results will never be credible without a decision on what constitutes the basic unit of study (*Parts of Animals* 1.1). Two possibilities present themselves. Either you take as the basic unit of natural inquiry "each substance alone about itself according to itself" (639a17–18),[13] or you take in its place "attributes common to all according to what is common" (639a18–19), and with this antinomy Aristotle pauses. The crux of the antinomy is the following. Natural science is either the study of individuals, or else it is the study of groups. Within this crux lies another. An individual is an individual in virtue of its membership in a group, or else a group is a group in virtue of what is held in common among its members. To these nested antinomies, Aristotle proposes the following solution: "it is generally likenesses [*homoioteta*] in the shapes of the parts, or of the whole body," that have delimited the genuses (644b8–9). Without likenesses, the antinomies about the basic unit of natural inquiry would be unresolvable. On one hand, without likenesses, there are no individuals, if individuals are thought of as spatiotemporally independent instances of a common substance. On the other hand, there are no groups since natural groups are indeed based on similarities. Groups are replaced by a limitless carpet of deviations, and for this reason, zoological work, as Aristotle conceived it, would be unrelieved tedium. It would never be finished

42

and therefore could never properly get started. So the science of organisms begins, before it begins, with homeoses. Failing the gift of homeosis, every animal and each part of every animal would have to be derived independently of every other, and before that, each trait of each part, one by one, for the entire field of life. Maybe this is the deepest dream of metaphysics; but it is doubtful whether, on the assumption of the primacy of individuals, without a prior field of likenesses, you could even discern a field of nature. Organisms are alike and species are alike in so many respects that you do and perhaps you must start with common attributes. Yet it is equally doubtful whether, on the assumption of the primacy of groups, you could avoid falling into dogmatism about common attributes. These have to be abstracted from the multitudinous likenesses that transect, almost randomly, the animal field. Shapes (*schemata*) are a common attribute, and yet what allows a science access to shapes are the likenesses among the shapes. To be recognized as a shape, in a part of a body or as a whole body, that part or whole, the shape, needs at least one analog.

1.4.2. *Morphology derives from likenesses.*

A millennias-long obsession with "form" can at last be tempered. Debate the meaning of form, update the ramifications of morphology, return to Aristotle, when you need to, overcome Aristotle, if it seems right. Here, Aristotle himself admits that a shape can be a shape, for ontology, only when it finds echoes across the spectrum. The order form–being–likeness needs to be reversed.

Taking these two related insights seriously — that morphology derives from likeness and the ontology of living things that seems to derive from form in turn derives from likenesses — you discover an esoteric origin within the official beginning. Zoology came about, in this influential inception, from an abbreviation of a much larger field. This is why it has explanatory power; this is what explanation was and remains. Nature, abbreviated, preempts a nearly infinite homeotic exercise. Even when you explain by abbreviating, the results of the procedure are credible only when you make the following presupposition.

1.4.3.   *Likenesses* (homoioteta) *permeate the natural field in a tangle that, in turn, allows likeness points to be selected and renamed, post hoc, "characteristics in common."*

The milieu out of which a scientific procedure can produce an explanatory picture of nature is a tangle, and it proceeds through acts of demarcation that Aristotle calls here, "delimiting the group," or more precisely, "horizoning off the genuses" (*horistai ta gene*, 644b8–9). Before this procedure gets started, before the genuses are cordoned off, however, the tangle has to be active. General attributes on which a category doctrine can be built are precipitates of the process of "horizoning off," and yet these generalities, as Aristotle himself says, are nothing more than higher names for the repetition of like characteristics.

Given its originary position in his natural philosophy, the fact that Aristotle gives no account of homeosis per se is surprising, since the intuition of likenesses had been a feature of Greek reasoning about the world since Homer. What could be more commonsensical than to say: were there no similarities, there would be no science, and also no nature, at least that you could recognize? A complex of similars is taken as a given, a bare fact for thought, and as such, it warrants no philosophizing, even if the science of animals, at its simplest, constructs shapes out of resemblances so that it can perform certain operations on those shapes, such as individuating and then grouping and therefore defining and explaining.

The assumption of a protolikeness tangle moves from the background into the foreground in *On the Origin of Species*, revolutionary book that works against Aristotle's conclusions in several important ways, and still Darwin, as I indicated, concedes in quite a similar manner that the starting point for the study of animate nature is homeotic, although this for him is due to the character of the history of life, the fact of heredity combined with the mechanisms of selection, and not due to a doctrine of shape. Repeating and extending Aristotle's insight, Darwin shows that the homeotic practices of the science of life are preceded by the multidimensional homeotic history of organisms. Species are resemblant. Offspring resemble parents; organisms in a line of descent resemble each other and through the line resemble the "common ancestor" (p. 97); across families there is "similarity of pattern" (p. 320), a founding fact for the subdiscipline of homology. Embryos are resemblant. They caught popular attention in the nineteenth and twentieth centuries because they make an uncanny picture: across the most diverse classes, embryos approximate one another (p. 323), seeming to suspend, for the period of gestation, historical distance, speciation, as well as differences in taxonomic rank (as Haeckel showed for instance in the phylum Chordata). Embryos of the most distant species and families, for the period of gestation, look like siblings. Stepping beyond Linnaeus's restricted principle, "like gives birth to like," Darwin strolls into other homeotic territories, raising the question of what he calls "similarity of pattern" such as can be seen in bone arrangements of foot, fin, and wing among human, whale, and bird. It is important to note that these similarities do not produce species. A species that resulted from homological affinities like this would be monstrous. Although not the result of a single birth line, homologs such as these do have a cause; a certain structure is retained through "successive slight modifications" (p. 320) from a common ancestor, along with gravity, so to speak, because the structure has never been selected against. Homology is generally taken as evidence of a common ancestor, an "archetype as it may be called" (p. 320). It is obviously as well a kind of homeosis that stands on the margins of heredity, suggesting likenesses beyond containing structures such as family or lineage or branch. Homology gives the appearance of a likeness that does not obey other hierarchies. In this regard, it stands uncomfortably close to analogy (pp. 314–15), which Darwin distinguishes from homology, not according to any intrinsic criteria, but on the extrinsic consideration of whether the likeness falls in a "line of descent" (p. 315) or between lines. Homology is likeness through a primal cause, heritance, and analogy is a likeness through an efficient cause, adaptation. Forearms are homologous in whales and bats and humans since they share a common history of descent. Fins are analogous in fish and whales, since they represent separate adaptations to a similar aquatic environment. The one "betrays the hidden bond of community of descent" (p. 315), the other testifies to a need for a particular function under similar conditions.

Nature, as seen by Darwin, is a partly structured, partly mutable homeotic field in which a naturalist first off differentiates among kinds of similarity and applies distinct values to them. "This is like that" becomes "These likenesses are essential." Despite the drive to differentiate, early evolution theory was certainly a windfall for homeotics. All biologists take their first steps as homeoticians and then, because of the objectives of the science, face a demand to convert the experience of similarities into an account of order in nature. More than perhaps any other science, evolution theory genuinely faced up to the problems in constructing a homeotic system. It is now apparent how resemblance becomes a problem because it cannot be limited through quantitative measuring; it knows no degrees. In response to this constraint, Darwin introduces limits into resemblance by separating it into kinds. Speciation, analogy, and homology, all belong to evolution. Two of them are hereditary and true, though functionally distinct, while analogy, standing outside the chain of primal causes, is already of lesser value. This is a fairly precarious distinction, at least at first, insofar as the first observable fact is usually a likeness, and cause is then applied to it or assumed to stand behind it. Likenesses appear before the cause. They can and often do lead to multiple associations, not only to the proper ones, the ones about which you can tell a coherent story from first causes, efficient causes, or from function or purpose. In Notebook D, Darwin hits on this very point. It plagues the naturalists of his day that "genus expresses as now used almost any group" (note 50,

pp. 347–48). The real problem, it should be said, is not perceiving similarities, but limiting their significance.

1.4.4. *Because of its tendency toward indeterminacy, "Everything is like*
everything in some respect" threatens to go over into "Anything
is like anything in any respect," morphing from a minimally
restricted to an unrestricted principle.

An unrestricted principle would be, as many have intuited, unuseful,
trivial, banal, or nonsensical, tantamount to a tautology, though not
the tautological foundation of anything, simply a vortex, a menagerie,
bad infinity, or chaos that might not even warrant a name. And so
before organic beings can be categorized, the natural scientist, going
several steps beyond what the breeder does and knows, has to tame
likeness's wildness. If, for biology or zoology, the order of nature
arises from affinities between natural beings, and the affinities stick,
so to speak, on the basis of resemblance, how to decide between resemblances becomes the pivotal question of method. The word "genus"
has been extended beyond its usefulness, Darwin risks writing. This
makes it seem as though a stricter use of the word would resolve the
crisis in definition. And yet when he rejects any quantitative determination for likeness, rather than solving it, Darwin deepens the crisis
for himself and for those who come after. To build any higher structure
on likeness, a strict criterion for deciding on the proper likenesses will
need to be found. Most of the time, Darwin chooses the criterion of
cause. He never to my knowledge chooses that other source, outside
nature, which has its own set of motivations — he will not even hint
that resemblance is a fact not of nature, but of mind.

Throughout *On the Origin of Species*, Darwin uses the word
"resemble" as an objective characteristic of natural organisms, as if
to ward off the subjective monster crouching in the shadows. In that
book, natural resemblance knows no "to whom." The shepherd of Glen
Turret and his life and imagination fall out of the equation. The truth
of resemblances is objective and self-evident. "The mule and the hinny

more resemble the ass than the horse," Darwin declares (p. 203), along with many more unqualified statements like this. This far along in the development of the theory, natural resemblance, though it may still pose problems immanent to science, has been separated absolutely from anything that transcends it, such as mental acts. Darwin avoids the mental constitution of likenesses not by confronting idealism but by avoiding it. A covert goal of his book then is to interpret the act of "resembling" on the surface of natural things as a special, but superficial coating so that he can eventually bring forward what supports it, the causal fact of "being related to," that is, heredity, which lends nature and likeness their "arrangement." Heredity lends resemblance its objectivity, nature its order, and science its certainty, although, to be fair, Darwin does once in the book allude to a cultural source for likenesses: "From the first dawn of life, all organic beings are found to resemble each other in descending degrees, so that they can be classed in groups under groups. This classification is evidently not arbitrary like the grouping of the stars in constellations" (p. 303). Culture comes out badly in this formulation. What doesn't survive is astrology, the old scapegoat of scientific enlightenment. Yet the paragraph is not only making a historical break and pointing out the superiority of naturalism. What links stars into a figure is not the physical fact of their positions in space, but another force that, although Darwin doesn't say it directly, his statement implies exists in the stargazers' minds or cultural practices. No doubt it is an overstatement to call the arrangement of stars in zodiacal signs "arbitrary." Stargazers inherit the habit of star patterns in almost as strict a lineage as they inherit their eyeballs. And lest we forget, natural groupings themselves are in important ways arbitrary by Darwin's own theory of variation. At the very least, the distinction between arbitrary and nonarbitrary resemblances is not so easy to make as this. Darwin's point is that the affinities among stars in Ursa Major do not make a bear in the same way that the affinities among paw and paw and claw and claw over bear generations make bears. The field for the former is the history of stargazers, the field for the latter is natural history.

Aside from this oblique reference, Darwin almost never considers other regions of resemblance besides organic nature. He leaves culture and mind out of the picture, although they persist at the margins of his vision, as for example in the passage above. It is apparent, also, that the so-called natural similarities also have to be perceived and collected according to inherited practices, and in some way, as well, it can be surmised, underlying these practices is a capacity to notice similarities, the capacity Darwin demonstrates dazzlingly in his notebooks. This capacity is not unique to Darwin or to stargazers. A butterfly has a similarity detector, faultlessly finding the right kinds of flowers. Why shouldn't the human scientist be situated in the nature he is studying? A butterfly in the dry season mimics a dead leaf, fooling the similarity detector of the birds or spiders that hunt it. Who detects the similarities among all these similarities and on this basis builds a similarity system? Who can be an evolution theorist? A being in whom evolved a special likeness organ.

How dependent on likeness theories of mind have been. The likeness mind's history has two orienting poles. Hume stands at one moment in this story, and Aristotle, once again, stands at another. Aristotle invests heavily in mind as a special kind of substance. For this reason, he eventually criticizes the theory of the *physiologoi*, repeated in Plato's *Timaeus*, that mind is sovereign over things because it is like what it knows (*De anima* 404b17–405b16). This theory says that to know hot, thought becomes hot, to know air, thought becomes air, and so on. Mind is the special kind of substance that becomes all others, and this is why what is is thinkable. Plato and Democritus thus maintained that we "know like by like" (*De anima* 409b27).[14] Aristotle, too, in *De interpretatione* asserts that the receptive aspects of mind are a homeotic zone: "mental affections . . . are likenesses [*homoiomata*]" (1.1. 6–9), but eventually he restricts this view, arguing that if understanding resulted from a natural sympathy between substances in this way, mind responding in kind to what is like it, we could not make conceptual mistakes, which we do all the time. Furthermore, if understanding were a material likeness process, knowing earth, for example, because *nous* was made of earth, how would we come to know the order of elements in a compound of elements? Further, are order and ratio also elements? Mind would have to be a special substance that could handle material objects as well as immaterial objects such as relations, structures, causes, accidents, and conjunctions of ontologically distinct types, and this meant unlike substances would have to be somehow like one another. Ontology thus needed to be maintained by excluding a homeotics that would vitiate it. In *De anima*, as he thinks over these homeotic theories, Aristotle also draws a decisive line between the perceptual part of mind and the understanding part, between *aesthesis* and *noesis*. He separates knowledge and perception, and with this division, homeosis is allowed into the *psyche* and gains limited autonomy from ontology on the bargain that it no longer challenges ontology. Perception is a likeness process, but only because it does not deal directly with substance. "When it has been affected," perception "has been made like it [its object] and is such as what affected it is" (*De anima*, Shields trans., 418a5–6, p. 34). A likeness here is distinct from the substance it is like, which is to say likeness is not substantial.

Today, it may not be controversial at all to present mind as a multivector field of substanceless resemblances,[15] but the decisive imprint of this pattern and a vast expansion over previous homeotic images of mind happened with Hume. To avoid god, Hume got rid of the world; to avoid the world, Hume got rid of principles external to mind; to avoid external principles, Hume invented and borrowed (from Locke, Berkeley, Bacon, Home, Hutcheson, and others) a set of immanent principles, among them "impression," "idea," "association," "resemblance," "contiguity," and "cause and effect." Then, in order to prevent immanent principles from referring to transcendences, he, sometimes overtly, sometimes covertly — though not always consciously, it seems — made all these principles reducible to "resemblance." It is not uncontroversial to say this. Not only the receptive, affectable parts of mind, but all of mind — the productive and active parts as well — become homeotic. Although multiple principles appear in his system, the dues Hume is willing to pay for a skepticism that scorches transcendence is reliance on resemblance almost to the point of its dissolution as a meaningful term.[16]

Images and their correspondences are by and large all there is to mind. The opening sections in book 1 of Hume's *Treatise* are a little treatise on mental modes of correspondence.[17] What are the correspondences among images, and where do they come from? "Copy" is a word Hume writes into book 1 to name one of the modes or mechanisms of correspondence. Ideas can be copies of impressions, whether impressions of sense or of the imagination; ideas can also be copies of other ideas; and complex ideas are made up of simple ideas, which in turn, as we've said, are copies of impressions. Hume's famous "copy principle" (1.1.2, p. 11) makes ideas correspond with impressions and ideas correspond with ideas. Objects are given to thought through copying. Copying is the modality of the given, because it is the relay by which the truth of an object transits mental space.

Yet copying is only one mode of correspondence in the treatise within the *Treatise*. When Hume moves from the question of the truth content of thought to the question of the continuity and persistence of mental experience, he introduces a second set of correspondences. As distinct from the single mode of correspondence between idea and impression, the copy principle, the modes of correspondence in the association of ideas are in total three "qualities": "Resemblance, Contiguity in time or place, and Cause and Effect" (1.1.4, p. 13). All associations of ideas happen through one of these three qualities. True ideas always copy impressions or other ideas. Experience associates ideas with one another in virtue of resemblance, contiguity, or cause between them. Ideas are copies, and experience is the association of idea copies. In this, the resemblance structure of image mind, oddly enough, resemblance enters the equation at two separate points, as the primary gesture in the mechanism of copying and, at first glance, as one of three qualities in the association of ideas.

That is to say, mind is in its ideas, in their production and their associations, and resemblance is in both. For the production of ideas, all relations are overtly resemblances. As was said, the famous "copy principle" holds that ideas exactly resemble impressions, ideas exactly resemble other ideas, and, in a little-discussed further instance, impressions from the different senses exactly resemble one another in at least one respect. When you touch a thing and see that thing, the two separate impressions have to have like parts (1.2.3, p. 28). Thus, there are three resemblance moments in the production of ideas. Then, after leaving the production floor, resemblance makes an important appearance as well in the association of ideas, which underlies both predicative judgment and the temporal flow of experience. Where the possible associations of ideas are exhaustively determined by the three qualities: resemblance, contiguity, cause and effect (1.1.4, p. 13), resemblance appears to be an independent quality on a par with the other two and yet, although they are presented as separate and equal qualities, contiguity and cause/effect will turn out also to need resemblance in their operations. Hume's is a picture of mind in which, whenever there is a question of fundamental principles, resemblance makes an appearance.

Begin with causality. How resemblance underlies cause is not immediately intuitive.[18] If you do with cause what Hume himself proposes, that is, "examine it to the bottom" (1.1.4, p. 13), you find, first of all, it has a nested structure. Causality is one of the three independent qualities by which ideas are associated. Contiguity is supposed to be another. And yet causality contains contiguity as one basic element of its relations. For there to be cause and effect, contiguity is needed (1.3.2, p. 54), along with priority and also necessity, although this last is what in Humean logic you cannot have. In a traditional understanding of causality, these two, contiguity and priority, are joined together by "necessary connexion" (1.3.2, p. 55). Now, whereas necessity is not discoverable in experience, correspondence very much is. What replaces necessity in Hume's experiential account of causality? Contiguity and priority alone cannot offer the kind of bond that would give even the appearance of necessity, in which when one pole of a correspondence is present, the other is consistently present as well.

This problem makes Hume pause. "Having thus discover'd or suppos'd the two relations of contiguity and succession to be essential to causes and effects, I find I am stopt short, and can proceed no farther in considering any single instance of cause and effect." (1.3.2, p. 54). Call this "Hume's breakdown," a pause in thought that might reveal something unexpected about causal type experiences. Just where some assumption about the being of causal events would have to be made, in response to his breakdown, resemblance reenters the scene. With necessity impossible to experience and so banned from the question, there is only a succession of events — worse, only successions of events, plural. What in this could give the idea of causality? The idea of causality lies within the ideas of priority and contiguity, within the notion of succession itself, or in one of its component parts. This is what makes Hume an analytic thinker — the answer to any question lies in the component parts of the question. Thus, you discover that although no external source for the apparent necessity in cause can be posited, there is a resource in the experience itself, but only if it is repeated. No single event can be considered causal, no one conjunction of affairs. Hume leaps to a second instance, a second conjunction, and a succession of a higher order.

Here is an extraordinary discovery, made at the pause in thought. To say that causality is the quality associating two ideas, the association has to be associated, or rather, another association has to happen that resembles the first. A double association is the beginning of an experiential account of causality. It routes, as you can see, through resemblance, and the resemblance basis of causality, as a likeness between two or more successions, has several ramifications. The minimum number of ideas to be associated for causality is not two, but in fact four. A second pair follows the first, and then, in turn, the second pair affirms the successivity of the first. That is to say, after the second time that one billiard ball sends another rolling, the first time becomes an example of causality. The experiential account of causality goes further. Humean causality is so iconoclastic that causality itself transits through the imagination, for which he says resemblance provides a "sufficient bond" (1.1.4, p. 13).

Hume's later definition of causality as "constant conjunction" refers back to the doubling of succession through resemblance. Let's put it in a formula: there is cause and effect where there is constant conjunction, and there is constant conjunction where resemblances double the event, as when one moment following another recalls a previous similar sequence. This doublet describes the experience of cause and effect — not the mysterious something between one ball and another, but the overt and illuminated echo of two colliding balls in two others. Causality occurs when two events are constituted through one another as alike.

A corollary to causality is identity, which follows a similar logic. "We readily suppose an object may continue individually the same, tho' several times absent from and present to the senses; and ascribe to it an identity, notwithstanding the interruption of the perception" (1.3.2, p. 53). Here is another characteristic of successivity that helps illuminate the resemblance field of mind. Perception is frequently interrupted. According to Hume, resemblance crosses an interruption of perception and gives experience the semblance of continuity above and beyond those events whose bonds we call "causal." Perceive, perceive not, perceive again, while the object disappeared, and then, after some interval, reappeared. If, when it returns, it resembles the original appearance, it has "identity."

1.4.5. *The identity of a thing is resemblance sustained over interruptions of perception.*

This is said of the resemblance field "mind." It could be said of the resemblance field "nature" just as easily, if "perception" were substituted with the word "heritance" or the word "species." The identity of a thing would result in nature when it was sustained, that is, resembled, across interruptions of hesitance or species.

Contiguity, the third quality undergirding associations of ideas, already figures in causality. Since causality is roughly speaking a combination in a particular order of contiguity, priority, and resemblance, and since priority is but a further specification of contiguity, you might deduce that the two fundamental qualities of all human experience are in the end contiguity and resemblance and that, further, they are independent and distinct, not reducible to each other. Our experience of time and space depend on contiguity, for example, as does our logic, in which premises are said to stand beside one another in logical space, when there are no intervening premises. Association itself relies on contiguity projected into a mental space.

The strange, nested character of the qualities of association comes to the fore again here. For a philosopher who begins with experience and ends with experience, and one who explicitly bans inquiry into the "original qualities of human nature, which I pretend not to explain" (1.1.5, p. 14), contiguity has to be the idea of contiguity, and so, as a quality of a perception, it only has to resemble contiguity. This is a very peculiar way of reasoning—but listen to where contiguity comes from. The imagination learns how to do contiguity from the senses, by imitating them. "'Tis likewise evident, that as the senses, in changing their objects, are necessitated to change them regularly, and take them as they lie contiguous to each other, the imagination must by long custom acquire the same method of thinking, and run along the parts of space and time in conceiving its objects" (1.1.4, p. 13). Contiguity of experience emerges from contiguity in experience, a twist in the mind that should be logically impossible. It is not, however. Resemblance makes this thought work. Contiguity, one quality of the association of ideas, is originally produced through a resemblance between an idea and an impression.

And there is another way in which contiguity relies on resemblance. Contiguity is always the contiguity of one object with another, and the objects are mental objects and thus themselves the result of copying procedures. The relationship of objects through resemblance also plays a role in the constitution of space. Space is predicated on contiguity; space is constituted through an experiential

operation — "distance will be allow'd by philosophers to be a true
relation, because we acquire an idea of it by the comparing of objects"
(1.1.5, p. 14). Comparing objects in turn relies on resemblance, making the structure of Humean experience more like a Klein bottle, a
closed surface that has no inside or outside, a multilevel array that
includes resemblance at key points on every level. Hume's is a thoroughgoing homeotics. One conjunction of ideas resembles another
conjunction: causality is a resemblance of conjunctions. Contiguity
is a comparison of objects, objects that themselves resemble impressions: contiguity is a comparison of resemblances. Although Hume
himself does not give a taxonomy of types of resemblance, he nonetheless comes directly to the point in the section on relation, where
it is shown by the *via negativa* that the conjunction of any two things
cannot not include resemblance. Here, Hume specifies that for his
philosophy, "relation" names something like a meaningful, internal
resonance that makes two objects "admit of comparison." He goes
on to describe the precondition for relation: "no objects will admit
of comparison, but what have some degree of resemblance" (1.1.5,
p. 15). Do not be thrown off here by the attribution of degree to
resemblance. Soon, Hume reveals that "degree" itself is a species of
relation, involving a comparison of more and less, and the subjects
of more and less, it seems clear, must display a minimal resemblance
in advance. Contiguity, too, is called here a species of relation, and
so in this way, too, it involves resemblance as its precondition. Even
contraries resemble — the most extreme example Hume gives of this
is existence and nonexistence, which resemble one another in being
about the same object, whatever may be and not be.

Review now the whole of mind, whose image-production
and distribution habits overtly and covertly share "resemble"
as a root term. Common to the most exclusionary of contraries,
shared out among contiguous things, intervening "betwixt" ideas
and impressions, ideas and ideas, fully enabling cause-effect conjunctions — resemblance . . . in a strict sense nothing in experience
happens without it. The specter of an absolute resemblance floats

through book i of Hume's treatise. If everything in mind resembles in some way, is not resemblance the quality of qualities, a separable thing that precedes and conditions all experience? "Universal resemblance" Hume calls it once (i.i.i, p. 8), but he does not pursue the intuition. In place of an absolute being, Hume imagines, as an essential complement to mind and its processes, an absolute quality, one that, no matter how transient the images in the mind, no matter how thin the vapors that condense into human nature, permits the other qualities to shine through, distribute, and distribute appropriately, conserving the correspondences among impressions, ideas, associations, conjunctions, in short: any familiarity among two or more phenomena.

"All perceptions of the mind are double," Hume notes (i.i.i, p. 8). In the logic of empiricism, resemblance is god—but it is a peculiar god, one who never left and one who always travels with a twin. Hume first makes mind into a domain for experience by opening a distance between impressions and ideas, by making experience double in that basic way. By no means can this distance ever close, in the Humean configuration, on pain of losing the distinctive character of mental life. The distance between impressions and ideas can never become too narrow, but it also cannot open up so wide that relations become unexperienceable. At the same time, Hume assumes that experience always consists and will always consist in this one set of operations. Resemblance for Hume is the settled, persisting quality that, in the mental workplace, allows for an orderly array of separate but interrelated mental objects, without any external reference and also without the dangers of total confusion and total dispersion across the mental sphere.

For a thoroughgoing resemblance theory of mind and a thoroughgoing resemblance theory of nature, put Hume's and Darwin's side by side: there is one shared premise, which comes with a shared qualification. Everything resembles everything in some respect, to be sure, and yet both agree, from different sides of the question, that mind does not resemble nature, and nature does not resemble mind.

Each of their theories depends almost completely on likeness as a heuristic and as an explanatory principle, yet each theory excludes the other as inapplicable, unnatural, or unknowable. In one theory, resemblance happens under its own unspoken law without mediation producing doublets, over and over, in the zone of thought. In the other theory, a historico-geographical pattern of similarities gradually displaces into new qualities, repeating aspects of originals in copies, at an absolute minimum repeating the likeness processes themselves (heredity, adaptation, speciation) without which life would come to an end. Thus, likeness takes over thought and living nature. The conundrum here is that from each side, Hume's and Darwin's, this is possible only so long as the two zones do not come to overlap with one another.[19]

After this reading of Hume and Darwin, the original assertion, that everything is like everything in some respect, should be modified and extended, in order to bring this one impediment, the absolute division of mind and nature, into a theory of resemblance. First of all, Hume's analysis of image production and distribution and Darwin's analysis of organismic reproduction and distribution resemble one another. They share a common presupposition.

1.5.   *To be something is to be like something.*

This new premise derives from the first premise, that everything is like everything in some respect, and yet it turns the first, most general premise against itself. "Everything is like everything" is already a sentence against itself, and though it may show a calm face to the outside, it is inwardly at war. The war, it goes without saying, is fought right on the surface of the line, between "is" and "like," and in the struggle, the soul of the world is at stake, as the Neoplatonist Plotinus might say. In this sentence and its siblings and children, likeness starts to separate from being, and when you think of "everything" under the aegis of likeness, the things that you comfortably think of when you think of what is alike — individuals and arrays and heaps of things — these things are no longer comfortably things. A more pre-cise way to say this, no doubt, though it comes closer to a tautology (a logical term that itself has to be redefined along homeotic lines), is the next premise.

1.5.1. *To be something is like being like something.*

"Being," you can see, is now encased in, bounded by, "likes," which gesture could indicate a historical unicum — its sources scattered across several centuries, from Linnaeus and his natural system to Hume and to Darwin, the "like" spreads like a stain or comes like a piecemeal invasion, crossing diagonally through established regions of being and their established sciences. A minimal consequence of the modified premise "To be something is like being like something" is that when you say everything is like everything in some respect, it now means that no individual thing is empirically or ontologically separate.

To be a thing, a thing has to be like at least one thing other than itself. In anything, two are inseparable, and so the character of "everything" changes from an accumulation of individuals to a peculiar, partial, and asymmetrical interpenetration, falling into doublets and lines, chains and fields and arrays. From a higher point of view, the process or technique "being like" (in all its multiplicity, with added restrictions in resembling, assimilating, copying, and so forth) is itself a matter of likeness. What it is to be like in any case is an approximation of what it could be to be like. Something comes close to being like without the need for actually being like. What-ever its characteristics, a thing or process is always "in the image of" something.[20] The Everything is a manifold of the kinds of somethings that include one another in varying ways. Since Darwin heard the shepherd of Glen Turret say he saw the mother in the sheep, it is hard to remain innocent about what it means to be a sheep. Being sheep implicates mothers, a branch of the tree of life, and also, though in different ways or manners, niches, closest relatives, farthest relatives, distant reflections in other regions of being, and so forth — all echoes of resemblances. At a minimum, therefore, it is wise to revise the concept of "thing."

1.6.   *A thing is a juxtaposition of at least two, constituted through their noncoincidence.*

Pierre Reverdy laid a cornerstone for the thought of things under the sign of resemblance. It doesn't matter that his indelible statement was about the "image." Things, in a homeosphere, are like Reverdy's images. An image, he wrote, is a "becoming proximal of two realities more or less distant," a *"rapprochement de deux réalités plus ou moins éloignées"* ("L'image," p. 1). This becomes the motto for surrealism, the epigraph to their lifework. An image for surrealism is a thing for homeotics. Were a thing like only itself, there would be no likeness, no discernible likeness, and therefore, under a homeotic regime, no discernible thing to begin with, because the distance could not be felt. If the distance cannot be felt, alongside sympathy or nearness, it cannot be a likeness, and therefore no thing. The same can be said in reverse, from the perspective of a world with things. In a thing world (as opposed to a likeness world), no thing can be just like itself, or else it would not count as a thing, just as an anomaly. For this reason, on account of the distance every thing projects between it and its similars, the world cannot simply collapse into a point or a uniform continuum. "This or that thing, what is it?" "What is a thing?" "What is it like?" "It is like this or like that — like this and like that."

1.6.1.   *A thing is a plenum of likenesses.*

2. *A thing is a plenum of likenesses.*

This is homeotics' challenge to ontology.[21] To the question, "What is a being?" there is a homeotic response.

2.1. *There are no real individuals and no real wholes.*

This thought can be unraveled in two ways.

A. There are no real individuals for the simple reason that an individual lives off other individuals, although this does not mean that a thing sits in a context with other things or exists in a network of meaningful relations. Rather, an individual results from constitutive attractions among multiples through their traits. Arrays or circuits of traits constitute and disperse a thing.

B. On the other side of this plurifocal attraction is a peculiar aspect of individuals, which, though not real, can nevertheless be isolated. An individual thing contains multiple elements, aspects, or qualities. It has an expanse, mental or physical, material or immaterial, across which it projects its self. What appears as individual is individual, to itself, and separated from others only insofar as it has extension — that it is itself to some extent, that it has extension into itself. Any thing stretches, stretches out, has magnitude. It has a physical or metaphysical expanse, or both, has duration, stretches in various dimensions at once; it is a zone. That is — to be a thing, there must be more than a single point.

The result of outward-radiating attractions among things, a thing is also the result of inward stretch into itself. It is better thought of as an inner and outer circuit, two circuits that mutually intercalate or insert within one another. On one side, as a circuit or array that goes beyond the thing itself, crossing individuals external to it of whatever size and shape, it draws its external array into a kind of group. One name for a group of outward-radiating attractions has been a "family."[22] If you think of a family less as what shares a common substance — blood or genes or history or psychology or experience — and more, again, as a circuit or array, you can imagine among a family's members similarities and affinities circulating along routes, distributing in ways that seem in some sense lawful and in some sense also incidental or free, in some sense predictable and in some sense idiosyncratic, even fleeting, and sometimes repeating at odd intervals. To be sure, familial similarities are not evenly or logically distributed over bodies or traits or times.[23]

The concept of family points toward a layer of experience that we hardly notice, and a look at this layer can teach how a belief in "things" may arise. What we call a "thing" is surrounded by a halo of partial things, traits, pieces, manners, affects, and so on, that are in some way kin to it. Penumbrae of resemblances surround and permeate phenomena. With this thought commences the dereification of the world. Penumbral elements make travesties of individuals. They are in it, and it is in them, by which I mean it is nothing without them. The very objective thing world that has been thought and rethought is not. "The surround" crosses the object, and the object is the surround, as a child is in a family and the family is also in the child. This reciprocal sense of "in" needs to be developed.

On another side, in addition to the things and partial things in the penumbra of a thing that make it a thing, a thing's own internal expanse is in it, and it in its internal expanse, making the expanse no more internal than the penumbra is external.[24] Whether its "expanse" is an intensive magnitude, such as the vividness of a color or the painfulness of a pain, or an extensive magnitude, such as the volume of a Platonic solid or the durée of a melody, a thing needs magnitude to stand up and be itself, and magnitude is in similarity. If it is "of" the one thing, the same thing, its magnitude has to be in some respect uniform and continuous; at least: it is not allowed to be the opposite, that is, a random aggregate. This pain you are feeling has to continue as this pain from one instant to another, however briefly it may last; that table has to continue as that table from one corner to the other.[25]

It is easier to show this for spatially extended objects. Hermann Cohen, who from the late nineteenth to the early twentieth century revised and extended Kant's critical philosophy, commented on this in *Kant's Theory of Experience*. "*Das Gleichartige macht das Mannich-faltige zur Grösse*" (p. 416) — "The uniform makes the multiplicitous into a magnitude" (my translation). This is in some way obvious, yet it gives an unparalleled insight into the meaning of "thing." An individual thing is synthesized through a process of making uniform, *gleichartig*, that results in a magnitude.[26] "Uniform" does not have to mean thoroughly homogenous. A magnitude may be made up of parts heterogeneous in materials and shape, and yet they show uniformity in some respect, to be counted together as an individual. A bicycle's uniformity is like this. Frame, wheels, gears, cables, and handlebar are not uniform in shape, material, or function, and yet whatever it is that makes them bicycle parts — fitting together, their role in purposive cofunctioning, and so on — they cannot include nonbicycle parts. A bicycle can't synthesize these into its expanse. No matter how many parts we count, they are all bicycle parts. The most commonplace way to think of uniformity is as sameness across a magnitude, where sameness is thought of as a high grade of similarity. One inch of a stone has a very high similarity to the next inch of the stone. This is what "stone" means. A thing is itself because its extents are similar to each other, materially or functionally, in appearance or in purpose — chain beside and similar to pedal (purpose), or stone beside and similar to stone (material). Following this reasoning, when we say a thing is an individual, we mean a thing has a minimum of magnitude, and across its magnitude it is similar to itself in some way or other, which may only mean it is at every point more similar to itself than to other things in its vicinity.

63

This homeotic assumption underpins ontology. In a post-Kantian ductus, an object is said to consist in an inherent, internal *Gleichartig-keit*—uniformity—a higher homogeneity within itself than across the divide between it and other things. No experience of an object without magnitude, no magnitude without internal *Gleichartigkeit*, an autohomeosis basic to all things.

A thing, then, is constituted by internal self-likeness across an expanse, no matter how small or how big, and by an external plurifo-cal likeness among other things. By rights, a thing should be inter-nally homogeneous and externally heterogeneous, discontinuous with its surroundings, but this is not strictly true. Once it can be established that a thing results from a union of itself with itself, as an expanse or a magnitude, it emerges that the very fabric of a thing's extension is crossed by infinitely many alien *Gleichnisse*, likenesses with what does not belong to it. A thing is like to itself because each of its microexpanses is like to its neighbor in a like way. A thing is also like to its likeness shadow because some of its traits echo some of their traits. A thing's internal consistency is not the same as its likeness to its shadows, but it is like it.

2.2. *Other things are like parts of the thing, and sectors of the thing, the spans that make it up, are like other things.*

This way of formulating the being of things brings up a serious ques-tion. Things are useful because they seem to divide experience into manageable units. The object, its individuality, uniformity, rela-tionality, and so on, reflects the needs of consciousness for orderly identity and difference. If parts or expanses of a thing are them-selves things, and if the thing itself is crossed by a plurality of other things, what is the basic unit of experience? Once likeness rejects the unity of the thing, you need to find another unit. And so it is wise to be asking, indeed, whether likeness has a basic unit. The unit of a thing is traditionally "one"—that is, the uniformity of a homogenous manifold to a limit at which the heterogeneous interrupts it. When likeness rejects this traditional idea of uniformity and difference, it leaves a question and an opening.

2.2.1. *The basic unit of likeness is a pair. Thing effects happen through a minimum of two that are not fully distinguishable.*

Likenesses array into pairs that are not uniform, and yet are more intimately intertwined than is usually comfortable. It is less than correct to call a thing "one" if any single trait has to echo a second trait somewhere within or without in order even to show up. An activity of enlikening happens within "the uniform"; *ab initio*, the activity has two poles. The proviso is that you cannot call the second pole "second," as distinct from "first." You cannot say which ancestor is the ultimate source for your brown eyes. Most immediately it is your mother, say, but hers are from a grandparent, and so on. This is one caveat. Here I am saying yes, the echoes of a trait line up into a series, and so which instance counts as the true first remains ambiguous, but I am also saying that in spite of our belief in causality, the order of the echoes is not ascertainable. The first brown eye is fully dependent on the second brown eye to become itself, an ancestor; the second brown eye is not a second to anything until the first comes along. For homeotics, it is just as much your brown eyes that call into existence the series you–mother–great-grandparent as it is your great-grandparent and mother who called your eyes into existence. And your eyes are dependent on their echo in a child or grandchild. There is much to say about this strange mode, distance without separation, intimate closeness without coincidence, firstness that comes second and secondness that comes first. These are the ways of the basic unit — the pair — in homeosis.

There are other modes of pairhood in other regions of being and other processes. We are more familiar with these. Semiosis, for example, also has the pair as its basic unit, but the semiotic pair follows a logic of substitution. In a sign system, the pair consists of a first position (a sign) that is for, in place of, or on behalf of a second position (either a sense or a thing) for which it can stand. Whether the sign precedes the thing or the thing precedes the sign — this depends on your position in the experience. Structurally speaking, all you can say is that in signification, a "second" points to a "first." The pair logic of semiosis can be called "standing for" or "aboutness." What's more, a semiotic pair always falls into a particular rank order. First is higher than second, to put it schematically. Whether "first" refers to sign or signified, it doesn't matter. The rank order can run in either direction. In average experience, it is one way: whether the sign be a social sign, such as a mode of dress, or a linguistic sign, such as a noun, when the mode of dress signifies class and the linguistic sign signifies a thing, class is higher than dress and the thing is higher than word. In the science of semiotics, the rank order runs the other way: the sign to some degree enables the signified. For semioticians, signs are higher and wield the power; they are the a priori of significa-tion. Whichever way it runs, semiosis is not essentially different in its value structure from mimesis, whose exclamation, "This is that," subordinates the mimetic image to the mimetized thing, the repre-sentation to the real. This is the perceived rank order when mimesis is functioning in average experience. In the science of "poetics," in contrast, mimesis is the higher power, the "first," an image, that picks out the "second," a real thing. Poetics or literary theory inverts the hierarchy, so that we sometimes say, yes indeed, the mimetic image is the condition for the thing itself. In both semiosis and mimesis, however, regardless of the direction that power flows, the pattern is similar. A near "this" subordinates itself to a far "that," or the reverse. A homeotic pair neither individuates nor subordinates. Its poles are coconstitutive, and still not the same, and not ordered by rank.

Note an important overlap between homeosis and semiosis and mimesis. A pair may be semiotically or mimetically near, even if spatially distant. This characteristic is even more pronounced in homeosis. Signs and images make their objects present, or that is the ideal outcome of the procedure. In other terms, more auspicious to likeness thinking, they bring far things near. The difference from homeotics becomes clear just here. Both signification and mimesis depend on the absence of their partners. Their power is weakened, their truth called into question, if the object itself appears. A likeness pair ignores space,[27] and yet its effect is not diminished if the things that are homeotically near are also physically near. Indeed, it may become more pronounced. Another way to say this is that mimesis and semiosis are constituted by the distinction between referent and object, while homeosis is constituted by the indistinction of the pair.

2.3. *A likeness happens where the poles of a pair become indistinct, where they support one another and abandon themselves. A likeness is in both resemblants and in neither.*

Every highly determinate thing, in other words, contains at least one point of indeterminacy, where it crosses over something else. At specific points, you can see right through one thing to another, and the reverse is also possible. Things become each other's medium without requiring a mystical "third." By extension, everything is potentially a medium for itself and for others, and that means also that no particular thing is mediatic in essence. What we call a medium may just be historically sensitive to homeoses; it may have made a habit of receptivity to traits of many other things. You could think of canvas and paint in this way, not to mention film and magnetic tape, and also writing and speaking.

From the perspective of things, likenesses are in them. From the perspective of likeness, things are nodes in a set of circuits, where likeness arrays approach one another; things are in the grip of multiple likenesses that spread their fingers well beyond them through the world. Because of this, it may help to suspend the perspective of things. This will also entail suspending questions about what things "contain" or are made up of, what they are in essence or in existence, as well as questions about their relations to other things and nonthings.

At first, when you make this *epoché* of ontology, you find that although a pair is the minimum unit for a likeness to come about and for a thing to constitute itself, there is no rule limiting likenesses to pairs. Likenesses fall into any multiple, into a circuit as long and circuitous as the history of carbon-based life or the color wheel or into an array as short-lived as an art movement or a single image. This seems like an empirical observation, but it is not. Two apples may overlap physically on a stem. A thousand, a million apples overlap in their traits, as do peaches, cherries, and so on. Soon you begin to intuit — let's call it resemblances permeating a multitude, a larger multitude of resemblances convoking a much smaller multitude of things. Now, however, the permeations themselves become targets of interest, starting points for a strange science — not a science of things, but a science of points where things almost coincide.

2.4. *Where likenesses are, things almost coincide. Likeness pairs are not pairs, but overlaps, and given that there is no limit to the number of overlaps at one trait, things and the traits that characterize them should be thought of as laminates, thicker points of the world.*

This means two things, really. First, as many things may overlap in one trait point as happen to do so. Further, a single trait that overlaps may be of any "size" — it may involve a whole "shape" or "form," a full body, a single simple idea, a complex of ideas and bodies, an epoch, or else it may take in a nuance of a color, one empirical nose, a stuttering question as it was asked, a mood that has no name. Do not think of traits as smallest indivisible units, as though they were atoms of experience. A trait has other traits as its traits. This does not mean that traits are infinite in the way space is, infinitely divisible.

2.4.1. *A trait, in order to be itself, refracts through itself a finite set of other traits, which constitute its character, and each of those constitutive traits is also made up of a finite set of arrangements or circuits.*

Moreover, traits that collaborate in a thing do not at all have to come from the same region of being. More than one region of being undoubtedly shows up in any one thing. A hammer shows the material trait "with handle" just as much as the social trait "for building." No doubt, these overlaps are truly bizarre. For once, you can say that the material is like the social, and the social like the material, without falling back on a causal or dialectical account. Further, the traits do not have to be spatially proximate, or even in related kinds of things. In red, an apple is intimate with blood, despite the skin barrier; in yellow, the sun approximates a sunflower, despite 150 million kilometers. When the spatial-exclusion engine is turned off, bizarre overlaps emerge. A homeotic view, as opposed to a phenomenological view, shows the interpenetration of strata to be fundamental. Overlaps, large and small, abrogate distance. The spatial expanse collapses at these points.

2.4.2.   *The likeness layer is spatially zero dimensional.*

Although it may be difficult to imagine a world without space — and certainly it is inconvenient for many beliefs — even where you want to continue intuiting things extended in space, the null dimension nonetheless shows up and begs to be counted. Homeosis carries on as if the law of space had been suspended. In every spatial intuition, there is a homeotic intuition as well.

Moreover, if you look again from the perspective of homeosis, space itself becomes a name for a quality of things — the quality by which things remain outside one another, despite their likenesses. And if you in fact turn this assumption around? If you dare to think of space as an effect of traits? Individuals are then concerned with one another, first and foremost, internally, where they overlap at thick points.

2.4.3.   *Thick points of the world can be called "traits," and traits happen in and through at least two.*

A troubling consequence of this thought is the following. In a world of independent things — toasters and dreams, dances and dragoons — that are homogenous within themselves, the problem of universals crops up. How can I justify claims about all things of a certain kind when my experience is always of this or that particular thing? Without fully separable things, however, in the null dimension, the homeotic layer, the world skin with qualitatively thick points does away with the problem of universals. If coffee cups overlap in cylinderness, say, if their shapes relate through likeness, and not through substance or idea or cause, then you may not have to tolerate the absurdity of a universal cylinder for our knowledge of cups.

2.5.   *In the likeness layer, circuits take up where universals used to be.*

In turn, a circuit is an artificially exploded view of a tightly packed homeotic overlap or interlap. I call it a "circuit" because it closes on itself, or almost. In any extension of the circuit, there is a reference to the starting point. Likenesses along a circuit go back around to the first, and the first to all the others, and so on. Thinking of cups, you could imagine one cup's handle as overlapping with another cup's handle and also overlapping with a nearby pot's handle, though in a different way and in different respects, and on and on around the panoply of the behandled cupboard of housewares, without losing the reference to the cup. You can envision these as connected around in a circuit, or you can see them as iterating out into a series.

2.5.1.   *A homeotic circuit has in mathematized ontological thinking sometimes been called a "series."*

How do resemblant elements relate to one another outside of things? A series is one answer — it was the answer given explicitly by amateur-turned-professional (and later denounced as quack) biologist Paul Kammerer, who adapted the series concept from evolution theory and extended it out beyond all reason to every type of experience.

His theory of series gives the most elaborated and rigorous picture of homeotic circuits.

Kammerer's reputation swung from the heights of fame and respectability to the nadir of discredit across his active work life, which began in 1902 and ended in 1926, when, in the midst of a public scandal, he killed himself. In his early career, Kammerer was simply good at breeding amphibians. An "Aquarianer," they called him. Since evolutionary theory — before and after the development of the modern synthesis — to its ongoing shame still cannot see natural selection directly, can only deduce it from premises and read it in remnants and traces, an experimentalist with success in the "vivarium" such as Kammerer could claim the attention of the day's leading theorists. William Bateson, for example, one of the early "synthesizers" of Darwin's macrotheory and Gregor Mendel's microtheory, followed Kammerer's results with interest, if also often with skepticism. No one had Kammerer's talent with salamanders. "Newts, lizards and toads," Arthur Koestler remarks in his book on Kammerer, could often be successfully bred for the study of heritable traits only by Kammerer himself. In 1971, Koestler made Kammerer his cause célèbre in *The Case of the Midwife Toad*, a book that defended the very last set of experiments, in which Kammerer finally demonstrated, or so he argued, the Lamarckian thesis: acquired traits are heritable. Heritable traits — this is a matter of homeosis, and it is also a matter of series.

Kammerer's evidence, it was discovered, had been faked. Kammerer insisted that a lab worker sabotaged the work,[28] but the scandal of Kammerer neither began with this debacle nor ended with Kammerer's suicide; it began much earlier, and developed more slowly, and still concerns us, not because of this late hoax or self-deception, but because in fact he made likeness a complete way of living and thinking.

Koestler recounts the life of Kammerer the researcher, complete with brushes with Viennese royalty. Alma Mahler was his assistant for a time, working with him on the molting habits of the praying mantis (*The Case of the Midwife Toad*, p. 20). However, the work was long and isolating, too long and too isolating for most to stand it. Fifteen years Kammerer devoted to proving Lamarckian inheritance (p. 25). Obsessively, he tracked organisms as they mated, as they laid their eggs, as the larvae developed, and as the organisms matured to reproductive age, generation after generation. His obsession was an intellectual crisis in slow motion. Along the way, he became more and more committed to the discredited theory, but this is less interesting. Peculiar desires and habits developed in Kammerer along the repetitive type of life. The pattern that took over, unlike the life patterns of his Viennese cultural consorts Mahler, Bruno Walter, and others, the pattern of attention tattooed onto him by his staccato practice, where perception gave itself again and again, in and out of years, in the closest of views, the smallest of doses, to miniscule divergences in essentially similar tiny bodies, drove him over the edge of evolutionary logic into homeotics.

Alongside his lab work, he kept a private ritual. Notebooks recorded mundane events, such as going to the opera, mentions in the newspaper, curious names overheard, odd encounters on the Vienna streets — events that showed the thinnest similarity to one another. He noted the phenomena down, categorized them, drew them out into longer and longer concatenations of echoes. Here is one in the category "numbers": "On June 15, 1912 I went to a concert at Beethoven Hall in Vienna and had a seat in the 18th row on the inside; on the very next day I sat in the great hall of the Musical Association, once again: the 18th row" (*Das Gesetz der Serie*, p. 24). Yellow dots on black salamanders at the Vivarium; words, names, gestures, numbers, personal correspondence, people, dreams, memories, accidents and deaths, and yes, seats in concert halls, along with other repeated events from his private life. You may call them "coincidences," but avoiding the slightest bent toward mysticism, Kammerer calls them "serial experiences [*seriale Erlebnisse*], which appeared before now to [the reader] as meaningless accidents [*nichts bedeutende Zufälle*]." He continues, in the book he wrote out of these private notebooks, *The Law of Series*: "From now on however he [*sic*] will learn to pay careful attention to them as the expression of a secret lawfulness within them [*als den Ausdruck einer darin verborgenen Gesetzmäßigkeit*]" (p. 35). Life was a honeycomb of unexpected similarities, and it produced the most sustained and thorough picture of the ways in which similarities form complex configurations.

2.5.2.   *Circuits are collapsible, and they also unroll. An unrolled circuit is a series.*

Why look at Kammerer and not at mainstream evolution science? A crackpot at the edge of a discipline says more about the discipline, about its limits and where they fall, and also about the secret desires and dreams that animate its middle-of-the-road practices and the most dearly held assumptions underlying them. Charlatans are not marginalized because they are totally mad, but because they reflect, in gross caricature, the real presuppositions that those in the center have almost forgotten, that they half-consciously intuit and prefer to keep hidden.

Belief in a "secret lawfulness" of phenomena is certainly not marginal. Such beliefs make up the *corpus mysticum* of any science, and the most sane scientists believe that the laws of nature are somewhere, somehow inscribed in the universe. Kammerer took an extreme position on this — no doubt less extreme in his own time, perhaps, but still well out of the mainstream. Through his laboratory work, he maintained the so-called "Lamarckian" position that acquired traits are heritable and added his codicil that experimental techniques can demonstrate this law by inducing it over time. He made sightless salamanders see (see the article "Dunkeltiere im Licht und Lichttiere im Dunkel," 1920), water-breeding salamanders breed on land, and land breeders breed in the water. He made — he said — these traits pass from generation to generation. Subtleties of variation normally trackable over great time periods became visible in only a few years, a time span in which an uncannily patient observer could make a career out of the findings.

They were more than findings, they were makings; more than makings, they were markers of a deep antipathy to mechanical explanations of evolution and, to add insult to injury, they had the makings of an inclination toward unnatural habits, a desire to free traits from natural kinds and allow them to live according to their own logic, with and also beyond Darwinian constraints of selection and adaptation. His amphibians are less experiments in breeding than living canvases, skin dabbed with spots by laboratory techniques and time, dark animals made light, light ones made dark, eyes drawn out where they hadn't been, and what's most unusual, all this so that the alterations would enter into the hereditary line and contrive an unseen species.

Any systematic work on likeness should take seriously Kammerer's attack on the division of the scholarly disciplines in *The Law of the Series*. He wields one weapon in the idiosyncratic "battle of the faculties" that crosses the book: the series itself. Series cut across modes of knowing, sciences, types of experience. The theory of series describes the shapes, classifies the kinds, and maps the spreading scopes of all the series as they cross — and disregard — the disciplines. To do this, it relies on two general, root modes of association among members of series that apply to all experience. These are *Gleichheit* and *Ähnlichkeit* — "equivalence" (in the mathematical sense of substitutability without loss) and "likeness." It is clear from the beginning, however, that although *Ähnlichkeit* might appear as a degraded form of *Gleichheit*, to Kammerer, being "equivalent" to something means putting likeness to work in a particular way. In the theory of series, equivalence is a function of likeness. And he adds a third term to the duo "like" and "equivalent"; that is "repeat." "About since the beginning of the century I have known that events that are equivalent in type and alike in appearance like to repeat themselves [*gleichartige und ähnliche Ereignisse sich gern wiederholen*]" (p. 19). Events in daily life are "gleichartig oder sehr ähnlich," "equivalent or very alike" (p. 20), and so they repeat themselves, or they repeat themselves and so they are equivalent or alike.

Which term is primary, repetition or likeness? A note on the figure "repetition": Kammerer uses it again and again, alongside likeness and equivalence, yet it is a pleonasm to say, "the equivalent and the like repeat themselves." We are accustomed to critiques of metaphysics that replace substance with repetition. But what is repetition except the happening of likeness? Throughout the book, Kammerer remains ambivalent about this obvious fact, as though the two, likeness and repetition, were . . . twins that cannot be separated. Indeed, it is true, the two are not the same, and they are unrecognizable without one another. Shall I say that the two are alike and they do not simply repeat each other?

2.5.3.   *Although it is supposed to explain how the real, how objects, how things physical and metaphysical happen, exist, "are" temporally, repetition is nevertheless an ontological parasite on likenesses.*

A fixation of European philosophy in the nineteenth and twentieth centuries — *répétition, Wiederholung, Gjentagelsen* — and now a common tool of critical theory, repetition supports the drive, with Europe since at least the baroque, to question the coherence of things and the consistency of events in history and experience; this is why it has been so popular. Repetition challenges ontology, but from within it. It is ontology's phoenix, rising out of the ashes of Aristotle. Whether in Kierkegaard's, Nietzsche's, Blanqui's, or Heidegger's versions, whether existential, psychological, cosmic, or hermeneutic, this view says: entities are constituted by their doubles; they are dependent on their past or on their future and in reality on both; the substantial spatiotemporal continuum is a fantasy; things and events are constituted through self-difference.

To be sure, repetition breaks the consistency of reality, makes continuity into a fantasy of metaphysicians, and yet . . . arguments from repetition continue to assume the primacy of beings, situations, events — individuals that could repeat and in repeating differ. The ontological picture is: even when repetition is constitutive of things, situations, or events, entities are still the primary unit and goal. The beauty of Kammerer's grand theory of series is that at key moments, he gives up this remnant of ontology for a provisory homeotics. He does say, tentatively—though with the force of insistence that only a private, personal, intimate experience can have—that "samenesses and likeness like to repeat," "sich gern wiederholen." Likenesses of different intensities come again seemingly by a will of their own. "Liking," a pleasure taken in something or a tendency or inclination toward ("gern") something, in this case toward likeness, is one of Kammerer's ways of saying that likenesses proliferate without cause. Likenesses go on on their own, and you experience them as if they, not you, were the agents of your experience. In contrast to repetition, which relays an entity through time and space, likenesses don't stop in entities, even if here and there they should traverse a being. Series keep rolling, undiminished, before and after the thing.

2.6. *Series proliferate; they depart from one another, return to themselves and cross others, dissipate, regroup, mirror, and scatter to such a degree that there is no such thing as a single series.*

Or so Kammerer proposes. There is no entity, least of all one that could repeat. Further, there is not even a single series. "If it is right to say that serial aggregations present something lawful or regular, it follows from this that the concept of a 'single series' is arbitrary—that the 'simple series' can only be a small excerpt of the uninterrupted cascade [*Folge*] of a total serial happening [*serialen Gesamtgeschehen*]" (*Das Gesetz der Serie* p. 55).

2.6.1. *The basic homeotic relationship will not be mereological, that is, the basic units of analysis will not be parts and wholes, but "Serie," "Folge," and the "seriales Gesamtgeschehen"—the "sum of all happening series." Label these in English "sequence," "consequence," and "persequence."*

A persequence is the kind of series that troops through all the other series, the total happening of all series in and through one another. In contrast, a consequence is what you can call a set of overlaps between two or more simple series. "Consequence" names the intercalation of a finite set of series. Finally, as if a single series could exist on its own, there is a heuristic category, a provisional name for a never-existing single object, the sequence.

Picture a tree of life, an evolutionary tree, one of Ernst Haeckel's — the monophyletic tree of organisms (Figure 2). The twig *Reptilia* is a sequence, a branch with multiple twigs, say *Vertebrata*, is a consequence, and the whole tree is a persequence of life.

The order of interaction among these fundamental homeotic units — sequence, consequence, persequence — is worth examining. From an evolutionist's perspective, sequence would precede consequence and consequence would precede persequence. You say: the tree is nothing without its branches, the branches nothing without their twigs; ultimately it is made out of twigs, a collection of twigs and their causal or quasi-causal relations. For Kammerer and for us, however, the converse is the case.

2.6.2. *All happening series are the* **conditio sine qua non** *for any single series, and thus the individuality of any series is arbitrary and artificial. A series gets broken out of the All for analytical purposes, but the proper attitude toward series is synthetic.*

It is simply an oversight that there are no codified synthetic techniques for a synthetic homeotics. Himself at times a victim of this oversight, Kammerer proceeds in a pseudoanalytical manner. He breaks the total series into pieces, falsely, for the purposes of demonstration, while here and there he touches on operations that could belong to a synthetic technique he cannot yet anticipate.

His intuition is cause for alarm. If series are constant, proliferating, in complex ways descending and ascending straight and diagonal and radiating through other series, what kind of "law" of series can be inferred? The reasoning seems circular or very close to circular. Any series, in order to happen, to stand out, to call for a continuation, for reaction, convergence or divergence, is preceded and underpinned by the happening of all series. In other words, the persequence is deduced from the way a single sequence proceeds, and then it can be assumed that the persequence drives this single sequence with all the others. Yet the reasoning is not circular at all, according to the law of series.

2.6.3.   *A series is by definition not sufficient unto itself and tries to make up for this by furthering itself in multiple dimensions. A series is not a closed figure, in geometric terms. Itself so long as it keeps happening, as ongoing serializing, as a thing that cannot get its elements only from itself, the total series happens in all directions at once.*

If you grant that persequence precedes consequence and sequence, how should you then describe the elements of a series, which Kammerer calls alternatively "Merkmale" or "Querelemente," "traits" or "transverse elements" (*Das Gesetz der Serie*, p. 58)? Here, homeosis and its peculiar sense of order takes center stage. Elements of a series depend on likenesses to be themselves; an element is an element in view of its likeness to its precedent and antecedent, as well as to its bilateral and diagonal siblings, and at the same time in view of some likeness to the ongoing series, the total series happening. Each element is a member of multiple series, and this multiplicity makes it like a series. In the order I have described, a single series occurs as an element in a series of series, and that in turn in and through a totally unfolding series. In a similar way, what Kammerer calls a "Querelement" gets its status as an element from its triangulation among multiple series.

2.6.4.   *A series element occupies an inimitable locale between other elements. Nonetheless, the element is an element in and through*

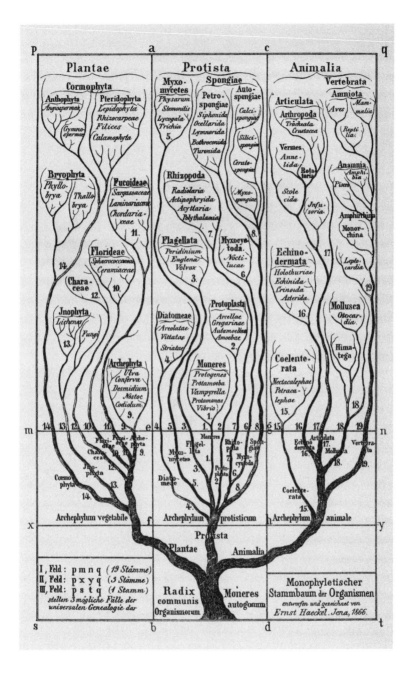

Figure 2. Ernst Haeckel, *Allgemeine Entwickelungsgeschichte der Organismen*, vol. 2 of *Generelle morphologie der organismen: Allgemeine Grundzüge der Organischen Formenwissenschaft, mechanisch begründet durch die von Charles Darwin reformirte descendenztheorie* (Berlin: G. Reimer, 1866), p. 463. Public domain, available from the Biodiversity Heritage Library, https://biodiversitylibrary.org/page/15099620.

a series, while the series gets its character from the coseries, and coseries get their status from perseries, insofar as perseries are no more and no less than the echoes happening among the furthering coseries.

Given this picture, analysis is a particularly bad method; there are no proper parts, and there is no proper place to begin cutting this or that element out of its row. Note that for a series, the regularity of internal relations is merely formal; regularity of contents is never proposed — it is not even possible.

2.6.5. *Series must happen, that is, they cannot merely repeat as though there were a law driving them onward, as though they had to (by law) serialize in like ways, which means also that their ways are never the same. Serial likeness happens on a bend or twist, more than along a straight line.*

The only thing uniform about the perseries is the overflowing, twisting serializing happening. That is why *regularity* of contents is impossible. *Geschehen,* happening, is a word that Kammerer uses often and that makes the difference between his theory of likeness and any realism, or for that matter any antirealism. The perseries should not be confused with a thing that exists, an object of possible knowledge for a subject, an agglomeration of independent entities (realia of the real), or a semiosphere, a set of signifying substitutions. The through series is not uniform; it is entirely dependent on continuing to happen, and series happen into the next echo, and the next series, and the series next to them, each of which can be said to refer to every other in some way without being in the least substitutable for them. Nor are series a matter of counting repetitions or of a merely additive notion of cumulation (although Kammerer sometimes uses the word "Häufung," "accumulation" (*Das Gesetz der Serie,* p. 24); they are much less a question of their form (as repetition, as heap) than a question of their contents; a series is what precisely happens when something happens, not the form of happening or seriality per se. This fact protects likeness from incursions of transcendence.

2.6.6.   *The law of series is a law of contents.*

This is to say, it doesn't matter that a reptile comes *after* a fish on some evolutionary sequence, but it does matter that a *reptile* comes after a fish, as opposed to something else. This is because reptile comes also *before* something else that depends on its specific way of happening after fish, and not on the mere formal fact that something comes after fish or that the sequence must continue by some external necessity. What matters is the specific conjunction of traits that are available for variation and that actually vary.

There is a mathematical definition of series that is intertwined with the foundations of number theory. From mathematics, borrow the axiom that no number is really independent — an individual ordinal can't be thought outside its series. And yet the most common formal definition of a mathematical series, "the sum of a sequence," stands far from Kammerer's definition, which says that "de[r] Begriff der Serie," "the concept of a series" is "a next to one another or after one another of equal or like occurrences [*gleicher oder ähnlicher Begebenheiten*] apparently without any cause that continues to influence them collectively [*ohne gemeinsam fortwirkende Ursache*]" (*Das Gesetz der Serie*, p. 24). Unlike the mathematical series, the homeotic series is not arithmetic — it has no sum, which means it cannot be seen as the function of a whole. A series is not a series because its elements are all alike in the same way — not, that is, to say it again, for formal reasons. Rather, each element is like its antecedent and successor, its twisted sisters and its traitorous brethren. Likeness happens locally to contents in a relation of "next to."

2.6.7.   *Events are not alike because they are next to one another, they are "next to" one another because they are like, and being like knows no "because."*

A Kammererian series rejects the logic of causality, which might look like it produces series, but in fact does not. Tradition is with you if you think of causes as linked up in a chain. Hume uses the chain figure often, and importantly, he uses it to explain how distant objects act on one another. "Tho' distant objects may sometimes seem productive of each other, they are commonly found upon examination to be link'd by a chain of causes, which are contiguous among themselves, and to the distant objects" (*Treatise*, 1.3.2, p. 54). The figure "chain" gives causality an image in which contiguity is allied with dependency. One link touches another, yes, but never contingently, by a mere touching; they touch under a robust constraint. No single link can on its own free itself from the touch that connects it to its partners. The kind of contiguity here is close to necessity — each link depends on the previous and is depended upon by the subsequent. Thus, "chain" also implies something that physical chains don't imply: transmission of effect. Contiguity, dependency, plus the added transmission of effect — the figure of a chain encodes several conflicts inherent in the idea of cause in modern thought. One of these conflicts is the wish for a moving chain, as fixed as it is motile, as responsive as it is dead and settled.

To deny flat out that there is action across distance contradicts our experience. On the other hand, to deny direct action at a distance has been necessary for counteracting occultism, Neoplatonism, idealism, and other modes of thinking. Distant objects are not supposed to work on one another directly, abrogating the space between. One modern concept of cause reconciled the need for action across a distance and disbelief in direct action that did not take distance into account — Hume's. Despite his skepticism about the reality of cause, Hume maintains that major things must be connected through a continuum of minor contiguities.

If you could break down the distance into intervening steps, if you found that a larger causal unit was made up of many smaller causal units, it would become easier to think action across a distance for everyday affairs, natural science included. This assumes that smaller causal units can be explained more easily than bigger ones. Hume's contribution to philosophy was to show that this is a deception, since you can never see or feel cause, no matter how small or how local (*Treatise*, 1.3.2, p. 53). Nevertheless, even at his most skeptical, Hume proposes that you substitute "constant conjunction" for causality, since that is all human consciousness can ascertain. Throughout, he maintains that what is conjoined constantly also has to have contiguity — the big expanses that conjunction traverses, such as between a planet and a moon, have to be divided into smaller conjunctions contiguous with one another.

Despite his skepticism about necessity, Hume denies there is anything in the universe that is not either a cause or the effect of a cause (*Treatise*, 1.3.2, p. 53). In the same breath, he asserts the priority of cause over effect, settling the question of time's arrow with a stroke (1.3.2, p. 54). But direction is not derivable from the figure of a chain — one-way succession has to be projected onto it, for a chain travels both ways. A further problem is that while "causal chain" is supposed to represent a series of minor individual causal events that make up a major event, Hume will never give up the intuition, which he says derives from experience, that no event can happen without a cause, including the causal chain itself, and so each causal chain, each major event and the minor, contiguous events that make it up, must be the effect of a cause. Causal chains don't spring up out of nothing from nowhere. Indeed, you or I cannot operate without the belief that a causal chain has an original cause, the cause of its continuity, so to speak. If there were no common cause for the sequence as such, "every link of the chain wou'd in that case hang upon another; but there wou'd not be any thing fix'd to one end of it, capable of sustaining the whole" (1.3.5, p. 59).

Turn now from Hume to Kammerer. Pivotal for the articulation of Kammerer's theory is the difference between a cause and a law, that is, between a chain and a series. Although Kammerer's book is indeed full of chain metaphors, he often strains the link between the chain image and causality. He stretches the already thin connection between chains and sequences: "wie an Stichworten der dramatische Dialog, spinnt sich an jenen Durchgangselementen die seriale Kette weiter"; "Upon the channeling elements, like the keywords of a dramatic dialogue, the serial chain spins its thread onward" (*Das Gesetz der Serie*, p. 58). A spinning chain (p. 58), a repeating chain (p. 104), a chain in which a single link "calls forth" the next (p. 105), a chain "of" imitation events (p. 134), a chain with "repulsive tendencies" (p. 161) — these are some of the chain images, clearly in tension with themselves, that Kammerer deploys. In this way, he imitates the chain image in order to bring it in line with the law of series, which does not have a causal logic. As also is the case in modern philosophy, where Aristotle's final cause and other types of causes fall one by one out of the reckoning,[29] the common word for "cause," *Ursache*, for Kammerer — means "efficient cause," which is often demonstrated through an analogy with colliding impenetrable bodies. The influential image of knocking billiard balls Kammerer also deploys, but he evacuates it, too, and turns it to another purpose, using it to describe "Verähnlichung," "making like" (p. 130).

Kammerer clings to the old metaphors for causality, chain and billiards, in part because a great worry haunts the book. With the law of series, either he fears he has done away with efficient causality or else, almost in revenge for the grave damage done to cause by the series idea, he fears causality will come back to take revenge on him. In effect, you could say it did. His death was the revenge of the ghost of causality. *Ursache* is the bane of Kammerer's imagination, the ideal of his better judgment, the elusive link in Lamarckian theory. Amid this crisis in fundamental principles, he nevertheless refuses to give in to easy metaphysical ideas of cause — he is like Hume in this — and, astonishingly, he then also refuses many empirical ideas of cause, as well. He plans to avoid at all costs settling for a "lifeless mechanism" (*Das Gesetz der Serie*, p. 43) underlying series. Where some causal theories, like Hume's presumably, are too mechanical, others lack all ties to mechanics and float in the air. Kammerer plans to avoid equally assiduously any supersensible cause for serial occurrences. The empiricist loves a lifeless mechanism; the metaphysician "dawdles in cloud-cuckoo-land of a mystical exceptional position of the human being in the all" (p. 52). A thought revolution happens in the phrase: "like occurrences... without a continuing efficient cause influencing the members collectively," "ohne gemeinsam fortwirkende Ursache" (p. 24). Like any real revolution in thought, it went virtually unnoticed.

As if to reassure himself that he wasn't just mad, Kammerer formulates variations of this important thought again and again:

> In light of the foregoing examples and groups of examples the series (multiplicity of cases) presents itself as a lawful repetition of same or like things and events [*gleicher oder ähnlicher Dinge und Ereignisse*], a repetition (a heaping up [*Häufung* — a mere accumulation]) in time or space whose individual cases, to the extent that diligent investigation can reveal, cannot be concatenated through the same cause with continuing influence among them collectively [*nicht durch dieselbe, gemeinsam fortwirkende Ursache verknüpft sein konnen*]. (*Das Gesetz der Serie*, p. 36)

With this statement, the chain of cause is definitively broken. An originary, motivating cause that instaurates a series and continues to maintain it, transmitted from one link to another, has no place in the law of series. A series is without common cause and thus without continuous effects transmitted along the reticulate body of the chain that could be traced to a single source. Later, Kammerer returns and adds force to the break with the chain: "We will discuss in this chapter possibilities that present themselves for explaining an apparently causelessly and nevertheless also not accidentally connected return of the same [or "the like"] [*scheinbar ursachenlos und trotzdem auch zufallslos verbundene Wiederkehr des Gleichen*]" (p. 93). Many cherished clichés are dispensed within these lines. Accident, cause's shadow since at least Aristotle, is no longer viable as a conceptual counterpart to causality.

2.6.8. *The modern paradigm of causality as efficient causality is incompatible with seriality.*

When Hume describes cause by saying "like effects necessarily follow from like causes" (*Treatise*, 1.3.15, p. 117), no one should be surprised at the need to include likeness at the core of the definition. If the effects of one cause are not like the effects of a like cause in a different instance, causality does not hold up. And yet this Humean description of causality takes likeness to mean "the same" and implies an immediate contiguity and transmission of effect consistent with repetition, not, however, with the series idea. Where causality is not appropriate for explaining seriality, repetition is not sufficient to make up a series.

A touchstone book for Kammerer, *Die Gleichförmigkeit in der Welt* (Uniformity in the world) by the *Denkpsychologe* Karl Marbe, offers an unremarkable formulation that apes Hume, except that it already takes a small step away from efficient cause: "among similar immediate conditions, similar things happen," — "unter ähnlichen unmittelbaren Bedingungen findet ähnliches statt" (p. 16). Marbe's formulation sidesteps causality and substitutes conditionedness, but it does not go far enough toward a unique theory of series to propose its own type of motivation.

What would it mean to explain the evolution of plants and animals by the law of series, rather than on causal principles or even on conditions of determination? Without a cause, how does a series begin, and where does it end? Its meaning or explanation has to be found not in a beginning or an ending, but in some other aspect of it. What, then, is the basic unit? Where would the value fall in such a picture? What can you or I hope to know or achieve with it?

2.7.   *To ripple over into a series, likenesses shun a single efficientlike cause whose "push" communicates across the series to each of its members, as though the members somehow formed a chain with a single attachment point or a tree with a common root.*

Thinking that there is an originating cause that communicates itself to all points in a series treats them as a group, not a series. This would be a mystical view. A good example of this is Haeckel's evolutionary tree of life. To his credit, you can say without error that Haeckel does try to depict what Kammerer calls the "ostensibly causeless being alongside one another and shared progression of the homeotic," the "anscheinend ursachenlose Beisammensein und Zusammenverlauf des Gleichartigen" (*Das Gesetz der Serie*, p. 96). Yet Kammerer is unwilling to attribute a shared cause for the series of nature, even one that gets communicated along a forking path, for this would turn the persequential all into a chain of causes or a tree shape. A homeotic tree has roots in the air. With biting wit, Kammerer says that attributing the rootless proliferation to a single root or cause would be like imposing "an orderliness willed by god that placed similar things somehow in similar shelves like a salesman lays out his wares, so he can get to them quickly" (p. 96). Not to be missed in this sentence is Kammerer's resistance to ontology, which he sees as a fire sale of creation: if it was worth creating to begin with, it would not be so orderly, uniform, and disposable.

2.7.1.　*A series is, by its law, a tree that buds outward from any point in any direction.*

To maintain the purity of the series law, to keep it separate from any interference from other laws and other modes than law, subtract two other possible explanations: accident, on one side, and superstition, on the other. Series, as I said, happen, according to one law, the multifocal, intercalary radiation of persequence. To Kammerer, these other noncausal explanations for happening, accident and superstition, lie outside the general law of seriality and have to be understood as forms of a will to know the future. In this one regard, natural science and common experience are siblings; "the ultimate goal of all scientific and popular collection of experiences: both want to predict the future and where possible control it in advance [*vorhersagen und womoglich vorausbeherrschen*]" (*Das Gesetz der Serie*, p. 331). In a late chapter on series and superstition, the argument about superstition is less that science supersedes it than that superstition precedes and prefigures science. Natural sciences operate on a similar model as superstition, just with a different standard of observation. Your neighbor says, "Spider in the morning brings care and woe," "Spinne am Morgen bringt Kummer und Sorgen" (p. 337); a researcher says that a spider spins a web anew each night in order to catch its fill the next day. If you want some certainty about what will happen tomorrow, ask your neighbor or a scientist, depending on your predilection.

Kammererian uncause is of a different order than accident or superstition.

2.7.2.   *Under the law of series, a nonforce actively refuses to allow change, actively deactivates causes, makes way for a nonprogressive element to transfer a retarding drift outward on a ring of ripples.*

Kammerer likes the metaphor of waves (*Das Gesetz der Serie*, pp. 114 and 120) to image transit without real change. Unlike a chain of caused events, the "allgemeine[s] Beharrungsvermögen," "the general capacity to persist" (p. 19), occasions pluriform undulations of virtually endless interaction — movements of likenesses that at the same time dig in their heels, *sich beharren.* If they didn't have this tendency to retard, likenesses would drift too swiftly and too completely.

2.7.3.   *The two main principles in the law of series are persequentiality (only the happening entirety is real) and holding on, retarding (Kammererian uncause).*

Likeness is more than enough to occasion a huge array of series types, shapes, and outcomes, arrangements of such internal and external variety as to require, in order to keep track of them, a schema of Sibylline intricacy. Kammerer has already argued that the *Ähnlichkeitskosmos* operates from the point of highest complexity and fullest undulation downward and inward, and also outward, too. You cannot distinguish the outward from the inward movement — in a likeness cosmos, direction is elusive. Series proliferate in space, as well as in time. At the most schematic level, there should be no distinction between space and time under the law of series, which have many more dimensions than these two alone. Yet Kammerer is never quite clear whether time is the standard for seriality, with space the standard for time, insofar as time is thought of on the metaphor of points on a line (*nacheinander* deriving metaphorically from *nebeneinander*), or whether space is the standard for seriality, with time the standard for space, insofar as the proliferation of series happens temporally (*nebeneinander* deriving from *nacheinander*) on an intuition of substitution. He treats the two, space (under time, simultaneity of sequence elements) and time (under space, contiguity of sequence elements), as coeval, and yet he always insists that series happen in space and time, as though spacetime and seriality could be distinct issues.

Take note of his ambivalence and hesitation about the priority of seriality over spacetime. What is time, if not a special series, analytically, and perhaps falsely, excerpted from the persequent spread and thus not a particularly special series after all—a fabricated master series with no more real privilege to act as a standard than any other? What is space, if not this also? By his own argument, the law of series prevents any single series from claiming a more privileged status than any other. In short, from the perspective of persequent seriality, space and time cannot remain special standards. Further, it also has to be true that seriality, by the law of it, is the vehicle for time, though Kammerer assiduously avoids this conclusion (*Das Gesetz der Serie*, p. 296). Under the law of series, time and space are two *Ähnlichkeitsserien* among others and lose their status as guidelines for what happens. If the law is taken seriously, space and time are an effect of series, rather than series' vehicles.

2.7.4.   *Spacetime fuses out of multiple axes of the persequent series, which is atemporal and nonspatial.*

There are not just two axes to persequence; its dimensionality is high, perhaps unlimited.

Kammerer provides a host of names for many dimensions of seriality. The first name he gives is "higher order." A simple series, if you abstract it and examine it analytically for a moment, gives rise to series of higher orders, which are potentially infinite, though in actuality, each eventually "breaks off," as Kammerer puts it, and the point at which a series breaks off is determined by a likeness factor endogenous to the series. At some not predetermined point, a secondary series no longer registers as like the primary series, from some perspective. At some point, the members of a series fall too far from one another on some scale.

2.8.   *Series are not effects of contiguity, but rather of proximity. Likeness holds sway in nearness. Over a field of nearnesses, likenesses precess until at some point they become unrecognizable.*

What is a "higher-order" series? Consequent series derived from a (fictional) first sequent series are named by Kammerer "higher-order series." The relationship of derivation or inclusion defines the ordinality of series. A higher-order series takes one or more of the elements of a lower-order series as the basis for building its own single or multiple series, making oblique reference to the lower series, in effect proceeding from it. Three traits (*Merkmale*), a, b, c, produce a series: $\{a, b, c\}$, $\{a2, b2, c2\}$, $\{a3, b3, c3\}$. Each of three portraits of Holy Roman emperors, say, carries a, an imperial insignia, b, a suit top with broad epaulettes, and c, eyes held in a faraway gaze. None of the three portraits yet makes a series of higher order. Once each of these traits gives rise to further series, however — $\{a4, d1, e1\}$, $\{a5\ldots\}$, $\{b4, f1, g1\}$, $\{b5\ldots\}$, $\{c4, h1, i1\}$, $\{c5\ldots\}$ — another imperial insignia ($a4$) transplanted onto a carriage ($d1$) with a driver in a red cap ($e1$); another suit with broad epaulettes ($b4$), on a soldier ($f1$), at attention ($g1$); and so on — here is that higher order. When portraits of princes and governors arise with their own insignia; when the nobility take on the style of wearing the broadest royal epaulettes; when merchants and court Jews commission images of themselves with faraway gazes, then a second-order series comes into its own (*Das Gesetz der Serie*, p. 58).

"Higher-power series," "Series höher Potenz," are different than higher-order series. "Higher power" describes the exponential enlargement of the persequent series through a movement to higher-order series (*Das Gesetz der Serie*, p. 61). A series of three three-trait groups in the first order gives rise, in the second order, to three series of three three-trait groups, and so the second order series are also third-power series of the third power. Power is the potency of a series to give rise to other series; the number of series it gives rise to is its potency. Thus the third order of these coseries has a power of six. According to Kammerer's explanation, orders develop linearly, powers geometrically. Whereas the relationship of order is one of derivation of series from "individual" elements, the relationship of power is one of unfolding series from the total number of elements in a lower series.

Members of a series are not coincident — that needs to be emphasized — and they are also not contiguous, like entities in the sway of causes and effects. What makes them proximal and neither coincident nor contiguous are the elements of other series that interrupt and articulate them. Other series donate the "in-between elements," the *Zwischenglieder* of higher-order series, through an interweaving of pulsing lines of recurrence. One series *a*, *b*, *c* donates an "*a*" element, while other series donate a "*d*" and an "*e*." Divergence of a series is not a matter of internal change, out of some inherent motivation, but a result of intercalating radiating channels of other series. Divergence of series is at the same time convergence of series. Radials take up and drop *Querelemente*, Kammerer's name, as mentioned, for the transversal elements — elements that cannot be separated from their place in a radiating set of contentful proximities — cutting across higher-power series in extraordinary arabesques while continuing to recur until they break off in other series.

In addition to series order and series power, Kammerer makes another important distinction and gives another set of names. There are "morphological series" and there are "functional series." To a morphological series, the elements are members, *Glieder*. To a functional series, the transversal elements are mere correlatives, and the seriality is merely functional. Take as an example the recurrence of the word "fish" across several contexts. "Fish," the semantic unit, is a member of a series. You see fish on a menu, hear someone say "fish" to a friend on the street, and watch a TV documentary about salmon. Or you find the same element in an evolutionary series: jawless fish, armored fish, jawed fish, lobe-finned fish, and finally, let's say, going over to tetrapods. No doubt this series ends in a transitional element, the four-legged fish, whose resemblance to its supposed predecessor, Agnatha, is stretched to a limit. Recognition of the proximity of "fishapods" to earlier chordates depends on the frame of reference; nevertheless, for Kammerer, all these fish and almost fish are all equally *Glieder*. They are in a single series and in multiple series as members. Their membership is based on the same relation to their context; they signify fish. They belong to their series on the basis of a shared signification.

Functional correlatives, in contrast, accompany all morphological series, but they do not generate series on their own. Consider a morphological series in which B follows A, and AB follows A and B. In the functional series that accompanies it, also called "correlative" or "concatenational series" (*Korrelationsserie* or *Verknüpfungsserie*) (*Das Gesetz der Serie*, p. 65), notice, for example, that in the variable A, the trait "acute angle" comes along for the ride, and yet the upper point of the capital letter "A" makes up a series element only inessentially. Angularity is essential to the letter formally, but not essential to it serially. Functional series are sterile.

Take another example. In the recurrence of the word "fish" in various contexts, a correlational series would be the letters "f," "i," "s," "h" — without which the word couldn't come to be and which is not, however, to Kammerer's thinking, a meaningful part of the series of occurrences of "fish." I will come back to "mere correlation" and the metaphysics of membership to which Kammerer remains partisan, despite the fact that his own arguments often mitigate against this view. From his conflicted perspective, the kind of likeness that builds up the word "fish" and its repetitions is not of the same rank as the likeness that builds a series of mentions of fish; semantic series are higher than syntactic series; real series are higher than unreal series. Syntactic likenesses thus continue to be underappreciated — Kammerer certainly notices them, and yet he diminishes them, admits them, then denies them a lawful place, even though there is no doubt that in fact, higher series all depend in some way on "meaningless" elements in what he terms "unreal series." In all instances, real series come out of unreal series, as German words come out of the German alphabet, arguably in a way that is at least as essential as series of meanings. It may even be the case that in reference to the series "letters," the series "words" are its higher-order and higher-power series.

Why, then, are the letters "f," "i," "s," "h" not meaningful members of the series of fishes? Mark for now Kammerer's recognition of the existence of unreal series, series without true membership, but still true series. He parses this also as a difference in the way transversal elements have of being proximate to one another. Members are proximal to one another by "attraction." Correlatives are proximal only by "affinity" (*Das Gesetz der Serie*, p. 66); membership brings consequent series into proximity in a more unavoidable way, while correlations are not sufficient to bring about higher series, and so another name for them might be "deficient series." Yet you don't have to accept the difference in the quality of series, as Kammerer describes them, the difference between attraction and affinity, in this case, as a difference in the relative value or truth of series. They are both series, as Kammerer acknowledges, and so they can be taken not as opposed, or higher and lower, but as elements in a series of series types.

2.8.1. *A truly homeotic view denies the existence of series ranks.*

So far, I have tried to sketch, in line with Kammerer, the generative activities of series, to understand how series produce other series according to their special law. In addition to the larger movements, however, the law of series has to account for the local variations within which likenesses light up. Within every larger musical composition, smaller tunes are playing. Kammerer calls these "metameric series." Real series do not have parts, but they do have locales or motifs that embroider patterns across them. To recognize a motif, cut out any segment and superimpose it upon another thus: *xy xy xy z* | *xy xy xy z*. In a "bilateral series," one type of metameric series, motifs mirror one another for a span in this way: *xy* | *yx*, or *xy xy xy z* | *z yx yx yx*. Metameric series tell you how a smaller segment or motif behaves in a series, giving you the mode of membership. Further, in addition to motifs (likenesses within limited variations), which are a form of "articulated membership" (*Gliedrigkeit*), another aspect of real series is "rowedness" (*Reihigkeit*). Any later likeness may display one, two, three, or more matching transversal elements. The number of like traits in series makes up its rowedness. When you see one child here, there a second child, there a third child, this series has a rowedness of one. When you see a woman with a green parrot on a bus here, there a second woman with a green parrot on a bus, there a third woman with a green parrot on a bus, this series has a rowedness of two (*Das Gesetz der Serie*, pp. 61–62).

Seriality is therefore at least septidimensional, reaching vectorially out into time and space, order, power, articulated membership, correlation, and rowedness. Then there is "polytomy," which transects almost all these serial dimensions (p. 63), an effect of higher power series in relation to one another. Athwart the "straight" series, likenesses crop up in relation to one another, occasioned not by the sequential proximity of members, not by reflection, you could say, but by refractions that arise only in parallel. Except for correlation, which is internal to seriality and yet somehow also external to it, the other six dimensions are equally liable to polytomy.

Throughout his disquisition on the dimensions of series, Kammerer is careful to emphasize that the relationships between series shapes are not in any way categorial. Series extend into what can be called "dimensions," but they do not fit into categories. Moreover, higher-order series do not contain or define primary series, and primary series do not subsume under or somehow "constitute" higher-order or higher-power series, as if from below.

2.8.2. *Series happen and their contents depend on what precedes, their form on what succeeds.*

You can see the dependence of the content and form of series on precedence and succession by looking at a single element from two perspectives. From the perspective of the antecedent, when an echo of an element occurs in another element, it can be said to follow the preceding because of its contents. From the perspective of the subsequent, when an element carries along a prior element, it can be said to continue the series in terms of the sequential form. Do not forget that the form of sequentiality in each and every case depends on the content that happens. If the content does not happen, which is perfectly likely, the form does not happen. That is to say, as well, the content and the form of series both hang on the vicinity in which any node happens, where likeness ripples outward and inward until the whole happening can be called the vicinity for any single series. Kammerer reminds us: "the course of a series empowers itself from the entire stream of happening," "der Serialverlauf sich des ganzen Stromes des Geschehens bemächtigt" (*Das Gesetz der Serie*, p. 60). Kammerer may be wrong to use such transcendental language here, the language of "empowering" and priority, since formally, the whole precedes the parts, and contentfully, the element and the series precede the whole, and yet formally, too, these are not parts; the whole is a "stream," and the only effect that is conditioned by the stream is the likelihood of more currents. Kammerer sums this up:

> To our eyes, whether it embraces the tables in this book or reality, the stream of serial happening appears, furthermore, to roll out [*wälzen*] widthwise, progressively increasing; effectively, it incorporates almost uninterruptedly the full breadth and depth of being. Since what we have called a simple series is nothing other than our own conceptual abstraction: the "departure series" [*Ausgangserie*] is first of all only an arbitrarily seized excerpt of being; second of all, it is a stage in the entire series succession that in no way exists at the actual beginning — but rather a stage into which the already countless preceding single series and series successions discharge. (p. 60)

A more definitive statement of the homeotic challenge to ontology is hard to find. Instead of an order of priority, transcendentality, Kammerer gives stages that issue into one another as if in looped flows, serially discharging and recharging with different contents. Instead of beings, there are interlocking stages that cannot be separated from one another. Here is a picture of the breadth and depth — "die volle Breite und Tiefe" (p. 60) — of being, which is to say that the empirical and the transcendental dimensions of being fall within the likeness array. In this way, a transseries cuts across ontological regions, not only the transcendental and the empirical, the a priori and the a posteriori, but also the tables in the book and entities in reality. This also underscores the fact that for us, circuits need not form up into a total confusion. Series are articulated and staged, flowing and flowing in specific directions, multidimensional, and even though any delimited dimension — rowedness, say, or polytomy — may evoke echoes across dimensions through others, a dimension is delimitable in the way that all homeotic phenomena are finite. The verb Kammerer uses here is "wälzen," which is associated with rolling somewhat resistant things outward and away.

Kammerer's anatomy of series is not the same as his law of series. It is important to recognize this. According to the law, though series themselves become exhausted when a certain likeness circuit peters out, the dimensionality of circuits, which are not equivalent to series, has to be unlimited. According to the anatomy, there are this and that kind of series that make up the bones, muscles, circulatory system, and the other dynamic strata of the homeosphere. The anatomy tells what kinds of series there are, but the law says there is no limit to the play of likenesses among them.

2.8.3.   *An anatomy of likeness is always provisional. Its categories need to be revised periodically, based on happenings. Circuits happen through and across established series types, shapes, and interrelations.*

The fate of likenesses tells the durability of the world. Series morphology is therefore followed by a reflection on longevity. In the "systematic" section of *Das Gesetz der Serie*, where the types of series are enumerated ("Serienarten und Seriengruppen [Systematik der Serien]" pp. 71–90), Kammerer responds in advance to the questions: What fate should any likeness expect to suffer across a series, into parallel, polytomic, higher-order, and higher-power series? How do you explain the duration of some likenesses into exponentially more rows and chains? What happens to the traditional distinctions among foundational modes, such as the distinction between thought and being? You can glean from the reflections in this section critical insights into the life cycle of homeotic circuits.

I encounter a long-lost friend. On the first encounter, and then each time after that, again and again off and on over the course of years, the series of encounters persists in part because the object persists, or so we commonly think. This kind of series happens as a combination of time, distance, social habits, and the persistence of the entity that is object of the series. This kind of thing Kammerer calls an *Identitätsserie*. Although the personal identity of the friend is not the cause of the series of encounters, it is an inalienable condition for it. In contrast, one day I meet someone who only looks like my friend. Or one day I read in a newspaper in a foreign country a name, "Greta," which is also the name of my long-lost friend. The printed name surely does not refer to my friend; this is doubtless some other Greta. Soon after this, I stumble across what look like varieties of her name, Gretel (in a bookshop), Grateful (on a song title), Gretsch guitars (on a shop sign), and so on. These likenesses arise solely in the serial juxtaposition and are not guaranteed by external factors, real or physical subsistence, mental or metaphysical persistence. This kind of series degrades much more quickly and soon diminishes to nothing, or more precisely, gives way to other series, Kammerer is convinced. These are *Ähnlichkeitserien*, likeness series (p. 71), which are fleeting and yet no less pervasive for that.

The life of an identity series obviously depends in part on the life of the object. As soon as my friend dies or moves away, I will stop meeting her on the street. Likeness series, in contrast, have different conditions for their continuation or ending. The "systematic" section presents two types of limitations on *Ähnlichkeitserien*: when and how likeness series diminish and finally end and what sorts of obstacles draw limits to their qualities or powers. Only toward the very end of the book does Kammerer broach the touchy subject of series endings. Endings for likeness series can be classified into two types: the scattering of likeness elements into spatially adjacent or temporally subjoined series to the point of dissolution and the interruption of a series by a causal interference (p. 426). The latter class is particularly interesting. Seriality does not do away with cause and causal explanations of natural and cultural events, according to Kammerer, yet the two live in antagonism toward one another. Either an event follows the law of efficient, motive cause, or else it follows the law of seriality, which is to say, as Kammerer does, the law of inertia, and never both.

When what you thought was a series and what you thought were likeness processes are discovered to have a motive cause—look-alikes turn out to be siblings, or their social context explains their similarity; genes generate phenotypes, nature has a creator—you demote them from one law to the other. Under these conditions, "Serialität geht in Kausalität über," "seriality gives way to causality" (p. 427). This is the second principle, a mirror principle, or almost, to the one that says events that have a motive cause can become starting points for series. Caused events can lead off a series or end it; nothing in the long middle of a series can be where it is, what it is, when it is caused.

This interchange between two systems of happening and two explanatory orders needs to be explored further. It is noteworthy that unlike Hume, Kammerer proceeds as though motive causality needs no explanation, while seriality does; whereas Hume shows that motive cause is never verifiable outside of series (regularity) and likenesses (like causes followed by like effects). Their two positions are not inversions of one another, but varieties of the same position, directed toward the same implied audience, bourgeois subjects under the sway of common sense and experimental natural scientists under the sway of experimental reason, though Hume and Kammerer show different degrees of adventurousness with regard to received ideas. Both Hume and Kammerer imagine an audience that takes motive cause as self-evident. And both are ready to become "Pfadfinder eines neuen Ordnungsgrundsatzes" as Kammerer puts it, "pathfinders for a new principle of order" (p. 428). Hume renders motive causality questionable, whereas Kammerer raises no questions about it while showing how in one specific region, it has no effect. In that region, causality is an obstacle; happenings near and far follow their own logic. Proliferating and radiating, approximating and equaling, transversal elements gather and disperse in homeotic vicinities.

2.9. *If the fundamental element of a homeotic layer is the pair, and pairs hook up into circuits, then circuits proliferate, radiate, and intercalate to make up vicinities.*

In the many tables that Kammerer uses to illustrate the likeness layer, patterns begin to emerge, almost in the same way that dots distribute in a halftone screen to make up images in a newspaper. From all the repetitions, all the series and supraseries, there emerge circuits that are their own patterns.

2.9.1.   *Complex homeotic vicinities can be called "images."*

This dimension of the image has been suppressed in mimetic theories.[30] Indeed, the only likeness possible in a mimetic image is that between the image and its dedicated outside, its object. Mimesis subordinates all likenesses to the ontological relation between image and thing. In truth, the two explanations of images are incompatible. An image may "be of" or "stand for" something, or, in contrast, it may allow traits to fuse out of the vicinities that cross it. And nonetheless, whether conceived as a representation of something beyond it or as a configuration of elements within it, images in both cases gather and distribute likenesses.

Toward a homeotic definition of the image: an arrangement of features whose echoes and reflections overlap with traits in the universe, an image only secondarily implies a figure, or the indication of such, contained by a frame, that makes direct reference to a figure outside the frame. The difference between "representational" and "nonrepresentational" art is not fundamental. The likeness vicinity, its singular arrangement of features, crosses all possible regions, including, but not limited to the region of image and the region of thing qua object. In this sense, a thing is also an image, already, before an image of it is made. Perhaps, like the fictional "primary series" in Kammerer's schema, an "image," arbitrarily lifted out of the persequent entirety, cut out, as it were, draws attention away from the weave of likenesses — draws attention away and allows some access to it at the same time. It is a cutting of the world and at the same time a patch on the world. And yet it is not right to call the outer limit of an image a "frame," since framing is just the effect of cutting one vicinity out of the persequent vicinity.

2.9.2. *Images are complex homeotic vicinities marked with the cut that removed them from the likeness layer, and this cutting and patch, too, belongs to a series.*

Images are marked with their removal, and yet they are not actually separated from the world in any significant way. A portrait, too, is in a series, an *Ähnlichkeitsserie*, as Kammerer would call it. Indeed, cutting out a vicinity does not subtract from the world, but adds a new overlap, begins a further circuit. Images are continuous with the world.

How does any single vicinity distinguish itself from the total vicinity, and why is the total vicinity not simply chaos? Roger Caillois, a generation younger than Kammerer and also a homeotician *avant la lettre*, describes homeotic vicinities as organized around "bizarre-privileged items in the universe" ("The Natural Fantastic," in *The Edge of Surrealism*, p. 350 n. 1). There is no better name for the heavily overburdened conjunctions of multiple series, places where circuits light up.

2.9.3. *A bizarre-privileged item in the universe, a BPIU, is a point of overlap that can be unfolded into a circuit.*

Caillois's nature congregates around eccentric elements, special concentrations of likeness effects where the world is thicker. BPIUs are those entities, double, triple, quadruple, that bring near traits from otherwise opposed categories, entities at whose insistence homeotic circuits light up in vicinities. It is a bold thought. Thinking it will prompt you to face a world without things, on a model that could be described as "aesthetic Spinozism," a world in which likenesses circulate and illuminate.

2.9.4. *Likenesses circumradiate.*

3. *Likenesses circumradiate.*

The homeotic theory of everything reaches a critical point with the introduction of the BPIU. Going back to the original premise, "Everything is like everything in some respect," it is apparent that following its own implications, it needed to be modified. The primacy of things needed to be rejected—independent, self-limited units whose relationality and higher-order constitution have to be described by a special science of the constitution of things, ontology. Under the experiment—taking likeness as the fundamental element of everything—it became more difficult to sustain the image of a world of things, even if those things had other things called "relations" that were in fact primary, for the not so obvious reason that there is and can be nothing essential in a thing that is not also at the same time and in the same respect like some other thing, not to mention like itself. What was called a "thing" came to resemble a plenum of likenesses.

This modification of the original premise moves the focus from a thing that is like over to the likenesses that resonate through it, the likenesses that, taken together, produce the impression that there is a thing. Thought from the perspective of a thing, from its form or function or its being, the conclusion was that a thing is a plenum of likenesses. This doesn't mean that a particular thing has to be made up of an enormous multitude of likenesses. It does mean, though, that however many likenesses come to constitute it, that thing is full to the top with likenesses, leaving no room for anything else. A thing is likenesses through and through, with no remainder. It depends on no substrate, hangs onto no structure, unless the structure be the pattern of traits that make it up, as repetitions and embellishments, as likenesses imitating other likenesses, and so on.

Taking another step away from the thing world, you can regard likenesses in their own right as having tendencies and inclinations, ways of proceeding and also of receding. Thought from the perspective of likenesses, a thing is no more and no less than accumulated overlaps, qualities piled up in some sort of registration — skewed, perhaps, but in touch through its layers in noncoincident overlaps that can, if the need arises, be unfolded. When unfolded, overlaps become series. Taken as series, overlaps spin out in directions and leap through dimensions, such that local crosses and clusters of series give rise to circuits or vicinities. Likenesses do happen in series, and series depend on them, but likeness's landscape is the circuit that dances over series and departs from them as ghostly patterns, epiphenomena atop the "total serial happening," as Kammerer called it. Likeness circuits are to series as rhythms are to meter; circuits peel off series and converge into realities of their own that do not necessarily respect series' sequentiality.

To understand the happening of likenesses in circuits, each node of which refers to all others, turn to a moment in which this was thought out on a grand scale in a context quite foreign to us. One of Plato's best readers, Plotinus, gives a detailed picture of the conditions under which likeness happens. It could be that in the wake of Socrates, attempts to systematize the theories of being, truth, and knowledge latent in his teachings led inevitably to homeosis, when the question was, "How do being, truth, and knowledge interrelate?" No doubt this happens for Plato, and for Aristotle as well, even though their main impulses were to negotiate and resolve philosophical problems.[31] For Plotinus, though, the main impulse of whose teachings was not so much to solve conceptual problems as to assemble a cosmos in which they simply didn't arise, homeosis is not so much explanatory as operational. Like a gear in a transmission, or better, like a lubricant such as oil, homeosis communicates the being, truth, knowledge around the system.

Turn to Plotinus and his word for vicinities of likenesses and the unique way they configure themselves into circuits. "Perilampsis," "circumradiation" (*The Enneads*, 5.1.6, p. 540; Loeb p. 30, line 28) is a mode of lighting in a penumbral way, an alternative to the metaphor of direct transmission and reception of light and an alternative to being, to "the One," which, in the system Plotinus developed with constant reference to his Platonist predecessors, cannot move, or change, or exude anything other to it. The nonexuding, unchanging One, a partner term to "being," insists on perfect unity, on remaining completely to itself, and is absolutely averse to anything else. In a word, it is absolute. The universe outside of the Plotinian "One," however, in response to the One's frigid neglect, exhibits its own peculiar characteristics, which include a kind of shining in semicircles operating precisely to avoid the One and its more direct mode of illumination, to avoid being. Likeness skirts being. The cosmos outside belongs to this mode of not being: not being one (as Plotinus writes, "For what could be, if it were not a unity?" (*The Enneads*, 6.9.1, p, 882). The cosmos circumradiates, "around-shines," and this verbal image of perilampsis pictures homeosis's most general style. The word appears at a key moment in the *Enneads*, when Plotinus needs to name the strange empyrean fiber of the many as, excluded and searching for its own mode, they semicircle the One.

Both a metaphysical principle and a real thing, the One is the source of unity for everything outside it, the soul and the world, as well as individual physical objects, along with everything in between. Anything that can be the object of perception or thought or the subject of thought or perception is in some way a unity, the argument begins.[32] Plotinus's intuition is primarily ontological: being means existing as an individual that contains neither more nor less than itself. A tree is one; it is all tree, and none of it is sky or horse. Above physical beings, other entities that exist by and large as multiplicities must also have unity — one example could be the collection of all existing beings, another would be images of those beings in the soul. Plotinus gives examples — armies and choirs and the soul itself, with its multiple faculties (*The Enneads,* 6.9.1, p. 883), multiple, and yet one. The concept of multiplicity here is more than one individual of the same kind. Multiplicity is thus thought of as an extension of unity; although the members of a choir are many, together, the members make up a choir, because each individual is a choir member.

To those raised on empiricist logic, the order may seem backward. For Plotinus, however, a chorus is not an aggregate built up additively out of singing people. Individuals derive from the unity of the choir, which dispenses the principle of individuality to its members. In this way, any many proceeds from a principle under which it is unified, and all principles refer back to the One as the principle of their unity. The One is real and primary; entities lie below and outside it, although they are also dependent on it, and so they are inside it, too, in some way, in an ambiguous zone that continuously troubles him ("no wonder it is not easy to say," he exclaims, *The Enneads,* 6.9.3 p. 885). The troubling question that persists is how the One is actually present among the lower ranks, giving unity to all entities at all levels and to the relations between them and to the whole as well, without diminishing its own oneness. How does it go out from itself without ever leaving itself? It must give without giving anything up; they must take without taking anything away. A One that dilutes its unity with multiplicity was never one ("the nature of the One, being generative of all beings, is to be identified with none of them" (6.9.3, p. 886. Thus, the many has to refer to the One, but remain ontologically outside it, although there is nothing ontologically outside the One. The One has to be the source of everything, although it may not depend on anything in order to be itself, to be one. Everything derives from and needs the One, and yet there are not fundamentally two kinds of things, the One and everything else.

The condition under which the One can lend unity to intellect, soul, and world is the same condition under which it threatens to separate itself too radically, becoming useless, setting itself adrift. What is unity that does not lend itself out? What is left of unity if it lends itself out? Out of this great battle over oneness — out of, let's say, the tendency of the world to dissipate, on one side, and the profound weakness, the utter terror of the One, isolated and cowering at the specter of its other, on the other side, circumradiation arises as savior — as protector of the One and redeemer of the many.

> We should say, then, that that which comes to be from the One in the intelligible world does so without the One being moved. For if something came to be as a result of its having moved, then that which came to be would be third in line from it, after the motion, and not second. It must be, then, that if something was second in line from it, that thing came to exist while the One was unmoved, neither inclining, nor having willed anything, nor moving in any way. (*The Enneads*, 5.1. 6, p. 540)

With this extreme prohibition on motion in the One, Plotinus goes in search of another principle, a nonprinciple with which to describe all that is not the One, strictly speaking. What yields, assents, stirs toward a secondary — this is what he is looking for, and it is what a theory of likeness also needs. Secondary things enjoy the community of the many, though, it should be said, never all at once. Seconds are in constant movement toward a second. Each is second to the other, each pair second to a second pair, and so on and on and on, bending, with each seconding, into an errant arc. For likeness, firstness has almost as little significance as oneness, and in this way, in the shadow of Plotinus's monolithic monster, there springs up a most sincere and detailed homeotic vocabulary.

Homeosis thrives in the One's neglect. Insofar as the One cannot have any motive toward the secondary existences, a secondary existence does not need the One, at least not as a plant needs the sun or a child a parent. It remains to say how one imagines this other existence near the One.

> How, then, does this happen, and what should we think about what is near to the One while it reposes? A circumradiation [*perilampsin*] comes from it, though it reposes, like the light from the sun, in a way encircling it, eternally coming from it while it reposes. And all beings, so long as they persist, necessarily, due to the power present in them, produce from their own

substantiality a real, though dependent, existent [*hupostasin*] around themselves directed to their exterior a sort of image [*eikona*] of the archetypes [*archetupon*] from which it was generated. (*The Enneads* 5.1.6, p. 540, translation modified)

Where the One does not lend its unity out, where it reserves itself to itself, its tendency not to alter leaves space for a different sort of mode, for elsewise than stasis and elsewise than alteration, elsewise than unified, and elsewise than principle. The contradictory movements in this passage — genesis out of stasis; encircling out of punctiform; radiance out of a vacuum — are envisioned not as antinomies, not as impasses or aporias, and not as dialectical movements, where negation delimits, circumscribes, and gives rise to an abstract countermovement. The pairs are not strictly contradictions — another logic is manifest. A metaterm in a predialectic, "stasis" means the absence of genesis such that nothing can arise from it, even its opposite in the mode of becoming. Stasis precisely cannot generate anything. The One is, in this way, not determinative of its outside. The One abandons the outside, which is then gratefully not determined by it. Not determined by unity, the outside is allowed all qualities except firstness, unalteringness, complete unity, and so on, and the figures Plotinus uses to describe the outside are: "secondary," and then "perilampsis," an existence in the One's neglect that shines through secondary, sympathetic, indirect, deflecting radiation.

Circumradiation is like the grace of a king toward subjects that surround him: through no action of the sovereign, in fact through his inaction, an aureole forms, a secondary glow in the sun's shadow. Power does not shine, it perishines. Circumradiation can be understood as a kind of halation, vibration, or skipping shift. Rather than a teletechnology, as is the usual mode of light, which gives rise to the idea of vision and metaphors of truth, rather than what we sometimes call a "medium," here, there is no medium and no projection of contents across distances, no communication of authority from high to low, no transmission from a secret interior into the open light of day. There is instead a plesiotechnology or proximity effect.

3.1. *Perilampsis lights around outside the source and is not directly traceable to its teletechnologic.*

The stuff of the secondary realm happens perilamptically, in circuits. Taken altogether, that stuff is a surrounding reality, a resonant and sympathetic reality of what Plotinus calls "hypostases" (*The Enneads*, 5.1.6, line 34), which are something more than stases and less than movements. A good way to understand this kind of perimovement is not as an overcoming of stasis into kinetic locomotion or metabole (not dialectical), but as a strange subtraction from stillness — a falling, or sliding, or shifting, a drift, or silting up, or slumping, or veering, or verging. A hypostasis has its being in another, and that in another, and so on — in a series, that is, where the circuit is "turned on" so long as the circumradiance is picked up by another circuit and another.

Circumradiation acts with respect to the One like "a sort of image [*eikona*] of the archetypes from which it was generated" (5.1.6, p. 540). An image of an archetype — how should you understand this? Another likeness steps in to explain it. In this treatise of *Ennead V*, Plotinus is describing the genesis of the three major hypostases of the One. Yet he first has to say how there could be anything besides the One in the first place, overcoming the paradoxes of the one and the many that plague him. Only then can he say something about the genesis and character of what is not the One. When he does, he introduces a series of figures, first one, "perilampsis," then two others that serve to unfurl its implications. What is perilampsis? Perilampsis is like an image of an archetype. To describe this relationship, another simile then is added: an image of an archetype is like the heat of a fire, which is around the fire, in sympathy with it, but not one with it. Perilampsis is like an image that is like an archetype that is like the heat of a fire. What is heat like? Perfume — here is the best and also the most troublesome image. Perfume — is the aroma in the source, or in what surrounds it? In a real sense, the source of the scent recedes behind the scent; the source does not appear to feed the scent directly, not through direct mechanisms, at least, since the source has a different character altogether that does not account for the scent. The source is not aromatic, it is sourcy, condensed, locatable, causal. You smelling the perfume is the effect of the cause, like being burned by a flame is the effect of fire. Heat, however, is something different, as is scent. The scent is diffuse, indeterminate, in its circuits occupying a position intermediate between cause and effect, neither one nor the other. On the sources of scent, Plotinus says, "so long as they exist, something flows from them around them, the existence of which a bystander enjoys" (5.1.6, p. 540).

Nearness that enjoys the existence of a source without being beholden to it in any stronger way — to develop this image, Plotinus will need a further comparison. What is the character of the nearness that allows for a mode of existence never to be confused with unity or source? Plotinus soon reveals the true complexity of this mode. For one thing, a spacer or buffer is needed between the higher, powerful producer and the hypostases themselves, so that the latter can remain near without touching or being contaminated by unity, firstness, stasis, and so on. Such a spacer or buffer is repeated at various levels of the system, a blank zone or separation that allows for a particular association. For instance, the soul lies around the intellect, separate from it, and because it is not in direct contact, "our soul, too, goes back up to it, supposing itself to be an image of it, so that its life is a reflection and likeness of it, and whenever it thinks, it becomes god-like, that is, 'Intellect-like'" (5.3.8, p. 564). Here, the special power of the circumradiant says how it proceeds, as a sui generis nonsource within the secondary, such that if you want to encounter the Intellectual Principle, the source, you have to first encounter the soul that resembles it and in resembling makes an image of it. Read the Plotinian braid of figures in reverse: perilampsis has been a figure for resemblance, drawing out some of the features that Plotinus and Platonists after him, in imitation of him, will continue to emphasize — separate, though near, diffuse without point of emission, transmission without transmitter, a juncture or overlap with the One without identity or, for that matter, without falling fully outside it as categorically other to it. How is it possible to be one with the One without being identical to it?

In the sixth *Ennead*, Plotinus spends a brief, though important moment on likeness. The One, toward itself and in itself, has no outside, has no other quality besides oneness, and it is nonetheless also productive of a zone that remains near it, though separate, illuminated under its own photologic. Separate and not distinct, the zone of circumradiation is home to relatives. A heat is more hot than another heat and less hot than yet another. One of the few definitions of likeness in the history of philosophy is given here, during an attempt to describe relationships among relatives. How do relatives relate? Likeness, Plotinus lets fall, is not a relation per se; rather, "the like is not the effect of that which is like it, but merely present, that is, the identity in what is qualified as the same" (6.1.6, p. 654, translation modified). He invents or exposes, in this moment of the text, a kind of identity outside the one that is not quantitative. Qualitative identity the circumspace accommodates.

Here is one way to characterize likeness in its plurality and quasi-uniformity, in its differing sameness. Likeness is most like . . . in a Plotinian milieu . . . qualitative identity. This is how the One, which remains itself to itself and quantitatively identical, can be articulated as more than itself without impinging on its status. Quantitatively solo, identical to itself in number, it is qualitatively in the company of the many, full to the top with identities. Identities of quality, then — this is one meaning of "one" outside the One, the articulation into circuits whose ranges or moments are qualitatively not different, so that the idea of qualitative identity remains, in an important way, consistent both with a thing that is loose with itself, a One distended and plural, spreading out, and at the same time a minimum, deeply conservative and ungenerous.

3.1.1. *Qualitative identity is the inherence of a first in seconds, and seconds become the medium for the first's identity for the life of its qualities.*

In this way, you are led to understand that the hypostases, as inherences of the One, enlikening the One, and provide its life, when intellectual acts liken the being of the Intellect, when in turn the soul likens the Intellect, and then things external to the soul, the things that the soul desires, in fact desire it in a special way. They liken up to it. Things raise themselves out of their sunken condition and liken up to soul (See 6.7, "How the Multiplicity of the Ideas Came to Exist, and on the Good," and especially 6.7.7, p. 811). Thus, the physical universe likens to higher modes of likeness up through the chain — that is, it holds together with the higher modes in qualitative identities. Sensation itself is no less than perception of "the sensible harmony" (6.7.6, p. 809), showing its own homeotic dynamic.

From Plotinus we inherit, if we are willing and open to it, a sophisticated homeotic vocabulary ("perilampsis," "qualitative identity," "image," "likening," "sensible harmony"). We also inherit a map of the whole of all likenesses with its qualitative identities on display — a whole of likenesses and a likening power that belongs to the products, and not to the producers, to the lower, and not to the higher, to the outside in its own way. He calls this at one pivotal point a "transparent sphere." For the theory of likeness, perilampsis modifies the concept "series" when it describes less a formal parameter of likeness than a mode of existing — as circulating luminance, without a direct relation to being. As an activity exterior to being, homeosis loops peripherally, in a general sideways, semicircular slip where — clipped, circulating, infectious, repeating — likenesses light up, resemblances trail resemblances, and qualities seep. You might think the Plotinian system is strictly hierarchical, more like a ladder, but the metaphysical whole (that includes the physical within it) can also be conceived of as a sphere, which, you can contemplate only from within.

A whole of qualitative identities, the transparent sphere, can be described as "beautiful." Talking about "intelligible beauty," Plotinus stays at first with the Platonic-Aristotelian hierarchy. The form is more beautiful than the material to which the artist gives form (5.8.1–2, p. 610). On principle, form is higher than matter — matter cannot be beautiful in itself insofar as it is unformed. That is, under this tautology, beauty, as you might expect from an author steeped in Athenian precepts, is synonymous with form. When it comes to the beauty of the whole, however, the beauty of the One or God as contemplated by the world mind, form has to be left behind as a criterion. The One does not have form in the way sense objects or their mimeses do, and the mind could never "perceive" God's form in any case. Because of this, Plotinus enjoins his audience to approach the one by "thinking through" the whole of qualitative identities:

> So, let us grasp by discursive thinking [*dianoia*] this cosmos all together as one, each of its parts remaining what it is and not jumbled together, if possible, so that if any one of these should occur to us — for example, the sphere outside the periphery of the cosmos — an image of the sun follows immediately and together with it all the other stars, and earth and sea and all the living beings are seen, as if all these were in reality to be seen in a transparent sphere. (5.8.9, p. 619; Loeb p. 264, lines 1-8).

Thinking through the transparent sphere means thinking it to its end and also thinking by means of it, from inside its viscous jelly. This is the first step toward describing the whole with all its qualitative identities — the universe will be encompassed with the tools of a being who must see through the whole in its vitreosity, a being who works at its highest capacity through *dianoia*, "through-thought." The perspective of the One is not accessible to mortals. This does not stop the dianoetic observer, however, from observing what the One perhaps cannot: how qualitative identities array about a transparent sphere. This should be as accessible to an empirical mind as it is to the world mind, and perhaps, because it is less obsessed with the One, more so.

For the next step, once this thought image takes hold, Plotinus asks that you superimpose a second globe over it without losing sight of the first.[33] The superimposition comes with a few requirements, however. "Keeping this image, take another for yourself by abstracting the mass from it. Abstract, too, places and the semblance of the matter you have in yourself" (5.8.9, p. 619). To tour the circumradiant universe dianoetically, you do something quite unlike *dianoia*, in fact, something more like thinking things away than like thinking in a discursive manner. Plotinus wants to think away the mass of things and the place of things and the matter of things. A more severe *epoché* is hard to imagine, and after it, what is left Plotinus imagines as a globe over a globe, which, rather than imply a vertical distance to be scaled and thus an ontological rank order, suggests qualitative proximity, a slightly displaced, overlapping vicinity that Plotinus calls "distinction by state without interval [*en stasei adiastato*]" (5.8.9, MacKenna translation p. 429; Loeb p. 266, line 20).

"Distinction by state without interval" — so Stephen MacKenna translates the Greek. Wherever things array about like this, in a bizarre vicinity, the size of the homeotic field and the number of likenesses become indeterminate. There are no intervals between instances and so no demarcation of beings or places as dianoetic contemplation would understand them, using percepts and concepts, say; now the spacing out that requires dianoiesis or that dianoiesis requires becomes forbidden. Distinction can be made only by state, insofar as the nodes arrayed around this sphere "are alike and at the same time each is separate, in a position without distinction, having no perceptible form at all," to translate more literally (Loeb, p. 266, lines 19–21). This *globus perlucidus vicinius* — Plotinus's layered globe — is the best description of a likeness cosmos yet. Plotinus's insight, whose spirit MacKenna captures, for all the inaccuracy that plagues his translation, holds the qualitative plurality together in a transparent sphere over another sphere; there, qualities, overlapping, indeterminate, huddle in an accommodating cross of distinction and convergence.

3.1.2. *Resemblances within resemblances, circuits within circuits, illuminate the transparent, layered* globus vicinus.

Overlapping circuits on a transparent, laminated Plotinian mantle produce more and less dense vicinities. They are not complex; they are implex.[34] Partially within one another, mutually inherent, able to illuminate only through each another, the laminates at the thick parts on the transparent *globus vicinus* mark areas of interference. A network makes distinctions by interval, and not by state. The *globus perlucidus vicinius* makes distinctions by state without interval, that is without space.

The overlapping, transparent globe is attractive for a theory of likeness because it captures neatly in an image the interlapping totality of qualitative identities. The globe extends perilampsis in all dimensions, generalizing it. Embroidered around the One in circuits, qualities bunch up, lay over, distinct by quality, and not by entity. The sphere has the potential to explain aspects of the likeness layer that were hitherto mysterious.

Now turn to two phenomena and three thinkers from the far future, unimaginable to Plotinus, without a doubt, and yet nurtured clandestinely by his *globus vicinus*. The transparent sphere outlives the problems of Neoplatonism and takes up residence, in its afterworld, in the oddest places. Take, for example, a phenomenon as obvious as a rabbit.

On Plotinus's transparent globe, you find a rabbit lit up in several respects — ears, whiskers, tail — overlapping with other rabbits and even other creatures where qualities are alike and holding itself apart where qualities are unlike. Keep the rabbit before your mind's eye. Imagine the transparent globes laying one over another layer upon layer with scarcely any thickness. Imagine on it a stain in the shape of a rabbit. There are several rabbits here, hundreds, millions — long ears overlap long ears, whisker shines through whisker, distinguished by state (floppy, pointy, attentive, asleep) without interval (lacking independent entities, falling into arrays of traits). Imagine the few circuits of traits out of which a rabbit would be minimally configured. The distinction by state without interval of the transparent sphere, what I have called "the likeness layer," applies here. Now take the rabbit and add something more, something incalculably modern — after the modern — a complicating and imbricating factor that will throw the natural kind, rabbit, out of nature. Add a duck. Before flying to conclusions, try to understand the result through Plotinus's transparent sphere. Leaning on the idea of qualitative identity, look at the enigmatic "duckrabbit," the figure made famous by Ludwig Wittgenstein in the second division of his *Philosophical Investigations*.

If you count on Plotinus to help gain a perspective, Wittgenstein's duckrabbit is not as puzzling as it seems at first, on one hand, and on the other hand, its problematic existence becomes even more problematic, because the effect is no longer restricted to a particular set of pictures, but is shown to be in fact generalizable to all "entities" where they overlap with others. For while it may seem clear enough how a rabbit overlaps with other rabbits, looping around a likeness circuit, piled up in layers on the transparent sphere, so that a plurality of rabbits is always also "one" rabbit where they lay over one another in qualitative identity, a rabbit, just as primordially, also overlaps with nonrabbits in many respects. Ears overlap with ears and whiskers with whiskers across a range of types. No doubt rabbits overlap with rabbits; the devilish addition now is that they also overlap with other things considered ontologically distinct.

First, consider the manifold of qualitative identities in simple rabbit-on-rabbit overlaps. This manifold may be less varied than when a rabbit overlaps with a duck, but the difference between the two is not so large as one would suppose. To state it under a Plotinian schema, there are indeed qualitative identities between duck and rabbit. They lie in some ways over one another on the sphere. The picture of the duckrabbit "shows" exactly where a few of these overlaps are. Wittgenstein's demonstration is a ragged corner of the Plotinian sphere poking into twentieth-century philosophy. The picture presents a difficulty for him only because the overlaps do not correspond to the relatively stabilized categories of zoological taxonomy that show up in college textbooks and children's picture books. Where a taxonomist might lay a wing over a foreleg and announce the indisputable distinction between duck and rabbit, a homeotician, writing in the ductus of Plotinus, lays ear over beak and announces a qualitative identity, taxonomy be damned.

The little picture of a rabbitduck in the right column of the page, printed in the German humor and puzzle magazine *Fliegende Blätter* in 1892, is drawn in the ductus of Plotinus (Figure 3). A homeotic circuit links up here in a world that has through some bad luck become resistant to Neoplatonist logic. Under these hostile conditions, the picture enters the corpus of theory. Something in the picture, something in the abandoned or prohibited logic that it represents, induced a strong reaction in the sciences that had superseded likeness or thought they had. Examining two of these reactions, you can perhaps calculate how far accounts of the figure fall from Plotinus and his twin homeotic motifs, perilampsis and the transparent sphere.

The picture was first taken up for theoretical purposes in 1899 by psychologist Joseph Jastrow, who believed it indicated a special power of mind. Later, in the mid-twentieth century, Wittgenstein took it up again, believing it gave evidence for a special power of "seeing." Neither saw in it an excuse to reimagine the world along homeotic lines, though both, I think, sensed that the picture escaped the logics of psychology and philosophy as then conceived. Wittgenstein took the picture as evidence for a multiplicity in "seeing" such that any "sight" was dependent on a frame or a game. To be sure, Wittgenstein's game was not the same as the parlor game for which the picture first appeared in the *Fliegende Blätter*. Here is the real clue about the analyses of the picture, how unlike the parlor game they really are: the weekly magazine's aim was satirical, and Wittgenstein's aim was deadly earnest. More than this, the intention of the magazine's editors was exactly the inverse of Wittgenstein's. Above the picture, the magazine printed a headline in the form of a question: "Welche Thiere gleichen einander am meisten?" — "Which animals are most like each other?" The formulation is extremely significant. With it, the magazine's editors show an unexpected hospitality to Plotinus. They do not preface the picture with the question "Which of two animals is the picture most like, a duck or a rabbit?" They do not ask a taxonomist's question;[35] rather, the question points toward a bizarre overlap. Which animals are most like one another? Which share qualitative space in the world, in our world? Wittgenstein, in contrast, repeatedly interprets the picture as a challenge to the univocity of sight, which is to say, he is willing to complicate sight, but not being. Sight as a medium can be two, or the picture itself can somehow be two, while the thing represented has to remain one. Trying desperately to insure that the two figures are essentially distinct, he attributes their confusion to an effect of seeing. In order to do this, he needs to assume that they are naturally distinct and that all interference between the two is the effect of human activity, an artifice, though as language it will become the chief artifice of human sociality. There are many hints of this assumption throughout the argument, but a particularly vivid one is the following passage. "I see two pictures, with the duckrabbit surrounded by rabbits in one, by ducks in the other. I don't notice that they are the same. Does it follow from this that I see something different in the two cases?" (*Philosophy of Psychology: A Fragment*, in *Philosophical Investigations*, § 125).

In some respects, yes, and in some, no, Plotinus retorts. A confusion always arises out of a fundamental distinction, the passage more than implies. The Wittgenstein passage nonetheless contains an important homeotic insight. It implies that for a single animal, in order to see it in all its distinctness, you may place it among a group of similars; you simply must not place it among differents. Rabbit is not only distinguished by being not duck, it is constituted out of something like a rabbit atmosphere. On its own, a mimesis would not be enough to tell which distinct being a being is or even that it is one. Mimesis is second to vicinity — a Plotinian view *après la lettre*. Now, if you extract the beast out of an atmosphere full of noses and tails that

Figure 3. Anonymous illustration, *Kaninchen und Ente"* (Rabbit and duck), *Fliegende Blätter*, October 23, 1892, pg. 147. Photograph courtesy of University of Heidelberg Library, https://digi.ub.uni-heidelberg.de/diglit/fb97/0147/image.

reinforces one qualitative identity over others, in an abstracted situation, the image surely becomes ambiguous. Among its own kind, that is, in its overlaps, along its circuits, it can remain itself. Wittgenstein says as much. Grouped up with other rabbits, through likenesses, the figure shows a rabbit; grouped up with ducks, a duck. To repeat, in the background of this investigation stands the assumption that a likeness circuit lights up in resonance with a surround, and this resonance helps determine what seeing sees.

The figure-atmosphere relation is not the center of interest for him here, though. Wittgenstein seeks to fix a relation between the two animals so that they are fundamentally distinct and their overlap is an afterthought, a product of certain manipulations, language as a way of doing things, with things it needs as objects of the doing. To set this in motion, he makes a distinction in the concept of likeness. From overlap, as Plotinus might call it, he rushes to the opposite end of the spectrum. "The head seen in this way hasn't even the slightest similarity to the head seen in that way — although they are congruent [*kongruent*]" (§ 127). It couldn't be clearer that this thought is contemplated from the perspective of a field of distinct entities. With the mathematical concept of congruence, he loses the possibility of accessing the phenomenon through Plotinian transparency. Congruence is far from circumradiance. Congruence is also the reverse of what the magazine proposes to its readers. For Wittgenstein, the points match up accidentally, and they remain distinct by entity, not by state. The picture has been excerpted from its duck-and-rabbit-filled atmospheres and painted onto the blank canvas of a philosophical inquiry, eyes lured away from the parlor magazine and its satirical question and its radical Plotinian suggestion. Under the condition of thorough abstraction, Wittgenstein experiences the congruent picture "as if the object had changed before my eyes" (§ 129).

A philosophy so willing to remove entities from atmospheres emits a special airless atmosphere for its investigations. In the airless zone, a figure consists in essential differences and accidental, though from time to time precise and surprising congruences — not in circuits of similarity fusing out in an atmosphere populated with ducks and rabbits, along with all of nature and culture, arranged in overlapping arrays by qualitative identities, like colors in a sampler fanned out in hues and shades. The irony here is that the airless atmosphere of this philosophy is a perfect context in which to see that differences among entities are in no way fundamental. In this highly constructed and purified context, the homeotic nature of the duckrabbit nevertheless suggests itself. The beast waits to be recognized for the nature it exhibits, and although Wittgenstein prepares for a surgical separation, the twins insist on staying together. To be a figure is to resonate with or to overlap with other figures in specific respects. These respects are in no way limited to the parameters of a natural kind, although natural kinds are one set of limited overlaps. Acknowledging the respects in which overlaps happen is crucial. In the duckrabbit, in this single picture, the respects are not only limited by trait — ear-beak and eye-eye; they are also limited by angle of view. Note that when you observe the duckrabbit, when you "see" overlaps in the two animals, or rather, when they light up in the likeness field that includes perception, the confusion depends on each figure's angle of rotation or angle of view. Wittgenstein does not mention this, but it is also fundamental to the singular atmosphere he calls "seeing." The rabbit is drawn as though looked at from slightly above and behind its face, while the duck is drawn as though from slightly above and in front of its face. These two positions imitate perspectival visions, although, given the limits of this kind of atmosphere or vicinity, the two perspectives cannot coincide for a single human at the same instant. For a pen-and-ink drawing, however, another vicinity altogether that by no means should be confused with seeing, it is not only possible but an integral part of the medium's game. Two animals, seen from two perspectives, overlap in pivotal ways and respects, and drawing overlaps with them. Or you could say that two animals emerge from the qualitative identities radiating through the atmosphere — the transparent sphere — of a drawing. Either way, drawing and animals overlap, as well. Accommodate your eyes to bizarre overlaps in nature, the sketch challenges viewers like this. The philosophical game, in contrast, asks readers to separate what is overlapping into distinct entities and then to play the game of accounting for their congruence. Wittgenstein approaches, but ultimately sidesteps the Neoplatonic solution, which, it is true, over the centuries had migrated out of philosophy into the occult, into art, and into bourgeois counterparts such as parlor games. It is perhaps no surprise then that a magazine should take up philosophizing, in a Neoplatonic key.

A bizarre-privileged entity in its own right and a litmus test of sorts for homeotic intuitions, the duckrabbit was first injected into the body of theory by Joseph Jastrow, a psychologist who, as a student, worked with C. S. Peirce at Johns Hopkins on threshold measurements of perception. A sentence in Jastrow's 1899 article "The Mind's Eye," whose final image quotes the duck/rabbit or rabbit/duck figure, says of this picture and others like it: "All these diagrams serve to illustrate the principle that when the objective features are ambiguous we see one thing or another according to the impression that is in the mind's eye; what the objective factors lack in definiteness the subjective ones supply" ("The Mind's Eye," p. 310). This is a different analysis of the duckrabbit figure, falling back on an ontological landscape different from Wittgenstein's, a scene in which the mind towers over the senses, much as the One towers over the lower emanations for Plotinus. Cognition can involve an emanation of the psyche out over objects. An object has objective features, without a doubt, and where these are well defined and simple, receptive perception is enough to capture them. Mind need not emanate when entities are distinct. When the senses give indeterminate evidence, however, mental vision steps in to aid in distinguishing the entity in question. The "mind's eye" lends a distinct outline to the ambiguous visual evidence. Jastrow confines this process to a small set of perceptions. Instead of an overlap of duck and rabbit, Jastrow envisions a projection of a mental image onto a perceptual image.

Jastrow gets no closer to the transparent sphere than Wittgenstein does, but like Wittgenstein, he acknowledges the role of atmosphere in these processes. An object, Jastrow proposed, may remain ambiguous for perception because it hides in a jumble of other objects. When thus obscured among an atmosphere, an object can be distinguished only by the active mental power of projective distinction. Another picture printed with Jastrow's article demonstrates this power on readers (Figure 4a):

Allow your regard to circulate around the picture. If it lands on a particular outcropping, as in Figure 4b, Jastrow indicates, you have experienced mental sight emanating out onto a confused perception.

The question wants to be asked: When your gaze stops on familiar features that make a face in the rock, are the features in the landscape, or in your mind?[36] What Jastrow calls seeing with the mind's eye can be called, remembering Wittgenstein's rabbits and ducks, "fusion of a likeness out of an atmosphere," which occurs neither in the mind nor in the landscape, but in the layers that include both, and not only these two.

3.2. *Likenesses light up out of an atmosphere, which in lighting up they alter. Likenesses fuse out of and diffuse into atmospheres.*

Likenesses alter an atmosphere twice, first when they light up, when they fuse out of it, and second when they go out, when they diffuse back into it. Atmosphere, however, is more than an inert ground (as Gestalt theorists imagined); it is active and available for unanticipated allegiances. The image of the rock face has many more sources to draw on than the one Jastrow prefers. It is not only the "mind's eye" that is involved here. The face fuses out of multiple layers of overlap. One source for the fusing out of the face, beyond mind, is Jastrow's writing. Jastrow has to work to point you toward the rockface that he fears your mind's eye on its own might not otherwise discover although at first he denies doing the explicit pointing out. "Wherever the beauties and conformations of natural scenery invite the eye of man does he discover familiar forms and faces (Fig. 1)" —

quite irresistible. We turn it about in all directions, wondering where the hidden form can be, scanning every detail of the picture, until suddenly a chance glimpse reveals it, plainly staring us in the

FIG. 1.*—The man's face in the rocks is quite distinct, and is usually readily found when it is known that there is a face somewhere. (For this view from the Dalles of the St. Croix, Minn., I am indebted to the courtesy of Mr. W. H. Dudley, of Madison, Wis.)

face. When several persons are engaged in this occupation, it is amusing to observe how blind each is to what the others see; their physical eyes see alike, but their mental eyes reflect their own individualities.

---

* In order to obtain the effects described in the various illustrations it is necessary in several cases to regard the figures for a considerable time and with close attention. The reader is requested not to give up in case the first attempt to secure the effect is not successful, but to continue the effort for a reasonable period. Individuals differ considerably in the readiness with which they obtain such effects; in some cases, such devices as holding the diagrams inverted or at an angle or viewing them with the eyes half closed are helpful.

Figure 4b. Detail of Figure 4a.

that is, Figure 4a ("The Mind's Eye," p. 300). Directed there, the reader finds a caption that declares: "The man's face in the rocks is quite distinct, and is usually readily found when it is known that there is a face somewhere" (p. 302). As Jastrow concedes, "The stranger to whom such curiosities of form are first pointed out often finds it difficult to discover the resemblance, but once seen the face or form obtrudes itself in every view and seems the most conspicuous feature in the outlook. ("The Mind's Eye," p. 301).

The article itself serves out homeotic perilampsis. Landscape, perception, and the "mind's eye" circumluminate through the sentences so that the image fuses out of the entire list of vicinities, Jastrow's words, the photograph, the rock, perception as it shifts through perspectives and various glances and reglances, as well as mental perception, the mind's eye, so called, which comes into transparency with its partners in a stroke. Reflect on the suddenness with which the face lit up and the scant few features it took to suggest the unnatural likeness crossing nature, culture, language, and thought. It is as though Jastrow's words had chiseled the rock while the rock fell out of memory where culture had been drawing faces. You may well have forgotten that the lighting up was triggered by a sentence, though you know it depended on a photograph.[37] Homeotics brings to mind the forgotten vicinities that must needs work together for a likeness to fuse out. You may have forgotten that the photograph is reprinted there out of context in a popular journal, and so it, too, is an echo whose reverberation rebounded through a memory, reexperienced, relayed out into a mental projection, and so on.

Going back to the duckrabbit, it is apparent now that the printed question, "Which animals are most alike?" is active in the event of the drawing, and it, too, overlaps with the figure. It shouldn't be left out. Printed above the picture in space, the question has qualitative identity with the picture. Without the question, the drawing might remain unseen, ungotten; without the picture, the question would remain abstract, unanswerable. That is to say, the question is one of the figure's overlays, and it is an accident that the medium is lan-guage, rather than, say, an image.

Wittgenstein's investigations, too, operate in the overlap of text and image. The homeosis does not occur in the picture or in a phantasmic encounter between the picture and "sight," but where a "remark" and the picture converge in essence. An anticipation of a game, a memory of a children's illustration of barnyard animals, fall into indistinction with the composite name "Entenhase"—resonat-ing with the picture and calling forth disembodied totemic animal heads. Together, phrase, game, memory engram, and drawing pro-pose an eccentric kinship among kinds. In this case, a word makes a contradiction into a truth. A Wittgensteinian "remark" places duck onto rabbit, likewise with Jastrow.

Simple facts become important in homeotics, especially because they are additive. Neither is the face simply "in" the rock, nor is the rock in the face, merely, just as the duck is not in the rabbit and the rabbit is not in the duck, simply or merely. Both are on the texts, and the texts are on the drawing and the photograph and the mind's eye, which in turn are on rock and rabbit. Circuits are overlaps. What pre-viously resembled a rocky river bend, in a picture that led your gaze toward the houses on the left bank, after reading the text, turns you to the right, in a story about a figure watching over the bend, totem advertising an archaic community or talisman protecting against an enemy in the distance, or idol grimacing down on a storm-driven river. Irreconcilable regions merge. As the likeness fuses out, sources and levels fall into healthy indistinction. This is perilampsis through a mul-tidimensional sphere, a perception, if you will, but with no subject and no single object. A resemblance fuses out of a multioriginal milieu that includes all that has been mentioned. A rock face becomes a rocky face, and nature puts on the mask of a culture carved by nature.

Ranging along this eccentric afterlife of Plotinus, you discover that the atmosphere-likeness relation is multiplex and can even be unpredictable. It isn't that other disciplines have not recognized this; they have, but they tend to reduce the multiplex by restricting it to one single field. Gestalt theory[38] and the psychology of perception place the atmosphere for the fusing out of figures in the psyche or the "mind's eye." Visual humor, in contrast, places the atmosphere in pictorial practices. The difference between these later homeotisms and Plotinus is one of extent: Plotinus shows how extensive the field is with reference to the broadest, most panoramic frame, in the transparent overlays ending in the circumradiation of the world. Where he does this, he threatens to leave the One behind like a desiccated pit at the distant center of a vibrant, erratic sphere, a tapestry of atmospheres.

3.2.1.   *For any figure, there are several atmospheres, not all of them immediately recognizable.*

Atmospheres come together and blend, so that the duckrabbit figure, to use that example again, can fuse out. The figure lights up through at least ten atmospheres that can be named, each of which is in various ways intermingled with some of the others. The duckrabbit lights up through the continuum of animal life; through its distorted reflection in the child's nursery, with its stuffed toys and storybook prints; in the nineteenth-century industry of scientific illustration; in the milieu of a certain strand of bourgeois kitsch; through the apparatus of empirical psychology; in the games of critical philosophy; out of the mad suggestions of Darwinian evolution; in the "mind's eye," whatever it is; and in the field of perception; as well as in the atmosphere of line drawing, which, wherever its roots lie, has been in large part since the Renaissance at least dedicated to likenesses.[39]

The duckrabbit counts as a bizarre-privileged item in history less because two animals shine through one another in it than because middle-class entertainment culture, psychology, philosophy, and art theory took it up as a mystery, reinforced one another with their successive gazes, and made it into an emblem of a problem. Problem aside, these are all atmospheres in which the figure now emerges.

Figure 5a. Giuseppe Arcimboldo, *The Vegetable Gardener*, 1590. Oil on panel, 35 x 24 cm. Invertible. Museo civico a la Ponzone, Cremona. Photograph by Eric Lessing/Art Resource, New York.

Figure 5b. *The Vegetable Gardener.*

Figure 6. Giuseppe Arcimboldo, *Vertumnus* (*Emperor Rudolf II*), 1590. Oil on wood, 70.5 x 57.5 cm. Slott, Skokloster, Sweden. Photograph by Eric Lessing / Art Resource, New York.

Figure 7. Giuseppe Arcimboldo, *Spring, Allegory*, 1573. Oil on canvas, 76 x 63.5 cm. Real Academia de Bellas Artes de San Fernando, Madrid. Photograph by Erich Lessing/Art Resource, New York.

They stand in close relation to the figure, as exponents of its refusal of being, and through the figure, they come into close proximity with one another.

A stronger cousin of the Plotinian sphere, laden with circumradiations, transparently piling up qualities, is this bowl of vegetables (Figure 5a). It, too, is a bizarre-privileged item in a post-Platonic history.

Plotinus could not have found a better illustrator for the *Enneads* than Giuseppe Arcimboldo, who, perhaps because he made art in a period still open to Neoplatonist thinking, or perhaps because of the age and development of natural philosophy in the era, could develop, to the highest heights, the kinds, scope, and quantity of qualitative identities. This painting — or these paintings — belayered by Arcimboldo, so apparently distant from Wittgenstein and Jastrow, share a gesture with the parlor game.

Like the duck and rabbit, these two figures, bowl of vegetables and, when overturned, face of a cook (Figure 5b), overlap and are not fully distinguishable. There is much to say about Arcimboldo's mid-seventeenth century and his own discoveries of homeotic effects. His "head" paintings are the best historical examples of circumradiating likenesses in overlapping circuits. Thinking of them as visual echoes of Plotinus and illustrations of the extended mode of circumradiance, peruse the homeotic vicinity full of circuits extending through these picture planes, quite illegitimately crashing forms, categories, regions of being, as still life invades portraiture, the raw invades the cooked, mutually exotic zones such as cultivated produce and sovereign power cycle through one another.

Confine your gaze for a moment to the representation of vegetables and the routes of specific colors. Any color is a qualitative identity. Say "orange," and a circuit of oranges radiates through both pictures, through the shadow of cheekonion, the curve of tangerinemouth, the inner kernel of eyeshallot. Say "green," and touch off a verdant aura fringing the clusters. In the likeness layer, color is the sign of a circuit.[40]

Notice, too, how these color circuits "light up," metaphorically and without any light, upon encounter with a word, "orange," "green."

3.3.   *Resemblances are neither in the psyche of the observer nor in the qualities of things; they light up in an encounter.*

Of developed theories, the closest to homeotics may be semiotics. Semiosis assumes a nonmental historical field, a zone with no privileged perspective. Least of all does it privilege the perspective of reason. Whereas semiotics is organized into structures, relays, networks of relata that build up and aggregate, generating, as they interrelate, a secondary plane of "meaning," likenesses, in contrast, are first and foremost fungible and unstructured. However, they make patterns. This allows an architectonic structure (semiosis) to be replaced with a historical face (homeosis). It allows homeotic truth to come forward, which does not move from a first to a second or build out a latticelike structure in defined dimensions. Only two theoretical operations seem possible with respect to homeosis: to trace patterns and to produce resemblances. In the end, these would be nearly the same — every pattern traced making a further resemblance.[41] But permit me to remark: likenesses are not about the components, the way signs are. For one thing, likeness is adverbial. Likeness "is as," proceeding by manner, and this presents a different challenge to modern philosophy than semiotics does. Semiotics substitutes a meaningful unit for the substantial unit of ontology; homeotics substitutes an adverbial mode for the meaningful unit of semiotics.

3.3.1.   *The adverbial mode of likeness is closer to mathematics than to meaning. The adverbial mode says how things are coindicated, without stating or implying that they ultimately unite somewhere else as a separate point of illumination.*

Another aspect of homeosis that distances it from signification, as well as from phenomenological intention, mental attention, aesthetic mimesis, or metaphysical causality, is bidirectionality. You can see this in Arcimboldo's painting (or paintings) of the bowl of vegetables / cook's head. They look at one another. Compared with intentional dispositions, likeness is invertible. It is as if whenever you said, "I perceive this object," you also had to say, "and this object perceives me." What is like something, something is like.

3.4. *Likeness looks both ways.*

A double regard, bowl at cook and cook at bowl, pulls the disparate, the distinct, into an overlap. A pear looks at a light bulb, and the light bulb looks back; my mother's face looks at my son's face, and his face looks at hers. This green leaf and that green dollar reflect through one another. An action, reflecting through as though moving through the transparent sphere, evokes a vocabulary from optics that may help sort out these new interactions. Mutual through-reflecting describes the partial and incomplete superimposition of traits, traits that come together through diaphany, a quality of qualities.

3.4.1. *Likeness poles are mutually diaphanous, and the result is a new kind of phenomenon, a diaphenomenon.*

In a diaphenomenon, traits look to and through one another, whether an observer enters their circle or not. When an observer is there, the effect may be eerie as though a private scene had been disturbed. Baudelaire captures the effect in a line in his poem *Correspondences*: "L'homme y passe à travers des forêts de symboles / Qui l'observant avec des regards familiers" (*Les Fleurs du mal*, p. 19). "Human beings walk through a forest of symbols / Who observe them with an intimate regard" (my translation). Whether observed or not, diaphanous symbols look at one another, know each other intimately, and when a human being is present, they know them, too. The likenesses regard the observer, anticipating the external glance.

Arcimboldo's faces regard you not with their eyes, but with their diaphanous zones, through which the most disparate aspects of the world reflect, or rather refract. Reflection in a transparent mirror — is refraction. The *sacrum imperium romanum* refracts through a face, Rudolf II, Holy Roman Emperor, painted by court painter and prop maker Arcimboldo — though "to paint" has a different meaning in his case. To paint in Arcimboldo mode is to rotate a bizarre prism so that traits can regard one another (Figure 6). The empire regards the emperor's features through its possessions. Refraction of things through persons, state through orchard, meadow through buds and petals, shades through shapes, power through products, words through fruit, outline through qualities: a domain — a domain of domains — puts on a face and confronts you with a mixed expression. This is not the Renaissance you know, but rather a surreal misbirth, the instauration of a nonspatial, antiperspectival mode, in the midst of the other, better-known revolutions in perception from around the same time. An optic, or rather a hypnotic, a panorama without a viewpoint, a single-point diffusion across a multifocal field, a world with its spaces collapsed, distinction by state without interval, a face, a transparent sphere — you have an Arcimboldo face.

Unlike the busts in the earlier series, *Seasons* and *Elements*, with which Arcimboldo began his cunning practice, this late picture, *Vertumnus*, confronts the viewer head-on. Earlier faces gaze to the side of the frame, toward the other paintings, apparently designated to hang together. Led by a looming chest hung on a pumpkin whose ridges carry your eyes upward toward the rostrum whose eyes, one a cherry, one a blackberry, cannot be said to be looking at the one looking at them, they are fruit, and *Vertumnus* is the epitome of Plotinian art. The fact that the eyes are not both cherries is a clue to their homeotic functions. Fruits can easily "represent" eyes, but they decline to do so here, preferring to carry other loads. The painting is a storehouse. Like the rest of the features, at the most simplistic, the eyes store nature's bounty in its diversity, rather than in its proper categories, one eye this, the other that, one of each kind, to complete the emperor's arklike comprehension of creation, which is one of a kind. The face is paradisal in this way — it receives all comers.

Compare it with the artist who looks out of the canvas in *Las Meninas* of Velasquez, the implacable artist of empire. Here, Rudolf II, painted a bit less than a century before Velasquez's masterpiece, is not a royal surveying his family. It is 1590, this painting has nothing to do with the baroque play of vision and visibility that marks that painting. Arcimboldo does take up the challenge of verisimilitude laid down by Da Vinci and his students and followers, with whom Arcimboldo had contact in his youth.[42] Yet verisimilitude, however much it informs the presentation of each natural object here, fails to characterize the painting as a whole. The bust is not in fact a mimesis of the emperor. What kind of artwork could be mimetic in its parts and not mimetic in its whole? The answer is another question. How can mimesis turn in on itself and become another mode? In an important sense, you see nothing in this image, nothing in particular — certainly, the likeness of the emperor is obscured, obscured and presented, through parts in likeness to things from realms interior and exterior, which in turn are turned, cut off, blocked, obscured, and then, to add insult to injury, the fruits are presented as what they are not. In this image, all the "fruits" of the empire, excesses given to power as gifts from nature, the fruits of all seasons pile up, a winter tuber with a straggling root, pearlescent spring blossoms, June green artichokes, ripe grapes and dried corn ears and autumnal fronds of grain — jumbled up and avoiding the alchemical metaphoric of Arcimboldo's earlier series, where the elements were distilled and separated as if into the bottles and jars of Rudolf's epochal *Kunstkammer*, as if the earlier painting series, *Seasons* and *Elements*, had been gathering base materials to ready them for transmutation into nobler things — then came *Vertumnus*. Nothing is transmuted in *Vertumnus*, except perhaps art.

The figure is vegetal-royal, no less plant than king, as mixed as it is pure, as silly as it is stately, as disorganized as it is subject to a rare kind of order, as broken apart as it is at the same time intricately bound together. Even the two orders, of nature and of sovereignty, as they were commonly imagined in the sixteenth century, fail to explain this contradictory aesthetic fully. The technique of *Vertumnus* does share something with alchemy — a material intuition, operable in the alchemist's elements, just as in the painter's paint — practiced at an analogous site, in the workshop on analogy with the laboratory.[43] In the production of this late painting, Arcimboldo also shares with alchemy a fascination with the composition of bodies, their potential to fuse into something higher, and a passionate desire to see the spirit, even if it has to lower itself into an embodied form. A thought comes: *Vertumnus* is a fusion of material and spiritual stuff, the immaterial power of the emperor, to produce abundance and receive it back in tribute to him, radiating through the material substructure of his rule, the capacity to provide for his subjects. The material conditions of rule, the needs of subjects and the cycles of nature, refract the immaterial side of rule, whether you call it authority, power, majesty, or right.

Shoulders back, chest forward, head tipped slightly back, as if on the brink of laughing — Vertumnus stands facing his portraitist, the court *conterfetter* Arcimboldo. The vegetal emperor's gaze aims beyond the artist, beyond the viewer, into a distance as extensive as his pose is regal. He poses as though fresh from victory in a war that cost him nothing, neck and chest ridged like a mighty colossus, like the *Augustus of Prima Porta*, decked out in a victory garland, *Imperator thoracatus*, the thorax of the empire. With regard to the attitude of its subject, this is not a typical Hapsburg family portrait, and it is not a political portrait, an *adlocutio* in which the ruler is shown addressing his court. Vertumnus holds his tongue (a barely visible bract of pomegranate seeds), taking cognizance, perhaps, of the truth of his majesty: it must not speak, in order that it may radiate. Appearing higher than the viewer, the head, which fills the upper half of the painting, draws a line to the horizon, geographic and historical, to the North Sea northward and the Mediterranean southward, generating the power of the last Roman ruler from his geographic reach. For such an expanse, political speech or even, as with other portraits of Hapsburg emperors, the signs and symbols of rule are not enough. To provide a contrast, in the portrait of Rudolf's father, Maximilian II, by Nicolas Neufchâtel, it is the emperor's finery — fur stole, gold tassels, and crystal buttons — that demonstrate his role. The distinction on the raiment indicates the distinction of the wearer. As with other Renaissance portraits of royalty or nobility, the tension between mimesis and allegory roils Neufchâtel's painting. Maximilian's sad, weary eyes, matched by unraveling ruffles at his neck, reveal a fleshy, fallen body. Despite these intimations of mortality, his body's physical bulk gives his authority its true weight. Judgment is coded into his right eyebrow, whose minute arc upward corresponds inversely to the magnitude of his word.

Perhaps because the Holy Roman Empire, as compared with the first Roman imperium, was so disunified, its domain riven by too many borders, its power gnawed at by too many princes, its normative force stolen by a pope — perhaps for these reasons, the new emperor, Rudolf, needed to incarnate himself directly into the flesh of nature. Perhaps Arcimboldo understood that new powers were needed. The father Maximilian symbolized rule by keeping the troubles of the empire out of the closed, gentile world of court, the imperator, instead of dying gloriously in battle, wearing down slowly among the infinite castle chambers. The son Rudolf ruled by taking the empire into himself, into his figure, ingesting its riches and its spoils, such that, as Marx says of natural man, nature became his body, stood proud by vegetables, fitted out with fruits, dressed in blossoms, and crowned with golden wheat.

"The dark green cucumber marks me, and squash / with its swelling belly, and cabbage bound with a slender reed" (*The Complete Elegies of Sextus Propertius* 4.2, lines 43–44, p. 351). The poem that according to Arcimboldo's friend Comanini provided the prototype for Arcimboldo's late painting describes the strange god Vertumnus vegetable by vegetable. However, Propertius's poem celebrates an antithetical mode, metamorphosis. In Propertius's poem, Vertumnus is a season god, the god of all seasons, of what makes seasons plural, the god of changeableness. He incorporates change in a single form, though a paradoxical one. Propertius's Vertumnus presents a terrifying, beautiful outline that varies from itself, a self-varying god whose unruly movement is emphasized in the play on the word *vertere* in the name Vertumnus. "You who wonder at my many shapes in one body: / learn the origins of the god Vertumnus" (lines 1–2, p. 349). The answer is the *versus*, the turning that characterized the seasons — Propertius's are not the fruits of summer or fall, but the fruits of turning, and Vertumnus is turning's special fruit (*uertentis fructum*, line 11). "My nature is opportune for all forms: / turn it into whichever you wish, I'll pull it off" (lines 21–22, p. 349). Yet whereas the poem focuses conceptually on turns, the painting is not interested in motion at all. Arcimboldo's Vertumnus is as still as a painting can make a subject, mortifying both nature and royalty into a tableau, each item of the season's yield frozen at the peak of ripeness. Arcimboldo was not interested in turning in Propertius's sense. The *Vertumnus* of 1590 could not be further from the mythic ideal of plasticity in Propertius or for that matter Ovid. In Propertius's poem, nature's products blossom and decay under Vertumnus's eyes; in Arcimboldo's painting, nature's products are his eyes.

The natural products that become the features of the emperor's face are depicted "from life." Decades of intent copying, tracing out the idiomatic lines of a narcissus or iris[44] culminate when what earlier was confined to the ornament of a frame or an incidental basket of fruit or the vines of a biblical grove migrates into the center of the picture, indeed, takes up residence in the figure itself. Think about the individual elements in the painting. Each item is representative of a single harvest at the moment of its fullest maturation. Your gaze is met by the cheeks, the right a peach, the left an apple, each showing a distinct ripe redness and filled-out tautness of its skin. The skin is not only its skin. Both ripe, each ripe in its own way, each in its own way fruit skin, and at the same time cheek skin. In this way,

Arcimboldo reels back in a circuit that has been left spread out until it overlaps again in its qualitative identity. When they are brought together like this, apple and peach, you understand that "ripe" is less a universal than a name holding together diverging aspects under a similarity that is not strictly sensible. Ripe cherry and ripe corn do not display similar sensible characteristics; rather, their place in a development is similar. Their place in a development makes them similar in one way; their place in a face makes them similar in others. Light comes from the left side, such that the shadow on the pear, right-side up in the front and center, touches its contour with a defining shadow and individuates it. From one perspective, this is not a face, but a fruit study, still life with fruit, grain, and flowers arranged to enliven — though frozen — an epiphanic moment, harvest, when nature fruits and fruit, that name, lays over a diversity of fruits. And yet they are more like atmospheric puncta in a weave of field and forest, which, stepping forward as a collection of independent, finite, singular facts, show tremendous individuation. At the point of the left earlobe, two green olives hang on a stem below leaves plucked at random along with them. One olive has not fully developed and protrudes, a brownish-red stub against which the green fruits manifest their success. Across and a bit lower, at the point of the right earlobe, a fig, not green, but purple, suggests the peak of sweetness, its sugary tangles enturned in wrinkles of wavy skin. Each separate spine of the chestnut cupule sticks up at the chin, flanked by bunches of barley, each kernel defined as itself and adding to the body of a cluster. Crevices in an artichoke splay downward toward a thorn, defining every petal as a cup that cradles the petal beneath.

You might be tempted to say the image approaches pure representation.[45]

But look at how this Vertumnus turns without turning into anything. A pear turned right-side up, a nose; a horizontal asparagus turned left, its slight arc lifting to a point aimed upward, another asparagus pointing right also with its arc up, together a moustache. Turned thus, asparagus and pear approximate a face's middle zone.

When green goods turn toward one another, this is one kind of turn. Cabbage leaf turns toward cabbage leaf — out of this mutual affinity there arises an alien shoulder. Cucumber turns toward turnip — now there are an alien neck and Adam's apple. The first kind of turning is when these fruits turn toward one another and make features. When an edible turns toward the front of the face plane, this is another kind of turn. These two effects, turning toward one another and turning outward toward the face plane, combine to make a face out of homeotic effects. A pear's calyx approximates nostrils: the turning does it. Turning toward or away — a version of approximating, getting near with a precise tilt until facets align. A swollen ripe apple draws near a thickened frond, and in drawing together, they draw near to a feature, though in ontological terms they remain distant. A homeotic reading of this bizarre-privileged item in the universe draws your attention to the alignments.

Alignment is one homeotic operation at work in Arcimboldo's late painting; at least seven further operations combine in Vertumnus, so there are at least eight in total. Let the sign for likeness be "~" — a common arithmetic symbol that sometimes stands for "similar to." In Arcimboldo's *Vertumnus*: features ~ natural things; natural things ~ natural things (circumradiation of traits through a vegetal "family"); turned to one another, aligned features of natural things ~ facial features; turned outward, aligned facial features ~ a face; face ~ a portrait; portrait ~ Rudolf II; Rudolf II ~ emperor; emperor ~ *Dei gratia Romanorum imperator electus semper augustus*.

I will have less to say about the later homeoses, since they move into the domain of what is traditionally thought of as representation, with its requirements for ontological indication, nondissemination, nondeviation, and unidirectionality, although the representational operations are also interesting and could be reduced to homeosis. What does it mean for a portrait to be like a face? Nonsensuous likeness comes into play, so that the planar, spiritless, fabricated object "portrait" can approach the prismatic, spirited, grown object / subject "face." As much as you may criticize these specific distinctions (planar / prismatic, fabricated / grown, material / spiritual), they are what keep the portrait from collapsing together with the face, and this difference allows the circumradiance to shine through the picture around into the face and into the physical body, as well. At the same time, asserting the difference between face (depicted) and portrait and between portrait and Rudolf (physical) permits the fantasy that an ontological transfer has taken place and denies the force of likeness in a way characteristic of representation. Remove the ideology of representation, and you confront the homeotic nearness of these two things, rather than their ontological distance. Mimesis has to preserve a material and spiritual distance, and that very difference supports, promotes, and exalts a spiritualist interpretation of life — the portrait is dead, acts by representing, the subject is alive, and acts by living. Yet this same difference cannot be explained except by likeness, a vicinity effect in which the emperor is already in his portrait and the portrait in the emperor, both living their death, dying their life.

Traits parted from their objects come into the vicinity of other traits and then, when they are in service of another, they become themselves. The curve of a peach or stone-round-dense-dark of a cherry turn away from their natural kinds, drawing out a further circuit. A peach curves into a cheek, and a cheek curves, peachlike. For the purposes of demonstration, you can tease apart these two events. It is not the things, fruits, objects, beings, but rather their contours and colors — traits — that approximate a face's contours and colors. Face and fruit meet in their contours and colors. Beware the phantoms of commonality and possession! *Their* contours, *their* colors — don't envision a transfer of property from one owner to another, as though in a contractual exchange, the face taking possession of the fruits, and nature, under duress, relinquishing its claim to them. Maybe the face does own the fruit; if it does, without question, then the fruit also owns the face. Mutual possession, from the perspective of the two owners, is not possession at all; the question of dominion cancels itself out.

Why would we say that the cherry is an eye, and not the eye is a cherry? Further, why wouldn't you say that the darkness of the cherry is the darkness of an eye, the glint of light off the highest curve of its shiny skin, bulging just so, such that a slice of white reflects amid the wine, the very habit of reflecting that the eye also has? Could not both the cherry reflect eye and eye reflect cherry and this doubleness constitute the nearness of eye and cherry that Arcimboldo encountered and expressed in the painting? We say, the two refract through one another, bending normal intuition in the process. To go a step further—the specific contour of the cherry's curve, where it is cut off by the countercurve of the peapod above it, such a cut and juxtaposition gives it the air of an eye—peapod interrupting cherry. I am talking here about the complex operations involved in the gift of traits. A cut interrupts the contour, and I say that it is the character of this particular cut as much as the curve and bulge and glint that makes this cherry like an eye.

3.5. *The relations between traits are also traits.*

An important distinction can be made between a thing qua feature (Vertumnus's cheeks) and the negative interactions where there is no thing, but only an interference, which is related to the turning and turnedness of aspects, cutting and turning toward a general alignment of features. Another important distinction can be made between single things that resemble single features, such as the cheeks again, and aggregates of things that resemble single features, the flowers that make up the cheeks in the earlier composite head *Spring*, for instance (Figure 7).

There is a situation in which multiple features liken up into one thing, in which everything depends on what you pick out as a feature. To speak more formally, I can posit that more than one thing may be like one thing, that is, a nut and cherry like a mouth, and one thing may be like more than one thing, a sheaf of wheat like a beard or an epaulette.

3.6.   *Traits may be of any size or consistency.*

Further, conjunctions of things that themselves have defining traits may define another thing through traits that are not prominent in the original things. This means that the defining traits of a thing may be erased or merge into the atmosphere again as soon as the thing is brought into conjunction with something else.

3.6.1.   *A gift of traits is accompanied by a withdrawal of traits.*

You can now make two statements about *Vertumnus* that apply in kind to the whole figure and to any part of the figure as well. First, one and only one thing looks like this. Only one thing has the right size, coloring, contour, and so on that, when these qualities fall together, homogenate out this face. This is the gift of traits. Second, you can also say now that coming together *in this way*, out of the precise degree of the turnings and the precise place of the interruptions, conjures up the face. Once again, this demonstrates the adverbial character of "like." Proof of the adverbial character arrives when, in different conjunctions, aspects of the "same" things come together and make up something utterly unlike. Here you are confronted with a brute fact: "traits" are not stubborn, atomistic ingredients that, when organized in a certain way, configure a thing.

3.6.2.   *Traits fuse out of, light up in conjunctions without which they do not exist in se*.

Loosening up traits from their carriers, and the magic — if you want to call it that — of fusing out of and into unhabitual traits when alien things approach one another applies just as well to your local harvest, and by extension to all of existing nature. The gift of traits produces a harvest. Arcimboldo finds / makes a likeness between nature and the sovereign, while nature, at least, independent of human needs and politics, is already crossed by its own homeotic layers. Nature's homeoses don't need human beings, but they are not closed to them, either. Nature approaches itself asymmetrically in what is sometimes called families, though the term "family" cannot be taken as explanatory, only as descriptive. For example, in the alchemical series, *Seasons* and *Elements*, with which Arcimboldo's madness for likenesses began, seasons and elements could be called families, "seasons" naming, let's say, everything that fuses out of a specific atmosphere of weather, "elements" naming, let's say, groups that approximate the classical qualities of antiquity — hot, wet, light, heavy. These archaic families — seasonal and elemental kinships — are on display in each of the early paintings. However, you don't need painting to display this. Similar grouping habits are exhibited in what we call "grain," similar habits in what we call "drupe" (apricot, cherry, olive) — any gardener knows this. What any gardener knows forms the basis for taxonomy and eventually also evolutionary knowledge. What a painter knows — that family resemblance is the basis for the gardener's knowledge — goes beyond this, to the supporting fact that likenesses are atmospheric and fusional and go well beyond traditional families, or you could say, as with vegetables, likenesses grow.

This is perhaps the significance of the harvest in Arcimboldo's paintings. In a double metaphor, natural products become emblems of the growth of likenesses.

3.6.3.   *Likenesses grow. Pears grow into apples, twigs grow into hair, nature grows into politics, faces grow into gardens — and all these grow into their observers, which take them into their fields.*

Incidentally, to talk of things briefly once again, when distant things grow through one another, a set of resemblances is lighting up. The more distant the things, the more powerful the image — or so said surrealism. Families of all sorts must grow and decay a million times a day; they do not require observers, only atmospheres. Circuits of likeness, internally intergrowing, become intimate, habituated, and at some point start to shine forth as individuated things, or as Roger

Caillois called them, "objective ideograms" ("The Praying Mantis," in *The Edge of Surrealism*, p. 76). You can also call them "faces," if "face" can be used in an unrestricted, nonbodily sense. As an unrestricted term, "face" can stand in for "qualitative identity," "circuit," and "transparent sphere," an extension and intensification of a Plotinian homeotic world. "Face" can tell the character of "world."

3.7.   *The combination of all lit circuits constitutes the face of the world.*

Arcimboldo's madness for likeness draws on this same madness for likeness as it preexists the artist in nature, in borderline natural-philosophical activities that result in the emperor's vast *Kunstkammer*, not to mention in techniques of likeness making in Renaissance art. The latter, however, Arcimboldo deftly betrays. Mere lip service is paid to the ideal of verisimilitude in faces, for whatever purposes power and class had needed them previously. Recognition of the emperor's face is secondary to recognition of bizarre overlaps among things and traits from far and wide, and in turn, to the resemblance that these can make, once arranged, once settled into a pattern, to a face. In short, in this art, a world of resemblances is simply put together, items brought nearer following their own impulses and put on display in the face paintings. On special display in *Vertumnus* is the potential to distribute natural likenesses in an unnatural way, or better, to emphasize the natural-unnatural distribution of likenesses in faces and fruit.

    The painting shows a long-run tendency in cultural work that expresses itself, after this moment, in empirical philosophy and evolution theory, as I have indicated, and also in the very technical basis of technologies, whose invention depends on a collagelike imagination that can put together the unlike to produce a likeness of a machine. If you want to talk about the larger family of invented things for which Arcimboldo's likeness field is the central node, the objective ideogram of its intention, I also should point out the largest family of which Arcimboldo's field is also the objective ideogram, namely, the world, of which it is also a part. *Vertumnus*'s most valuable act seems to be the condensation of antagonistic ontological regions, two (produce and power) and a third (art) and thus to indicate, in the thickest of overlapping points, the homeotic nature of the world.

3.7.1.   *The world is an asymmetrical array.*

4.   *World is an asymmetrical array.*

Visualize, if you will, a field with a few simple marks:

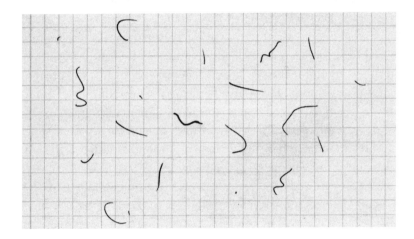

Inadvertently, resemblances light up among the marks, mark turns toward mark, kinships crop up among the traits that make out those marks, and traits of those traits also find close kin nearby. For now, think of these marks in terms of just a few traits, even though you know you are abstracting, and for important reasons, homophany does not allow for abstraction, if to abstract means to step away from the tangled mess of characteristics.

Perform a test on yourself on this field: What here is atmosphere, what likeness? How do you receive the particular array of marks and their asymmetrical distribution? In one line of thinking, in psychology and aesthetics, you might call these marks "figures" and the graph paper supporting them you might call their "ground." This well-established schema, the Gestalt idea, assumes that the ground is not a part of the figures, and yet at the same time it is the source, *ex negativo*, for any figures' individuation — the ground is for them, but not of them. To the Gestaltist,[46] ground is ontologically distinct from figure. Ground is not figure. Conversely, figure, as what distinguishes itself from ground, is the source for the nonindividuatedness of ground, though this inverse effect is often left out of the discussion. Figure is thus not ground. These simple opposing principles, each of which contains its own determinate negation, are not logical principles. They are principles of sensibility — their relation is a fact of perception, not a fact of reason. They demarcate each other in a visual field, and they do so highly symmetrically, figure / ground, ground / figure. If the symmetrical demarcation fails, you are left not with a paradox, but with a perceptual confusion, which leads toward asymmetry, and tipping toward asymmetry brings a homeotic process into view, along with a different mode of negativity that attends it. You can look at the figure / ground as either a Gestalt phenomenon or a homeotic phenomenon.

To see this, and to see how the homeotic admits or allows for the Gestalt interpretation, start with "figure." In classic figure / ground discourse, it is rarely mentioned, though always the case, that the figure in question is recognizable as a figure. The spectator is assured that there is a figure and the figure is never figure in general but this or that figure. As an example: in the famous silhouette ink drawing of a vase and faces (Figure 8), figures emerge from the ground, and then they merge with it again, becoming figure and ground of each other in turn. This is what fascinates in the vase-face image. It is a Gestalt image times two.[47] And yet the ground, or better, the atmosphere out of which faces and vases emerge is not just in the picture; the ground includes the vast, undrawn, echo chamber of faces and vases that have already fused out in their traits — nose / curve; forehead / vase; mouth, lips and chin / vase; face as a sort of contour, vase as a vessel that excludes its outside — specific collections of traits fused out from among the atmosphere of all other faces and vases that could be accessed by memory or culture. Thinking homeotically shatters the idea of perception into a thousand shards. Vase-face is no longer simple ground and figure and no longer merely a reciprocal and highly symmetrical interchange, but two figures that reciprocally interact, each of which has to become recognizable out of a much larger atmosphere that dwarfs them before they can be either confused with one another or distinguished from one another.

This image makes it easy to see the homeotic presuppositions for Gestaltism. If you had never encountered a vase or a face, the figure / ground distinction would not operate. Without this likeness to draw upon, no Gestalt would come forward. A larger field, the field of all vases and nonvases, far out of proportion with the excerpt before you, makes up the atmosphere out of which a vase "fuses out." If you call it "fusing out," the dynamic relation between confusion and resolution becomes apparent, as does the disproportion between the figure and the field or pool or atmosphere out of which it emerges. What Gestalt theory understands according to the figure / ground concept pair, homeotics understands according to atmosphere and likeness, where there is a large confusion and a tiny, transient fusing out.

A Rorschach test works on a similar model. Homeosis precedes all possible Gestalt relations in a Rorschach image, which presumes a homeoplex, a vast array of likenesses that can couple and decouple, depending on the vicinity in which they repeat. The likenesses are not in the inkblot, and yet to be sure, in another way, they are in it. A test subject's encounter with a particular inkblot activates a set of resemblances — stains corresponding to human figures, parts of human figures, animal aspects, patterns, and so on. These resemblances exist between the inkblot's indeterminate stains and other instances, among which an atmosphere arises. You encounter an inkblot already in a field of memory images, cultural inscriptions, moments of fantasy, dream, where histories of the obsolete and forgotten resonate. The existence of stains and the field or atmosphere

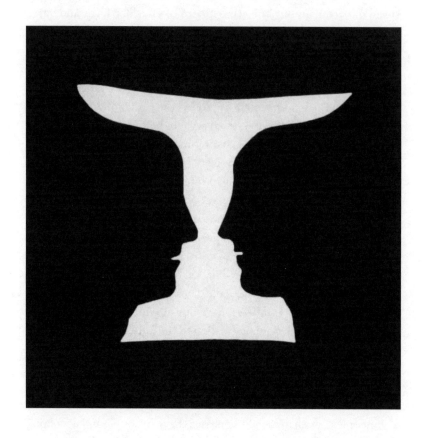

Figure 8. A "Rubin Vase" (optical illusion) from Edgar Rubin, *Visuell wahgenommene Figuren: Studien in psychologischer Analyse, Part 1* (Copenhagen: Gyldendalske, 1921), Image #3.

is mutual, called into existence together; one would not exist per se without the other. If you are thinking in Gestalt terms, the blot would be the ground, and the figure would come to prominence when a closed outline pushed back the blanket of indistinction that tries to hold onto it. If you are thinking in homeotic terms, an inkblot would hold a vast array of resemblant traits, including all those not immediately present, that could fuse out of this particular atmosphere, should they, through memory or some other field, come into contact with correspondences. Inkblots are less a test of an individual psychology than a historical barometer of the human homeotic alluvium at different levels.

One reason to prefer homeotics to the psychology of perception is that psychology is prejudiced against traits in favor of forms. Rorschach insists the blots are in reality made up of forms, and the task of the psychologist is to lead the patient to those forms, a process Rorschach calls "Deutenlassen von Zufallsformen," "the letting be interpreted of accidental forms" (*Psychodiagnostik*, p. 3, *Psychodiagnostics*, p. 15). The forms are simply there; the interpretation is added by the test subject. It is true that Rorschach sees the particular forms as accidental with respect to the blot. They have not been drawn by a human hand or imprinted from nature. That does not mean they are accidental with respect to the test subject or to psychology in general—quite the contrary. The contents of the forms, so to speak, are filled out by the patients themselves, but the form of forms—that they are there and that they are forms always in every case—is a basic tenet of psychology. "Forms" are the elements of cognition, and the particular forms are necessary in view of the psychologist's and the subject's own histories. Any form will be tolerated, so long as the association to a form is familiar to both the subject and the psychologist, so long as the form already resides in their (immediately overlapping) likeness fields. Forms in an inkblot used in a Rorschach test emerge in the overlapping psyches of subject and scientist. It goes without saying that a form that could be experienced by the patient alone in a wholly private way would be as intolerable as a form that only the clinician could experience. The form has to resonate in the likeness fields of both — a major and ignored presupposition of this brand of psychology.

Rorschach does not develop the likeness character of his experiments very far, though he does allude to its importance. At one point in his argument, in order to talk about the resemblance field that makes possible his test, he quotes the 1916 edition of Eugen Bleuler's popular *Lehrbuch der Psychiatrie* (Textbook of psychiatry): "Perceptions arise from the fact that sensations, or groups of sensations, ecphorize memory pictures of former groups of sensations within us. This produces a complex of memories of sensations, the elements of which, by virtue of their simultaneous occurrence in former experiences, have a particularly fine coherence and are differentiated from other groups of sensations" (quoted in *Psychodiagnostics*, pp. 16–17). Leaving aside the metaphor of physical storage and retrieval (the ecphoria or activation of engrams), consciousness, in Bleuler's picture, performs acts of diffusing and fusing out resemblances. Rorschach continues this line of thought when he defines the primary operation of the test, "Deutenlassen von Zufallsformen," as "associative integration of available engrams (memory-pictures) with recent complexes of sensations" (p. 17). How "associative integration" works is not specified, but Rorschach, and Bleuler as well, envision an operation that brings the inkblot into concordance with forms stored in memory so that the two fields may be integrated. And so, although the theory limits its objects to "forms," an extrahomeotic locus, the specific forms are determined by likeness processes.

How a particular form fuses out is interesting. Rorschach asks: On what basis does this form appear to the patient, and not that one? He does not ask the ontological question par excellence: Why is there something and not nothing? He asks why this likeness and not another. In place of the great either / or of being and nothingness, he recognizes a small one / another of like and like. In Hume, to the question why this association happens and not that one, the answer is still something like a scale of being — vivid impressions are truer, higher, than paler ideas. Vivid impressions guide the emergence of ideas. Truth is a matter of the intensity of being. In Bleuler's textbook on psychology, reactivated memories overlap with current sense perceptions, an old pattern resonates with a form in the present, just as for Rorschach, the blot suggests a memory engram, and a memory engram attracts one form or another hidden in the blot. Blot assimilates to engram; similars resonate. And so, although indebted to Gestalt theory, which attends to the figure / ground experience and forgets about the larger atmosphere and likenesses that must preexist it, the psychology of perception, in the work of Rorschach and Bleuler, although they focus on forms as the basic element of psychic experience, also attends to the real atmosphere of perception, the vast array of traits available for association.

4.1. *An atmosphere is an ongoing archaic merger in which traits drift, awaiting diaphanous partners.*

Gestalt theory and the psychology of perception help show how a homeotic field can be misunderstood as a repository of figures or forms, but they also show how even these depend on an impulse toward likeness that precedes form or figure. With this in mind, suspend the terms "ground," "figure," and "form" and conjure an atmosphere graced with archaic homeons:

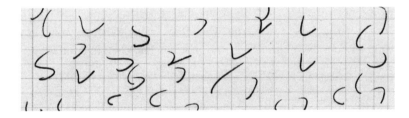

Now you can do your own test, a homeotic and not psychological one: let a few archaic protohomeons fuse out in a basic atmosphere—let an asymmetrical array congeal. Abjure figures, forms, and beings for your field—accept only traits. Traits are not simply given, and they do not preexist the process of fusing out. A trait may single itself out among a host of other traits, or it may not, and yet traits are there only once they fuse out.

The role of language should be noted. When you name some trait — call these homeons "hyperbolae" — when you name the trait, the word "hyperbola," itself a mess of resemblances, will resonate with and single out some traits, hyperbolically, curving beyond itself in sympathy with marks and countermarks in a homeotic-linguistic compromise (see Premise 6) that projects its own patterns. Names are catalysts for fusion. However, put the naming act aside for now and regard the mark field and its activities. As with stars in a horoscope, one hyperbola orbits near another hyperbola, and their traits begin to exchange looks:

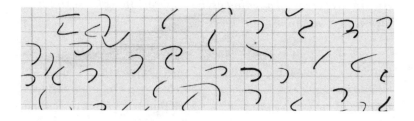

In an environment in which hyperbolae can approach one another, when they do approach, their traits become their traits. In the approach of indeterminates, traits light up. Curve with curve, "tail" with "tail" — the reverse is also true: when their traits exchange looks they can be said to be approaching one another. The phenomenon is bidirectional. Traits become their traits when they approach one another and the traits repeat. Likewise, traits repeat when they approach one another homeotically. Recall that in a multidimensionally indeterminate atmosphere, where traits alone light up, nothing else gets established, nothing else is expected — no figures, as the Gestaltists thought, and no forms, as the psychologists of perception thought.

As part of this homeotic test, restrict your vision, allow a minimum of traits to resonate, repeat. Suspend, temporarily, the following perceptual categories: direction, color, weight, density, relation, distinction. Imagine a minimum, "hyperbola." Ignore the countless other traits amassed in these same hyperbolae — line, point, slip, hook, fat, not white, not nothing. Note that infinite negative traits attend any fused-out trait — as its long tail. Negative traits such as lack of hair, or "not opossum," also float there. A trait clutches a negative infinity to it like a lifeline. Trait "means" the temporary suspension of this infinity. A trait is a face whose infinitely varying body is every other associable trait in indistinction.

4.2.   *A trait is a face whose body is the world.*

In the above sketch, a useful caricature of a real atmosphere, imagine there are no empty spaces, populate every span with hyperbolae in all directions and dimensions. Then visualize an excerpt, a cut out from the replete atmosphere:

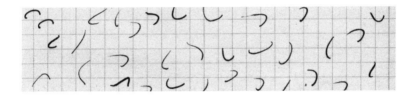

Assume that (*a*) ⸦ in this excerpted field calls out to, looks at, faces (*b*) ⸡ in the first field. You could name, arbitrarily, many subtraits that would justify this selection, but for now, take only one: relative thickness of line. Through the thickness of these two lines relative to the other hyperbolae (skinny ones, which form their atmosphere), these two messes of traits (*a*) and (*b*) face each other, singling themselves out as "thick hyperbolae."

4.3.   *Likenesses look around — this cannot be described any more precisely or in other terms. Traits look for one another.*

Although the process itself is autonomous or semiautonomous, you can still enter it, trigger it, play on it, pray for it. Here, my text is the prayer that calls up the pair that looks each toward each in the following format: there occurs ⁊and then ⸰ when my text adds emphasis to their mutual look in the phrase "thick hyperbolae." The phrase looks toward the marks. A psychologist of perception would call these forms that are "integrated" by memory "engrams applied to accidental forms." It matters little which field hosts the likenesses — memory, paper. Call them together through memory engram, through the history of a specific figure (à la Aby Warburg), through wordgram, illustrative diagram; measure the two hyperbolae, plot their curves, express them in a mathematical formula — each of these fields allows the pair to resonate its way out of a congeries.

4.3.1.   *Calling out a likeness takes the place of pointing out a form.*

Pointing out a form, the operation that when talking about inkblots Rorschach calls "deuten," requires a conjunction of a phenomenon and a meaning. A form must appear and have a meaning in a context in order to be pointed out. In the context of a life, of a psychology, a form plays some determinate role, it goes along with, qua form, a function. In contrast, for a likeness to be called out, a chain of correspondences only has to come into alignment, and there is no need for them to have a meaning or a function — in fact, a certain degree of meaninglessness attends the fusing out of a likeness, and though it may find a function, that function may not yet have been born.

Modes we don't normally think of as connected or connectable appear in the unexpected alignment of correspondences. Consider the act of taking a measurement. At least two domains not naturally connected come into alignment in this operation. Measurement assumes a qualitative proximity among measuring techniques and things to be measured. Measurement produces this alignment. When you measure something, the act of measuring, before it begins, calls out a similarity between the measurer and the measured.[48] While there are technical terms for this assumed proximity — "conversion of units," "comparison to a standard," "orientation in Cartesian space" — such technical terms lie like veils over the operation. One fact can't be denied. Measurement can never substitute for the things measured. And yet the act of measuring assumes that something within an object is measurable, and that measurable aspect becomes the object of a measuring technique, in a particular way at a particular juncture, when you measure. You can see this most clearly in one particular kind of measurement, measuring a length, whose ideal object is a line. In order to measure length, two lines have to come close together, as if from opposite universes, one marked off in regular intervals and one receptive to marking in a like way. The marked and the to-be marked, the divided and the to-be divided, share a likeness as lines and become like one another in divisibility and markability. The measured line becomes like the measuring line with respect to markability. By means of a made overlap, line on line, a measured line imprints its likeness on a bare line. A bare line cannot be supplanted by the measure, but measure and line do come as near to one another as two things can be, in measurability. Or better, line and measurement come together in an associative integration that has its own face, its own character. Proof of this: weigh a bushel of corn with a ruler. Measure the length of a board on a scale. The attempt fails because when it comes to lines, the homeotic sphere lights up with respect to rulers, Cartesian axes, dimensions in neutral space, and intervals, not masses, gravity, pressure, or displacement. For a ruler or a Cartesian axis to be "useful" for something like weight, a habit of likenesses (a standard, a vicinity) would have to be established. There is no reason it cannot be. Keep in mind that I am not talking about the practical activity of measuring a line or weighing a weight, where a habit of placing a coin on a scale produces certain effects; I am talking about the constitution of a paraphysical and perhaps even prephysical association called "measuring."

Why do you turn to measurement when confronted with a line? This is not nearly the only disposition possible. We commonly turn to measurement because lines have been likened up more regularly, more frequently, and with more emphasis than other pairs of things. The likeness process called "measuring" has become, through repeated enlikening, quite likely to be repeated.

4.3.2. *The "standard" of any homeosis is another, and groups of homeoses tend to reinforce one another in progressive integrating associations.*

One homeosis refers to another homeosis; all homeoses consist in this transversal reference. A likeness is crossed by another and others. When you reconstruct a "first time" in which a homeon fuses out of an atmosphere, it can only be a heuristic. There is and was no first time. There are only more and less established, more and fewer like likenesses. Here is another difference from psychology and Gestalt theory. Compared with a well-established likeness with many precedents stretching back in a long cline, a young likeness only ever barely comes together. The fewer references a likeness makes, the lighter its touch. A pairing suggests itself. An association loosely brushes. In contrast to the necessitarian dialectic of figure and ground, a homeon does not depend on its difference from the atmosphere, and so the atmosphere does not need to be uniform, as a ground does. The atmosphere may interfere with the likeness as much as it wants to or can. An embryonic homeon bleeds into the atmosphere.

4.3.3. *A "first" likeness barely emerges, faded among a plethora of almost and not quite likenesses.*

The likeness world is asymmetrical in this other sense, as well. Imagine a pure homeotic vicinity, for the purposes of the theory — pure in the Kantian sense, uncontaminated by anything of another order. Although beings, forms, and meanings are excluded, the pure homeotic vicinity includes everything, or almost everything. The adverb "almost" helps express the asymmetry you find all over the homeoverse. In English, "almost" implies an approach and an approximation as well as a dissociation and a despondence, a pararelation, mixing a negative with a positive, that filters through a zone both other and same. Since nothing holds it together and it holds all traits within it, a quasi-pleroma, the homeoverse may well contain within it self-identical, uniform units, but not as the whole of the All or as the basic element, rather as this or that efflorescence of the quasi-pleroma. A being is an accident within the approximum.

4.4.   *The homeoplex is almost, mostly all and all mostly, an approximation to itself.*

Return to the homeotic test purified of form and being and any other explanatory schemas besides likenesses looking at one another. Take these squiggles from the test field, lines with a few traits, hyperbolae with direction, thickness, and a pronounced tail. They liken up, approximate, look toward one another, fuse out of the vicinity of indistinctly directional, tailless hyperbolae, whatever other random marks aggregate around them. Yet the squiggles can only reject what they are not after at least two of them have already come together to affirm what they are, what they are like. They affirm by approaching and approximating and in distancing from other likenesses, rejecting not their opposites, not their determinate negations, but rather their closest kin and the closest kin to their closest kin, one pairing barely coming to prominence among a set of further candidates for pairing up with. The kin stay close — almost in, though mostly out, a little more out than in, all / most — asymmetrically. The outside comes adjacent as soon as a pair lights up. Evoke this or that pair, and a minimal likeness diffuses through the vicinity, making up a set of almost pairs, just as memes diffuse through culture and accrete a family to themselves or as genes diffuse through a population and organize phenotypes.

    Now something more general can be articulated about the homeoplex, and more hopeful: it can never be used up. Fusing out of an atmosphere, no matter how long it goes on, is not the progressive determination of the All. Fusing out throws a segment into confusion for the sake of a few pals, in the same way that a cloud casts a shadow on the ground so that the surrounding landscape can disappear into brightness.

4.4.1. *When a homeotic pair lights up, a cline or continuum of gradations enchains, a figure (a trait with traits) establishes itself, a species, a language, a style, an industry amasses, and when this happens, each time it happens, a new indeterminacy unrolls alongside it.*

Now conceive of a likeness as a restricted indeterminacy among an unrestricted indeterminacy. A restricted indeterminacy, one likeness, a species of butterfly, say, thrives on its internal indistinctions at the same time as it hosts itself within an unrestricted indeterminacy surrounding it. A "new" species can fuse out of an old one, as though out of an alien atmosphere, one restricted indeterminacy shifting its fusions around. The homeoplex is made of more and less restricted indeterminacies. Since in it nothing is ever fully determinate, nothing is ever fully indeterminate, either. Nothing can become a "being" or "nothing." What is clear is that one indeterminacy, such as a particular species, can act like another indeterminacy, such as the greater kingdom of organisms. Either can become an atmosphere for further likenesses.

4.4.2. *A species is also a family. A likeness is also an atmosphere. The tree of life is in some ways not unlike an organism.*

Given that homeotic overlaps happen not just horizontally among putative equals, but also hierarchically among putative lessers and greaters, the asymmetrical landscape is pocked by severe confusions. These are real confusions, not merely epistemological ones. There are epistemological confusions, too, of course, but this is because thought is also homeotic. Beings overlap, and knowledges overlap, as well—all / most, almost.

You can easily get lost among the overlaps. As an interim measure, to get oriented, you can make homeotic composite.

A homeotic composite doubles the moment when a variation becomes a species, when a two goes over into a more and then into an all / most. Homeotics is good at incipience. In its optic, there is no "evolutionary logic"; instead, traits do their do-si-do in the quasi-logic of the transparent mirror.

We need to understand at last the transparent mirror! In its haze, an image reflects over another image, bringing two into proximity. A transparent mirror does not reflect, it refracts. Snell's law describes the relationship between the angles of incidence and refraction when light or other waves pass through a boundary between two different media; to understand a transparent mirror, you invent a Snell's law of likenesses. With a Snell's law for this aesthetic Spinozism, a particular atmosphere would have a particular refraction index, given a specific history of fusings and refusings in its vicinities. An elementary-school art class would have one of the highest refraction indices, a primordial aesthetic soup at the instant after a new big bang. A simple system would have a low index, given the higher constraints on variability within such a system. The economy in Marx's *Capital* would have, at most points, a very low homeotic refraction index, for though capital is complex, it is also simple with regard to indeterminacies. It is, in short, dialectical. That is to say, the machine of capital places huge constraints on variation. And yet wherever there are two or more of these low-likeness systems, say, the machine of capital and the system of reason, or the evolution system and the fashion system, the homeotic index rises sharply and overlaps multiply, because, of course, the systems themselves overlap. How can capitalism be thought of without evolved organisms in their niches? If they were thought together, as overlapping, before long, indeterminacy would begin to increase again (as if you could compare or measure this), or rather, indeterminacy spreads among and between established likenesses, and as it spreads and like but not identical likenesses become established, variability tends to rise, which is to say that the likelihood of a fusion goes up, the vaguer and thus more enterprising the incipient likeness regime.

4.4.3. *History happens in the transparent mirrors of crossed homeotic fields.*

It is easiest to see this dynamic in the history of technical objects. Take a simple technical system, which you can call a "device." It is customary to think of a device as a mere piece of equipment. In truth, a device is a combination of two different kinds of things from two different regions of being. A device is an arrangement of parts brought together under a specific set of purposes; it is something "devised" with a claim on some end. It may be that a device is the concretization of an invention that brings together a new combination of features for a new purpose. It is also the case, however, that a device is always for producing like effects. The effects that are wanted, the purposes, are a repetition of old purposes with a new twist, but never far from a previous iteration, and the effects are also expected to repeat into the future. Production of like effects is not only the aim and outcome of photographic devices or printer-scanner-copiers. All technical objects exist in a chain of likenesses and in order to produce likenesses.

This chain, extending into the past and future, is actually two chains. In any device, at least two clines cross one another: a cline of parts and a cline of purposes. A technical object is what happens at the point of approximation between parts and purposes. When the parts draw together, they draw near a purpose, and the two become a family, as unholy as the marriage may appear. They start to become like one another. A bar becomes like the stone it is supposed to help lift, or rather, it becomes like the lifting and lifted stone. The bar as lever describes the movement of the lifting — the two overlap. A device is the transparent mirror in which two clines refract through one another, parts and purpose. Hold up an iron bar. Here is the part. Sight a stone to be lifted. Here is the purpose. Bar and lifting approximate for the first time in a device.

If you think of the chain of likenesses extending into the past, the bar has many analogues and forerunners. In light of its purpose known as "lever," the bar is already an approximation of the long disymmetrical cline "lifting" (action trait, with inherent purpose) to the cline "wedging tools" (parts of a process). Leg, hand, torso, core muscles, earth's gravity, iron's weight, inertia, with tipping, leaning, suspending — the parts of the process can be described pragmatically. This is what you *do* when you lever something up. You lean your weight and augment it by extending leg and torso and back muscles against the lever, which transmits and increases the force in opposition to gravity and inertia, as one side goes down and the other goes up. The same parts of the activity can also be described homeotically, as traits, as fusions in a mode of approximation: leaning leg, pushing hand, pulling torso, attracting gravity, lifting, and so on, all of which you have seen or done before. Leaning enlikens to leaning, pushing enlikens pushing, hand enlikens the figure that hands get into for a particular purpose. Doing is enlikening (see Premise 7). In doing, these process parts mimic precursors at the same time as they overlap with a purpose, which is what dictates their specific arrangement. A purpose is a desire for a like effect, a part a like means to a like effect.

The particular technical object called "tool," then, in this new definition, has its parts, and those parts are homeotic. The homeotic parts line up in the cline of the tool's evolution — a historical field that, if it were a photo album, would show snapshots of the ramp and the wedge, as well as the earliest cranes. The album displays the cline of the parts. The cline of purposes is something else entirely. Purposes that can liken up with lifting vary from low to high lifts, from light to heavy lifts, on compact or ungainly objects, and so on, with a view toward the architecture produced, which varies along with the purposes. High to high, low to low. The building is a likeness of the purpose / part overlap.

What's more, there will be other buildings of this height. The final cause of lifting is never one single lift one single time or one single block that wants lifting. No action ends with itself — no action ever ends: it anticipates a second action like it in order to become itself. No purpose is ever to itself alone in human affairs. A cross of clines is always "for" another cline. Never one lift alone, but a string of lifts, never one lifting device, but a string of lifters, never one object to be lifted, but a catena of lifted things. Particularly evident in technological history is that nothing happens alone. The primal impulse of all technohistory is to make and scatter species.

Planning also plays a role in technohistory, a fairly important role, as you would think. In the history of devices, planning has a role similar to that of art in social history. Art is the homeotic milieu *tout court*. For a plan, be it written, drawn, thought, or dreamt, the lever, stone, weight, pyramid, skyscraper, dwelling, place, purpose are imitated in advance as a sketch, so that things and acts in time and history can liken up to them. Art, in this narrow sense — as sketch, as blueprint — is the premier forum for approximation. A building lights up in resemblance to a plan. A plan lights up in resemblance to an imaginary building. From the pair, the one. A likeness gives itself for something to emerge. This does not happen in a vacuum. The emergence of a likeness is also a defiance and a distortion of the homeoplex in its current configuration. A building where there was none, a device to do something you always hoped to do, a new group — a family, species, series — is always a fusing out and at the same time also a violation of the pleroma, when it converts a dimensionless interreticulation of clines into a pseudoentity, a gathering of traits. When they gather together, the gathering of traits always reduces homeotic dimensionality, because in effect, it makes an excerpt of the chaos appear as an orderly thing, as if a single "device" that stood out in a history was not already crushed back into the world fabric like a fiber into felt. A thing or a group (a thing is a group) is an excerpt of the ongoing clinic confusion.

If it seems as though clinic confusion, the approximating primordial pleonasm, the alternation of restricted and unrestricted indeterminacies, depends on a principle of difference, hold yourself back from this belief. Variation should not be confounded with difference. Variation is the flip side of the clinic tapestry. Patterns on the recto fuse out of the mess of variations on the verso, and yet they are not formally distinct from them. The threads that group up into patterns on the front trail off into indistinction on the back. Or if you like, the crane that lifts the stone block to the highest point of the temple wall, the developed lever that positions the building's highest point by means of its own height, is the recto of a fabric whose verso shows the ragged ends of all the approximations and attempts in the history of levering, what is sometimes called, in the thrall of progress, "the past."

4.5. *Variation is the "almost" that correlates with homeotic "overlap."*

When a trait overlaps with another to make a likeness, that trait can also be described as a variation of the other, since like is unlike same. Like is almost like, a like trait is almost and not quite another, and thus it counts at the same time as a variation.

    The interpretation of likeness as variation entails one huge consequence. Under a principle of variation, the substitution of one thing for another, the trade of one trait for another is never allowable, since like is unlike same. And thus a principle of substitution, such as the one involved in any classification system, is as inappropriate as a principle of "nonsubstitutability" such as the one involved in any theory of difference. Two traits are neither substitutable nor nonsubstitutable; they are almost, alike, variations of one another. In technical philosophical terms, homeotics rejects the identity of indiscernibles, as well as its inverse, the nonidentity of indiscernibles. What results from the refusal of these two absolutes is a world of asymmetrically distributing homeoses. In the homeotic Rorschach test, after the sideways-facing hyperbolae fuse out, downward-facing hyperbolae would emerge, and so on. Right hyperbolae and then left hyperbolae, one after another, come together (not spatially), into a cline. After the hyperbolae concatenate a resemblance field, variations may gradually lead toward other shapes — "after" in the sense that one work of art is made "after" another, in the image of and diverging from, or in the way that you are "after" your ideals and so you approximate yourself to them.

4.5.1. *Homeosis names the constitutive nearness of everything.*

The rays of homeosis pass through history without resistance, to light up in foreign climes. A homeotic approximation diffracts along multiple clines, clines transect climes, climes diffract clines, which radiate into unforeseen, varying, crooked patterns.

What can be done with the constitutive nearness of everything? Who has a picture of it that will illuminate the situation? To follow up on this, return once again to Neoplatonic thought, where likeness was more at home. Radek Chlup, in his introduction to Proclus's thought, proposes the word "hologram" for the asymmetrically distributing homeotic world that gets built across Proclus's writings. "The Neoplatonic universe resembles a hologram: each sphere of knowledge mirrors all the others and is convertible to them" (*Proclus*, p. 12). It is significant that in Neoplatonism, which in broad outline is an extended argument for a nonphysical world, this nonphysical world, at its most systematically presented in Proclus, can be described as a closed, hologrammic, refracting domain—a set of transparent mirrors. The conjunction of mirrors and convertibility of spheres, in Chlup's rough and canny summation of Proclus's nonphysical world, describes a universe in which every thing and every sphere is constitutively near. Each sphere, in Proclus's system, is convertible into another, in the sense that no sphere can be fully delimited from another, not because one sphere is just as good as another, but because all spheres partake of each other's goods already and by design. The spheres in question—cosmos, world soul, soul, *intellectus agens*, *intellectus passivus*, descended One, One beyond everything—overlap. None of them is completely separate, and none is completely substitutable by another either. The kernel of the problem, then, as Proclus shows us, is how to understand and more importantly how to live within Plotinus's invention: a separation without difference, an overlap without identity, convertibility of all into all unevenly through a transparent mirror.

Proclus's *Elements of Theology* synthesizes decades spent commenting on the Platonic dialogues, with constant reference to Plotinus, his precursor in the systematic exegesis of Plato by a couple of generations.[49] Recall that for Plotinus, there is a name for the activity of an interrelational sphere, "perilampsis" (see Premise 3). In the direction of this thought, Plotinus is also talking about "hypostases." Every level of being has its hypostases, all the way down to physical substances. Clearly, this ontological ladder is lopsided, the One towering over the rest. Recall: "And all beings, so long as they persist, necessarily, due to the power present in them, produce from their own substantiality a real, though dependent, existent around themselves directed to their exterior, a sort of image [*eikona*] of the archetypes from which it was generated" (*The Enneads,* 5.1.6. p. 540). This is how the conjunction of transparent mirrors looks from the inside. Hypostases have a double gaze for Plotinus. They take in their before and after, they are outward facing and backward facing at once, they are the thinnest scrims, two-sided screens receiving and transmitting substance, looking back and fore at once. Hypostases' receptivity to the One and its power is their power, a different kind of power than the One's own. In this consists their radical asymmetry. Hypostases have a special urge, a "power which must be in them," that the One, to its shame, does not have. The One faces itself. Like transparent mirrors, hypostases face both ways, are radically transmissive of their outside. When he describes the double gaze of hypostases, Plotinus is already moving into a different metaphoric, beyond the picture of "perilampsis," with its semi-ring form and its oblique referent in a sun. And this metaphoric, hypostases that face both ways, transparent mirrors that catch and overlay substances, finds an echo two centuries later in the double gaze of emanations in Proclus.

Proclus belongs to the group of Plato interpreters active between the third and fifth centuries CE who, like Plotinus, along with his student and biographer Porphyry, as well as Porphyry's rival and the figure many consider biggest in Proclus's thoughts, Iamblichus (*Proclus*, pp. 17–18), followed roughly three main impulses in interpretation. They systematized Platonic thoughts for the sake of their rational coherence; they went beyond a philological approach to Plato's texts in order to discover, elaborate, and systematize the thoughts; and they were Pythagorean enough to consider this more than an exercise in logic or philosophical imagination. They also had to say how one could live in the coherent, stratified, fundamentally unequal world they built upon the Platonic hints and suggestions they developed into a complete cosmos.[50] Proclus's name for this elaborated whole for living was "theology," and in addition to the many commentaries on Platonic dialogues he wrote, plus some exegeses of others' texts, with one on Plotinus, he wrote two main systematic theologies. For the study of likeness, look at the commentary on the dialogue Proclus considered the pinnacle of Plato's work, the *Parmenides* (a commentary that was also a crucible for the thoughts developed in the probably later, monumental *Platonic Theology*) and the condensed and very suggestive theological work, *Elements of Theology*.

Propositions 29 and 32 of *Elements of Theology* contain Proclus's reinvention of the minor, but crucial Plotinian metaphoric of "hypostases" that look asymmetrically "both ways." His reinvention puts the crooked double gaze of hypostases directly in terms of likeness. Extramission and remission, *proodos* (§ 29, line 1) and *epistrophe* (§ 32, line 1), Proclus's names for the double gaze, both happen "through likeness," "di' homoiotétos" (§ 29, line 4, § 32, line 4). And so where Plotinus's model was candescent — the world outside the One was about an exchange of light and power — Proclus's model is extrusive. The hypostatic world is about the jutting forth of derivations across a median. Plotinus, in order to have a multiplicity from the One, but not of it, came up with a secondary illumination circling the never-diminishing flame, perilampsis, an alternative mode that the One neither contains nor rejects, but tolerates, refusing it, and by refusing it, allowing the

periphery its unique, dim, circulating candescence, which nevertheless still points the way back to the original fire. Proclus's model is
refractive, not reflective, though still almost perfectly spaceless, just
as the cosmos also was for Plotinus. At least until you reach the very
low level at which formed matter occurs, at all other levels of being, for
Proclus, there is no space in the likeness universe at all.[51]

Proclus introduces into the Plotinian universe an altered set of
names for the fundamental communications among the spheres of
being. Extramission and remission, *proodos* and *epistrophe*, are metaphysical movements that make new vectors of likeness available;
however, these new vectors are stained by a peculiar and powerful asymmetry; the laws of equivalence, which guaranteed the even
transmission of the One through all the spheres in Plotinus, gets
suspended. In the Proclan holosphere, the reflexivity, symmetry,
and transitivity of Plotinus's cosmos are replaced with refraction,
asymmetry, and divergence. This marks a subtle, but important shift
in the trajectory of Platonism in the early Common Era, a crucial
revaluation of cosmic moments. Proclus's system depends on many
asymmetries. When you look into the matter, you find asymmetries
permeating the hologrammic universe; at a minimum, five basic
asymmetries can be listed:

1. There is an asymmetry in function: a higher level "generates,"
   but a lower level "likens."
2. There is an asymmetry in look (refraction): the One looks
   toward itself, but the derived looks back toward the One and
   at the same time looks outward toward the hypostasis — the
   two-way gaze.
3. There is an asymmetry in inclination: likening to and being
   likened to are not equivalent. This is most clear when you
   realize that the One, when it is likened to, remains one,
   whereas the multiple remains multiple. Without a principle of symmetry, this imbalance does not need further
   explanation.

4. There is a general asymmetry in the number of traits: a lower level likens to a higher level, but it is only ever like that higher level in some respects, never in all respects. From the perspective of ontology, you would say something is lost. From the perspective of homeotics, you would say a certain resemblance lights up.

5. There is an asymmetry in transitivity (divergence): *B* likens *A*, and *C* likens *B* means that *A* is also like *C*, and yet "like" is unlike in *B/A* and *C/B*. You can envision the uneven transitivity at work here in the following way. A grandchild is like its grandparents, and this way of likeness is unlike the way in which the grandchild, as a child, is like its parents, who are in turn, in an unlike way, like their parents. The child of the parents and the grandchild of the grandparents are arguably the same entity, and yet they are unlike to the extent that they are like each of these two precursors. And they are also alike, but only through their others.[52]

Doubtless, it is important to look more closely at the asymmetries in Proclus's likeness logic.

Ignore for a moment the two most common cases of likeness in Plato-inspired philosophy: the good as imitable and ideas as copyable. The imitable good and copyable ideas are not less important than homeosis, but they are probably derived from it. Both the good and the ideas are concerned with their transmission into lower realms. Before they can be transmitted, however, they have to be constituted, and likeness operations constitute the good itself and ideas themselves, as Proclus teaches us.

He shows that likeness is involved in the primordial constitution of everything, including the One. To see where the constitution happens, recall the One and the destiny it takes for itself. The One has to go beyond itself in order to stay One. Thus, it is no simple unit, to itself alone to the exclusion of all else. It wants to be One, without fully excluding the All. This requirement appears paradoxical, and it is not, so long as the One's mission obeys the rule of nonparticipation. The One can go beyond itself so long as it does not participate in anything else and nothing else participates fundamentally in it; in this way its oneness will never be violated. This does not mean, however, that the One has no outside; indeed, this could not be the case. The argument says that a One with no outside, with no alternative, could not be one, because it would have no determination at all. The One would become the indeterminate, would fall away into the *apeiron*. The One's mission is thus truly in conflict — it needs its outside, and it cannot depend on its outside.

Proclus's solution to the conflict comes in an image. The One has a to itself and also — because it cannot, like a regular part of a plurality, have a toward another — it also has a "despite another." The One is one not with or through the All, but despite the All. Proposition 4 in *Elements of Theology* says there can be no plurality if the One is ever for a single instant for another, since in that case, the One would bleed out into the world. "For the One, if identical with the unified, will be infinitely manifold, as will also each of the parts which compose the unified" (proposition 5). "One" is a possible name for the highest thing, but there are others: "cause" (proposition 11), "good" (proposition 13), and "unmoved mover" are also names for it (proposition 14). Proclus insists that these other aspects, originally Aristotelian and Platonic, are neither parts nor accidental characteristics of the One, but rather logical corollaries. To be anything is to be determinate, and in this way, the One is the cause of everything else. To be good is to be homogeneous and complete (proposition 8), and to be a mover without moving is to be the object of reflection of all moving things (proposition 14). The mission of the One thus can include the extramission of everything and the remission of everything toward it, given that the extramitted and the remitted have categorically different powers. Extramission and remission allow for the birth of reality from the One and the return of reality toward its neglectful parent, and the cost of this is cosmic asymmetry.

Before Leibniz, there was Proclus, where a monad is possible only on the basis of a prior dyad between a remission and the henad that emitted it. Henads are the lead moments of series, which are to-themselves refractions of the One; monads are unitary for-a-series emitted remissions of henads. Henads and monads converse through asymmetrical likenesses. Proposition 28 lays out one half of the principle: "Every producing cause brings into existence things like to itself before the unlike" (line 1). Qua cause, each higher instance, each productive level (excluding matter and the body, which are passive causes) is the cause of a likeness. Such strange causation involves two minimum tenets: no extramission comes without a remission, and the remission is like to the extramission, but not the same as it. Within likeness, there is a fundamental unlikeness upon which the One bases its claim to absolute separation. That is to say, within "extra-mission" and "re-mission" lies "mission," a riven, self-conflicting moment. You can say that "mission," this underlying motive, means likening, but only where you conceive of likening as not equal in both directions. This is the asymmetrical, approximate stuff of the universe's bonds — like before unlike, unlike within every like. The product cannot be identical, and it also cannot be unlike before it is like, or else the One would not produce unity, unity would not produce coherence, coherence would not produce consistency, consistency would not produce contiguity (space and time), and so on, as you go down the ladder of being. The slight preference for likeness in the universe guarantees this somewhat orderly displacement of moments. If unlike predominated, in contrast, anything could come from anything, and the possibility of even a minimal order would evaporate. Proclus's likeness principle takes the tiniest step out of chaos and thus explains the real and ideal worlds and their interrelation.

4.5.2. *In a Proclan universe, the scales are tipped ever so slightly in favor of likeness.*

Look how this changes things. For there to be anything at all, being and the One are not the primary requirement. Slightly more important than these, slightly outweighing being, emanations, one-ness, and unlikeness, is the moment that prevents either difference or absolute identity from taking hold—likeness, in a quietly explosive remark, is said to be the force that produces the whole system. The One's mission is to foment likening, and likening does not—cannot—come from the One itself. So where does it come from?

Hidden under many layers of discourse in *The Elements of Theology* lies an obscure navel of the text: "likeness [*he homoiotes*] generates the products out of the producers" (proposition 29, line 6, translation modified). The sentence is astounding. Not the One, not the henads, but homeosis is the generative moment. This fact alone is an enormous surprise. Yet it is also true that the homeotic is generative in two different ways. While on one hand homeosis is responsible for the existence of all metaphysical products, in a perhaps even more shocking codicil, likeness is said also to be responsible for producers qua producers. A producer is generated out of the secondary products that remit to it. What does likeness produce? It produces the followers, the secondaries, the monads, and the series of degenerate moments. It also produces, retroactively, the henads and one could surmise the One (proposition 32). The place of likeness in the Proclan version of Neoplatonism thus needs to be stated.

4.6. *Likeness is a first-second. It produces an asymmetrical bond between a series and its henad and between a henad and its monad, between a multiple and the One, between the One and its determining outside.*

For Proclus, likeness is the secret counterforce that de facto generates the whole (the All, together with the One, their togetherness). Although you might think that remission happens after extramission, this is not true. The inverse is also not true, that the second retroactively constitutes the first, as though the owl of likeness took wing at dusk. The two bloom out of the likeness operation immediately together without hesitation or independence. Homeomission takes no time at all; remission overlaps with emission. The corollary of proposition 25 teaches this.

> Cor. From this it is apparent that the principle most remote from the beginning of all things is sterile and a cause of nothing. For if it generate and have a consequent, it is plain that it can no longer be the most remote: its product is more remote than itself, and itself is brought nearer by the fact of producing another, whatever that other be, and thus imitating that cause which is productive of all that is. (proposition 25, lines 5–9)

He seems to be saying here that only the One can be a cause, and nothing in the principle farthest from it — that is, the physical world, the world of perception — can be generative. But look at how this is expressed. Remoteness is the barren one, nearness the fecund. In a universe of nearness, the remote (in time or space or metaphysically) is "sterile and a cause of nothing." That is, the most unsterile, the most productive, is always in the nearness. And what is the principle of nearness? It is what stands apart qualitatively without interval, as Plotinus put it. But it is better to imagine this completely backward: the One overlaps completely with its emanations and is truly and actually indistinguishable from them insofar as they are like each other and like the One. Another way to say this is: a distinction between being and likeness is not possible. This is perhaps why, as a purely epistemological matter, homeosis has never been fully separated from ontology.

4.6.1. *Likeness is immediate and overlaps with being.*

That likeness overlaps with being, however, makes it difficult, if not impossible, to account for unlikeness, and Proclus is very concerned about this difficulty. What is like has to be unlike, as well, in some respect, or else it would coincide with being completely and there would be no cosmos (and consequently no One). How is what is like also unlike? It helps to see "unlikeness" and "likeness" as the homeotic names for emission and remission. As an e-mission, a hypostasis is unlike, while as a re-mission, it is like. Or, better: the contents of likeness are slightly "higher"; the like is nearer to its object than the unlike, and this discrepancy within each and every refracting, transparent mirror gives life to the universe. What, then, is the content of unlikeness — is it slightly "lower"? Indeed, this is one way Proclus discusses it. Likeness explains the relation to higher contents, unlikeness names the admixture of lower contents.[53]

Within a likeness, in order that a two be alike, like will take precedence over unlike by a hair's breadth for the moment of enlikening. Taking precedence is a matter of orientation and emphasis, not a matter of quantity. And therein lies the universe's precarious balance — alike by a hair, for a time, by orientation or emphasis, balanced over an abyss of unlikenesses that could at any time swallow up the correspondence. Proclus works out the positive moments of this precarity in his commentary on Plato's *Parmenides*, a work that, along with his commentary on the *Timaeus*, formed the core of Proclus's Platonism. Almost all of book 2 of the commentary on the *Parmenides* is an attempt to show the importance of the question of likeness and unlikeness and to untangle the knot in which Plato tied up the like and the unlike. It is a Gordian Knot, but Proclus has an ingenious way to annul it that does not involve cutting and thus destroying it.

Discussion of "the like" is confined to a brief early interchange in Plato's *Parmenides*, before the thicket of argument grows too dense to see in this bewildering dialogue. That does not diminish its critical importance for Proclus, who elevates what falls under offhand attention here into a principle of cosmic import. In the brief interchange, the young Socrates attempts to confound Zeno, himself a renowned peddler of paradoxes, with a paradox of his own about homeosis, referring obliquely to one of Zeno's stances against multiplicity, namely, the Parmenidean assertion that "there is one alone." To support the statement, Zeno has argued that if there is real plurality, everything will be both like and unlike, and this is a contradiction. Proclus's concealed doctrine of generative, but asymmetrical likeness is born from Socrates's refutation of Zeno's argument. To put it concisely, likeness is a different kind of thing, a different kind of idea. It cannot be subject to the law of noncontradiction, as other forms have to be. Reference to such a contradiction cannot refute a likeness principle, because its logic knows no "either-or." Proclus pays careful attention as the young Socrates turns Zeno's argument against itself, while Socrates, inadvertently perhaps, as far as Plato was concerned, but nevertheless with large consequences for Proclan theory, looses the terrors of asymmetrical likeness on the philosophical world.

If you are an atomist, the following is true for you: things are alike, and they are also not alike. The atomist argument, against which Zeno and others took strong stands, speaks against monism and for pluralism on one basis. Things are like and unlike in a particular way: they are elementally like and unlike in combination; that is, atoms are by and large alike, and their combinations are different. Likeness becomes unlikeness when fundamental elements mix.[54] For the atomists, the concept of an encompassing One is unintelligible. In response to the atomist position and to its complement, the Eleatic position of Parmenides and Zeno, Plato insists that there are both plurality and the One (whole, untouched, metaphysical, and so on), and in different dialogues, he tries out different schemes in which the two poles could come to occupy the same totality.

One of these schemes is homeotic. Socrates's genius in Plato's *Parmenides* is to liberate likeness from an old, false argument, demonstrating to the inventor of the argument, Zeno, that things can in fact be both like and unlike, even down to the level of the basic elements. In his translation of the dialogue, R. E. Allen reconstructs the old argument, which is merely implied in the text, deducing what must have been Zeno's first premise: if there is plurality, things will be both like and unlike. Allen, in his commentary, then gives a second Zenoan premise: opposites are nonidentical, and a reconstruction of Zeno's conclusion: therefore, plurality cannot exist (*Parmenides*, p. 93). Socrates's rejoinder to this implied argument begins at 128e, the first play of which involves Socrates in a game of reenvisioning the cosmos. If plurality necessarily involves like and unlike things, there must be ideas of likeness and unlikeness that share out to phenomena the characteristics like and unlike in an orderly manner. If the idea "Like" and the idea "Unlike" remain separate and distinct, the qualities they engender among appearances may mingle as much as needed.

Zeno's position is much simpler, however, and Socrates stumbles here on even ground. Calling likeness a characteristic opens Socrates up to other dilemmas. The most poignant of these is the following. Likeness is also expected to explain how characteristics are distributed, as well as how appearances and ideas occupy the same totality. If likeness is the mode in which ideas provide their gifts to phenomena, then likeness cannot be an idea like other ideas. If it is the functional relation between ideas and phenomena, it must be a third type of thing. Normal experience confirms this — we don't say things "have" likeness in the same way they have magnitude or color. Rather, likeness is one way color or magnitude appears in a thing, the way a "-ness" — any characteristic — comes to characterize it. One way to say a thing is purple is to say it is like a purple thing. Weighing one gram is a fact of being like the standard gram. Going a step further in this logic, if like is the way ideas and phenomena interact, and if there is an idea of likeness, the logic is graced with what looks like an elaborate tautology — likeness is like because it is like.[55] The problem with this is not that it is an empty statement of identity. It looks more like an infinite regress, and this regress forms the basis of Parmenides's crushing response to Socrates.

Parmenides responds to Socrates's invention of ideas of likeness and unlikeness at 132d. There are two holes in the fledgling philosopher's proposal. First, he has failed to address priority: if like is like like, then ideas and phenomena are equal in rank. Second, he has ignored the regress itself. Likeness, if it requires a third instance to determine itself, can have no content in itself. Each instance has its essence outside itself. There is no single "what it is to be like" if the idea of like needs to be like something else again. Proclus asserts himself as a philosophizing commentator just here. The first lapse in

Socrates's account, the question of priority, implies equality between the like and the likened, which Parmenides and Zeno reject. The second lapse, the question of regress, implies an asymmetry in the relation. Proclus answers the first question with his hierarchical picture of the metaverse. The One "is," the hypostases "are like," and each hypostasis is "only like" its immediate superior, which Proclus interprets as "ontologically less than." The second question, however, he answers with a simple affirmation of the question. He accepts the likeness regress; indeed, he refuses to believe it is a problem. In his systematic, it is fundamental that each likeness calls upon a third instance to give it its character.

Proclus performs a subtle operation on Parmenides's intransigent logic in his commentary on the dialogue. The first order of business, he proposes, is to say how likeness and unlikeness relate to one another. Proclus makes a dizzying array of distinctions—proposing, for instance, that there are two kinds of coincidences of like and unlike. This proposal is decisive for the theory. The first kind of coincidence of like and unlike is a plurality without any unity, where what the two have in common is having nothing in common. He says this relation between like and unlike "refutes itself" (English, p. 103). If what like and unlike have in common is their unlikeness, then they are alike in being unlike and in no other way. First of all, this kind of manifold has no unity whatsoever, and nothing can be said about it. Second, it betrays human experiences of objects as well as the All, experiences of order, and so on—it betrays the very terms of the thesis. In this schema, it turns out, things are "both like and unlike and neither like nor unlike," "kai homoia kai anomoia, kai oute homoia oute anomoia" (p. 103 / Greek, p. 726)—so, a double contradiction. This is the extreme pit into which the logic of likeness falls, a dissolution into quasi-chaos.

Proclus has two arguments against this schema: it leads to too many absurdities, and under the dialectic method, it produces premises that do not follow. Here he isolates "the movement of Zeno's thought" (p. 104) to show that it is one of two possible definitions of homeosis and it is too absurd even to raise as a counterargument.

Why is this? For the simple reason that Zeno treats like and unlike as contradictories, when they are not. They will be, for this system, contraries. They become contradictories in the unfortunate "movement of Zeno's thought," but only through forced manipulation. Contradiction is the sledgehammer of low minds. Proclus demonstrates this by showing that Zeno has substituted the wrong terms. Like and not like are contradictories, Proclus reminds us, and unlike and not unlike are contradictories. Like and unlike, in contrast, are contraries — they lie on a continuum, which means that at all times there is a little of each in the other.

Proclus clarifies Zeno's thought for him and thereby leaps into a likeness logic, and yet he does not jump off the precipice altogether, as close as he may come. Homeologic tends to consume everything around it, and Proclus wants to hold onto metaphysical levels or grades and thereby keep some things rigorously distinct. His reading of Socrates's argument begins by separating the like and the unlike from the characteristics likeness and unlikeness. Like Socrates, he wants to hold back the ideas from phenomena that can be called like or unlike.

What is a contrary? Proclus may be thinking of Aristotle's dictum: "All contraries must either be in the same genus or in contrary genera, or be themselves genera" (*Categories and De interpretatione*, p. 38). It is important that contraries be contingent on one another. For contraries, it is not necessary that one be true always and the other false always (p. 37). Further, it is not true that if one exists, the other necessarily also exists (p. 38). As with sickness or health, good or bad, contraries can come and go, and — this is crucial — they may coexist in the same thing. Indeed, they must belong to the same thing under Aristotle's substance ontology. They cannot exist on their own, since what they do is characterize entities or types of entities, tracking the transformation of their properties between extremes. Sickness and health characterize the extremes of a body, justice and injustice characterize the extremes of a soul. What is significant is that contraries are at home with "and," while contradictories know only "or" or "but." The poles of contraries sit contentedly side by side in a variety of ways, within a genus, in contrary genera, or as genera themselves. Note that it does not make sense, in this schema, for contraries to be in or between a genus and a thing. You cannot say that an action is just and at the same time that the class of actions to which it belongs is unjust. The question answered by the concept "contraries" is: What kinds of traits can an entity carry? How extremely disparate can they be so that the entity remains itself and stays within its class? Contrariety tells the extremes an entity can bear before it decomposes or becomes something else.

Proclus's task will be to describe the intense dynamism of like and unlike in a hypostasis without the ability, mistaken as it would be, to separate the two absolutely.[56]

To do so, Proclus positions likeness / unlikeness, the two intermingled contraries, as an idea of intermediate rank. Neither highest nor lowest, likeness / unlikeness becomes identified with the power of a demiurge whose job it is to forge the relations among ideas and phenomena.

> There is then a demiurgic Likeness and Unlikeness, the former analogous to the cause of the Limit, the other correlative with the Unlimited. The former brings things together (which is why he says [Plato in the *Parmenides* at 132d], "The like is like to the like"); the latter is separative, delighting in procession and variety and movement, and at the extreme is responsible even for contrariety. The essence of each of them is immaterial, pure, simple, uniform, and eternal; and their powers correspond to their respective essences, those of the former, as we have said, being aggregative, unifying [*sunagogoi*], limiting, and tending to uniformity [*monoeides*]; those of the latter are discriminating, diversifying [*alloiotikai*], leading to indefiniteness [*apeiropoio*] and duality. (*Proclus' Commentary*, p. 110 / *Procli Philosophi*, p. 734)

A likeness has both faces, unifying and diversifying, tending to uniformity, but not reaching it, and tending to indefiniteness, but not reaching it. To say, as Proclus does, that likeness and unlikeness are analogous to limit and unlimited is first of all to raise them up among the highest genera, among that privileged group of ideas that move freely among and help determine both phenomena and other ideas. To give them the epithet "demiurgic" is a clue to their peculiar status, since the Demiurge's powers depend on characteristics not available to the god himself, the ability to move freely between gods and mortals, for instance. It is analogous to much higher categories, and it is also analogous to much lower ones, and as high and low, it is best described as an "intermediate form" that occupies no clear place in the hierarchy. Why not go further and say that the homeotic layer does not belong to the hierarchy of being and is thus a unicum in the metaphysical universe? "Consequently the power of producing both like and unlike things must belong to all the Ideas. But if this identical power is common to them all, likeness and unlikeness cannot be identical with anything in the universe" (pp. 109–10). They are pivotal to the system and at the same time not of the system — pivotal, ubiquitous, and atopic; an anarchic power, a leveler of heights and raiser of depths, a paracategorical.

At this stage of the argument, a new puzzle arises. On one hand, un / likeness is the milieu of ideas through which ideas both come to be themselves and avoid coinciding with each other qua ideas. On the other hand, the power of producing like and unlike belongs to all ideas, circulates among them, distributes to each idea its own little dominion of echoes and refractions, a domain that is not exclusive because of authority or rank, but rather due to the fact of likeness, because of the closeness of characteristics and at the same time due to the fact of unlikeness, because not all characteristics are close.

It will be easier to understand the status of these intraideal workings if you divide homeosis into a power and an effect. As an effect, likeness is located in the descendent, in the lower echelon, in the second, the product. *Homoios* thus describes an effect that is not at the origin, not authoritative, but rather refractive, which may be considered a version of receptivity, if the receptive also passes on, receives and projects, lets pass. The homeotic is indebted, but as indebted, it has a special grace, the freedom not to possess its traits. As a power, likeness is, strictly speaking, located in the ascendant. The demiurgic power of like / un (*kai homoiotes demiourgike kai anomoiotes*, p. 110 / p. 734) lends from higher to lower, and yet at the same time, it also spreads out, among ideas and among the phenomena. Ideas and phenomena coemerge, and this accounts for the multiplicity of authorities [*huperkosmios*] in the system, as well as the multiplicity of subservients (*egkosmios*, p. 128 / p. 759). The vertical relation of lending / debt and projecting / refracting depends on horizontal relations in each level. A sun never lends its rays to one single leaf. That star would not be the sun. Only because they can be alike can a restricted plurality of ideas explain the unrestricted multiplicity of things. Only as the echo of a multiplicity of things, equally, does a restricted plurality of ideas hold any sway. Are there then two homeoses: one to account for rank relations and another to account for member relations?

This problem of rank and membership is addressed later in the commentary. Proclus returns to Socrates's manner of speaking about un / like. Socrates speaks about them in the plural. "But let us, if you please, look in another way at the cause of his speaking of likes and unlikes in the plural. This Likeness, the Form itself, exists in the Maker of the whole, and it exists also in the other intelligences, both those above the cosmos and those that are within it" (p. 128). Already the distribution is unsettling — the idea of likeness exists in the extracosmic demiurge as well as in the intracosmic intelligences. It seems to be everywhere, and most surprisingly, everywhere the like is unlike itself.

> Suppose that our argument, then, is to find whether all these essential Likenesses are the same as Unlikenesses, and there is nothing so remarkable in his using the plural, not the singular. For Likeness is not singular in its action, but as numerous as are the ranks of intelligent beings proceeding from the Demiurge, so numerous may be regarded as being the workings of this Form, when we consider that it is active in each intellect in its appropriate fashion, supracosmically in the intelligibles above the cosmos, and encosmically in the ones contained in the cosmos. (p. 128)

4.7.   *Likening is not singular in its action.*

All Proclus's argumentative powers are trained on this moment, because a fracture in the logic of ideas cannot be tolerated. What is the relationship between supracosmic and encosmic likenesses? How do they approach one another in a nonsingular action? They are undoubtedly analogous and probably identical, and if they are identical, there is, once again, no possibility of rank order distinctions among metaphysical entities. They are not identical, however — this much has been established. They are, rather, alike. And so if they are as unlike as they are alike, then an asymmetry in any likeness, a factical unlikeness inherent in every likeness, is required. Likeness is numerous — Proclus states this with no subterfuge. Its taste for multiples is in fact insatiable. When Proclus claims that for every idea there is a further likeness, he also says that the likeness idea as a whole is homogeneous with itself, "holon homochroun esti pros eauto" (p.119 / p. 747), just as likeness provides the homogeneity of any idea. As an idea, likeness is like itself, merely and fully, which is to say never fully different and never the same. As homogeneity, it freely varies because of its basic self-relation. Instead of autoaffection, this idea suffers an autoaffliction. It plagues itself. Likeness, as idea, as intermediary for ideas, as medium of supracosmic and intracosmic contact, as the nongiven power to steal back, after being ejected from the One, something of the One's character, must partake of itself and of unlikeness. Itself is unlike itself, which is to say, like, but not in all traits. This self-relation has to be generous (p. 125). That the generosity — giving another, then another likeness — is endemic to all likeness relations is proven in Proclus's commentary by the fact that through all the discussion of likeness, it is never even suggested that likeness derives from or is determined by anything higher. There is no primal mark or skin around it to restrict its variation and spread as the only instance in the system that is not an emanation of the One.

4.7.1. *No one can say where likeness comes from.*

Being mysterious forms part of likeness's personality, just as being not singular forms part of its complexity. You can read it as a rejection of transcendence. Nothing transcends likeness that could distinguish within it, once and for all, the exact proportion of likeness and unlikeness, and nevertheless, both are always at work.

4.7.2. *The way of likeness transits through unlikeness.*

The negation at work in "unlike" is expressible as "not quite," where "not quite" is a mirror image of "almost." Not quite is not a lack, but rather the expression of likeness operating freely within its negativity. This species of negativity accounts for the double valuation of the aesthetic in the history of European thought. The aesthetic has been both truthy and deceitful, and further, it has been so close to the truth as to imperil the possibility of distinguishing it, like a best friend you can't quite trust, since you've placed so much trust in them to begin with that you have lost all measure. This is the way a certain tradition has appropriated likeness — lies are like truths. If you take seriously the approximating character of likeness, its not quite and also its almost, there are better words than "truth" and "lies." Things converge, and things diverge; verging is happening continually and at all levels.

What happens to distinctions in such a world? Nothing and everything. Whether there is such a thing as scale, and thus such a thing as rank, and such a thing as value in a likeness world is a question. The answer is yes. There is something it is like to be bigger and something it is like to be more powerful and something it is like to be better. Since like transits unlike, however, there is also something it is like to be both bigger and smaller, as an airplane is like a dragonfly, a planet like a pea. And since like transits unlike, there is something it is like to be both better and worse, as a god is like a human. No comparison is absolute. "World" names the constitutive verging of all on all. In every scale, there are elements that ignore the rule of scale and produce monstrous overlaps.[57] For instance, an embryo displays the asymmetrical verging of all ancestors onto one another, including the farthest, most "primitive," and in some ways the almost wholly unlike. "Culture" names the constitutive nearness of practices no matter how eccentric,[58] and culture thereby nears nature as what becomes accultured, made into tools, consumables, fashion. A table is like a butterfly, a tree like an umbrella. Science names the verging of ideal forms and standards of measure on phenomena that are as unlike to them as a raindrop and a spectrometer. "Mind" names the verging of image and object, language and image.

4.8. *The homeoplex is like a closed, overlapping, finite plurality.*

Proclus wanted a name for the verging of all on all, a motive for the lower levels to stick around, to remain captured by each other and by the One's magnificence and for the One to care, to share out its magnificence to its hypostases. He got a name for it, "homeosis," a logical description of it, the interpenetration of like and unlike, and yet, since the structure of the universe was already given to him by the Platonic tradition, his task was to say how the machine worked, to iron out the difficulties. He could not say why the Demiurge should have made the world in this way, as a closed, overlapping finite plurality. Say you decide not to accept the Neoplatonic schema of One and hypostases. You still need an explanation, for this world, why its items don't let go of one another, move on, differ, become ontologically independent, why it doesn't give in to metaphysics or entropy. Where does homeosis come from?

4.9. *Homeosis remains from yielding.*

5. *Homeosis remains from yielding.*

If the homeoplex, at any instant, is like a closed, overlapping, finite plurality, it is left to clear up the hazy matter of "becoming." How did it get this way? How do parts of it shift, go over into other combinations, relocate and realign? It is left to clear up the matter of becoming, in particular, because of a conflict in the picture of homeosis. Closed — you can say that the homeoplex is closed, that traits overlap, that any instant of the universe is a finite configuration of traits — a face. You can also say: likenesses happen. They light up. It is left to clear up becoming because of the tension between reconfiguration and stasis in this picture. Becoming is an obvious way to account for happening in a closed system. It is left to clear away becoming, however, because rather than arriving into being from nonbeing or transitioning between one state of a being and another, a likeness happens in a field, immediately and without plan or reserve. Rather than becoming what it is, a likeness fuses out of an atmosphere.

What is the homeotic correlative of becoming?

A likeness happens when two traits approach one another, when, through some power or operation, they find themselves nearer rather than farther. Circumstances conspire, you might say, when old "becoming" is out of service or when it is brought to a halt, when it gets diverted or suspended, when one thing is restrained from becoming, when a trait is caught in the magnetism of another. Instead of a thing becoming what it is, traits are suspended with respect to one another. Call this "the double glance" of thing; you can also account for it in terms of motion. "Become" speaks in a metaphor of movement. What becomes arrives after transiting to a destination, on a will to arrive, already having arrived beforehand in its intention, in a fateful trajectory out of potentiality into actuality. When you try to think a homeotic counterpart to becoming, you begin by jettisoning many of becoming's presuppositions — substance and properties, space and time, and motion as well. Turn it around — when homeosis happens, something refuses to move; something says no to distance, avoids going somewhere other than where it happens to be. Likenesses result from not moving.

Two theorists who would likely not admit their thinking had a deep affinity, Wittgenstein and Bergson, nevertheless each independently took small steps toward a theory of homeotic happening distinct from becoming. They came at it from different extremes and did not fully recognize they were doing so. When Wittgenstein wrote down his fragmentary investigations on "aspect change," he did not expect to find the answer to his question, how does a change of aspect happen, in a text from half a century before. When Bergson wrote his antidualist treatise, *Matter and Memory*, he certainly did not expect to discover that the question he was asking was not the question he was in fact answering. He was overtly asking how a particular understanding of time could overcome the Cartesian duality of soul and body. What he proposed, however, became in advance an answer to Wittgenstein's question of how aspect change happens. Wittgenstein has a sophisticated vocabulary for homeosis that includes "seeing-in," "seeing-as," "image-object" (*Bildgegenstand*), "aspect" (*Aspekt*), "lighting-up" (*Aufleuchten*) — with which he comes close to an understanding of homeotic change. Bergson has a sophisticated account of change, and yet he has a deep antipathy toward likeness, a necessary accompaniment to his wholesale rejection of empiricism. Because Wittgenstein leaves hardly an inch for the question of change, the question rings out for him with the urgency of an alarm. Because Bergson wants to avoid likeness almost at any cost, a strong model for homeotic change sneaks up on him.

Wittgenstein makes overt thoughts on likeness in his remarks on James Frazer's *Golden Bough*,[59] but the theoretical core of his likeness thinking is still the section of the *Philosophical Investigations* on "seeing-as," what is sometimes called "aspect perception."[60] In 1949, when Wittgenstein showed his friend Maurice O'Connor Drury the duckrabbit picture, Drury reports him saying: "Now you try and say what is involved in seeing something as something; it is not easy. These thoughts I am now working at are as hard as granite" (*On Wittgenstein*, p. 136). "Seeing-as" may have been as hard as granite — and it is significant that Wittgenstein finds a simile to express this, reminding us of the deeply homeographic way he has of expressing the hardest thoughts — "seeing-as" may have been impenetrable, but *Aspektwechsel*, its counterpart, was too slippery to catch hold of.

The duckrabbit picture, a parlor game raised to a model for psychology by Joseph Jastrow, was used by Wittgenstein in the critique of psychology in the second part of the *Philosophical Investigations,* the *Philosophy of Psychology: A Fragment*. Here was a limit case for a representational theory of mind. More bothersome perhaps than the two in one was the fact that the two switch back and forth almost at will. The picture-object as an example of "seeing-as" was troubling evidence for "aspect-shift." Both of these terms go back to an *idée fixe*: two fundamentally independent entities occupying separate ontological positions. This assumption is the source of the problem. Another exemplary picture-object, the drawing of a cube that looks two-dimensional at one instant, three-dimensional at another, also suffers from the assumption that it must either be one or two. About the fictional observer of this cube Wittgenstein writes: "And if for him the flat aspect alternates with a three-dimensional one, that is just as if I were to show him completely different objects in the course of the demonstration" (§ 179, p. 213).

Is it? Assuming completely different objects results in the concepts "seeing-as" and "aspect-change." Further, analysis, as a technique, works only when confusions can be reduced to differences. In the order of being, there must be one entity or two. In the order of experience, of course, there is one picture with aspects that alternate. Why do experience and being diverge here in this peculiar way? One could argue that the (perhaps philosophical) presumption of separate and distinct beings is the condition for the alternation. In any case, the apparent divergence causes the philosophical irritation that calls forth the concepts. An act of philosophical imagination projects an outside to the image, a strictly governed zone in which only independent entities may reside. A single image gives birth, so to speak, to two images, the picture and its outside, one on display, the other hidden. A preprojection colors the intellectual enterprise, a double image of a confused picture "representing" an unconfused world.

Were Wittgenstein to assume the coconstitution of the two entities, duck and rabbit, through the all-too natural overlap of traits, the philosophical task would be different. Take the picture at face value: the "two" beings in fact share every one of their constitutive marks in the first — and only — image. On the page, every duck line is also a rabbit line, and vice versa. This is a simplification, no doubt, for the figure is not only a confusion of duck and rabbit: in the duck hide the duck's ancestors, in the rabbit the rabbit's. Duck and duck ancestors also share constitutive marks. Rabbit and rabbit ancestors share constitutive marks. Evolutionary history is etched into each and both, and so is the history of drawing. With a slight shift in perspective, when he brings forward these picture-objects whose aspects shift, Wittgenstein is on the verge of proposing a schizoid cosmos in which aspect shifts are primary and "completely different objects" are incidental or even illusory.

One could choose to think that the cosmos is double, rather than argue the harder line, that not the cosmos, but "seeing" is double. But Wittgenstein, opting for a solution not far from Jastrow's, ascribes the effect to "seeing-as," not to "being-as," as Heidegger had done in another context. Wittgenstein attributes the figure's doubleness to the seer, not to the picture or to the object. "That is what I treat it as; this is my attitude to the figure" (§ 193). For reasons that have a deep philosophical history, it is easier to believe that dispositions are constantly shifting, that faculties are multiple, or even that language is multiple than to imagine that states of affairs are multiple and even shift.

> The change of aspect [*Aspektwechsel*]. "But surely you'd say that the picture has changed altogether now!"
>
> But what is different: my impression? my attitude? — Can I say? I describe the change like a perception; just as if the object had changed before my eyes. (§ 129)

Several possible explanations are offered in this tiny polylogue — either the "picture" has changed or the impression, the impression or the disposition toward it. In the way we speak about it, he says, we treat it just like we treat any perception, ignoring the contributions of perception and ascribing the effect to the object in itself, even though, he implies, such an ascription is impossible. When it appears most vividly that the object has changed ("just as if"), this is the moment when it is most clear that it is only seeing that has changed ("as if").

However critical he may be of some of these possible explanations, every possibility is presented here except the homeotic one. The terms are "sensation," "perception," "apperception." Each may ultimately be a game of language — "surely you'd say" — and even then, it cannot be the case that the object has changed. When Wittgenstein wonders whether children know they are pretending when they "see-as" or whether they as a matter of course think the objects themselves have changed, he opts for neither. "And does the child now *see* the chest as a house?" (§ 206). This thought is followed by: "And if someone knew how to play this game, and in a certain situation exclaimed with special expression 'Now it's a house!' he would be giving expression to the lighting up of an aspect" (§ 207). This is another way Wittgenstein characterizes the happening of aspect change — "the lighting up of an aspect." Notice that the attribution of being to the pretend house is the expression of a situation, a game. With this, he touches on a pivotal characteristic of homeosis.

Lighting up, *Aufleuchten*, is orientational, not absolute. Under certain conditions, in a "situation," a child gives special expression to an absolutely normal happening. And yet he sticks by his questions, asking again the same question he had about children pretending, and perception, as well. Why do we react to the lighting up of a new aspect as though it were a change in the object? Why do we respond as if the object had truly become something else? "But the expression in one's voice and gestures is the same as if the object had altered and had ended by *becoming* this or that" (§ 209).

Wittgenstein gives his own reason, here, for eschewing the old concept becoming. To take the object as having become something else would mistake psychology and language for ontology, and this would be a form of metaphysics or magical thinking. And yet none of his schemes for understanding aspect shift satisfy him fully. Aspect change stays mysterious in the philosophy of psychology. First it is a matter of perception and its changeability. Then it is a matter of language games and their variability. Later, the ghost of a more overtly idealist solution comes out: "The aspects of the triangle: it is as if an idea came into contact, and for a time remained in contact, with the visual impression" (§ 211). What is impressed in an impression, he wants to ask, so that it takes on the aspects of a triangle? What is an aspect, and more importantly for him, where is an aspect?

While he does not find a suitable explanation for lighting up and the mysterious objective-subjective character of seeing-as, Wittgenstein does bring forward the phenomenon of aspect change and consider it central to experience. Three intuitions give definitive shape to the phenomenon. In § 247, an explosive thought: "but what I perceive in the lighting up of an aspect is not a property of the object, but an internal relation between it and other objects." This is a clear alternative to the linguistic or facultative understandings. Earlier, in § 244, there is another explosion: "The likeness strikes me, and its striking me fades." Lighting up, which happens as a result of the internal relations among objects, happens outside the self — and then it strikes, exists in its striking. Further, it is bound to time in a particular way. In § 237, an exclamation on the fact of fleetingness: " — Ask yourself, 'How long am I struck by a thing?' — How long is it new to me?" These three intuitions suggest a close kinship between lighting up, aspect change, and the embeddedness of an object in a reservoir of other objects. From this you can draw several conclusions, tangential to Wittgenstein's project, but essential to ours.

5.1.   *A likeness lights up when an aspect shift occurs.*

No likeness stands there awaiting reception. Perception of likeness happens when a shift of aspects happens. Perception is the subjective side of aspect change, which in turn is the objective condition for the illumination of a likeness, and the aspect shift on which illumination of a likeness depends rests on the thing's connection to other things.

5.1.1.   *An aspect shift occurs in a reservoir beyond a thing itself or things themselves. What you perceive is the facet of a larger shift.*

Two apparently singular, independent, and distinct objects fall into confusion, and through this they can be taken as an index for the reservoir turning, shifting, confusing, and deconfusing beyond them. When it happens, it happens fleetingly. The tripartite phenomenon — reservoir shift, aspect change, lighting up — crackles through homeotic experience.

5.1.2.   *Likeness strikes and is next to nothing outside the time of striking.*

The question of how *Aspektwechsel* might happen is met by a complex response, as tentative as it is illuminating. A likeness lights up during an aspect change resulting from a shift in a larger reservoir of object relations, and the lighting up is temporally restricted by the time of the shift. Further than this the *Philosophical Investigations* does not go. It is as though Wittgenstein, despite gathering the materials for an investigation of likeness, hit a wall made out of his own terms.

Wittgenstein's wall was Bergson's doorway. One stopped at the intuition of a reservoir, the other began from it. *Matter and Memory* lies, *avant la lettre*, in the murky underside of the *Philosophical Investigations*. Bergson looks unashamedly at the whole, decrying atomistic objects and their counterpart, analysis. "Not with impunity, either, can we congeal into distinct and independent things the fluidity of a continuous undivided process" (p. 123). Analyze it, and the reservoir withdraws from view, a warning to analysts such as Wittgenstein, who, had he synthesized his own reflections, might have become Bergson. Synthetic philosophizing promises to keep the reservoir in view by answering the question that Hume, for example, leaves unanswered — Why does one idea associate with another? Why does this association happen, and not that? And the more disturbing question: How is any single association related to the entirety of the reservoir?

Bergson's name for the reservoir in this book is "memory," which he says demurely is "just the intersection of mind and matter" (p. 13), that is, a zone in which images can lie closer to one another than in nature. *Matter and Memory* is a book about images. Memory is image, matter is image — matter is a "self-existing image," "une image qui existe en soi," as he calls it in the new introduction to the seventh edition in 1911 (English, p. 10; French, p. ii). This explains the urgency with which he distances himself from empiricists and associationists. Memory, the place where images meet, comes with its own special theoretical demand. "What we really need to discover is how a choice is effected among an infinite number of recollections which all resemble in some way the present perception, and why only one of them, this rather than that — emerges into the light of consciousness" (p. 164). Thinking from the reservoir to the aspect shift, this becomes the paramount concern. It is the question of *Aspektwechsel* asked from a different perspective. The simple fact is that for any perception image there are many memory images that resemble it. The fact is simple, but its consequences are not. Bergson needs a rule for why these image associations arise, rather than those. Note how different this question is from Leibniz's paradigmatic philosophical question: Why is there something rather than nothing? The principle of sufficient reason does not touch memory. Something less than sufficient reason, something more than chance has to govern its combinations. This is where Wittgenstein left off in *Philosophy of Psychology*, asking for a sufficient ground — Why now the duck and now the rabbit? He cannot answer because of the underlying atomism of experience, which Bergson rejects. Why this likeness instead of that? "But this is just what associationism cannot tell us, because it has made ideas and images into independent entities floating, like the atoms of Epicurus, in an inward space, drawing near to each other when chance brings them within the sphere of mutual attraction" (*Matter and Memory*, p. 164). Empiricism is an inward atomism, and for Bergson, atomistic presuppositions block the possibility of accounting for experience.

In its most general impulse, the plan for *Matter and Memory* is to project the distinction between subject and object onto time instead of space.[61] In place of inside and outside, Bergson — well in advance of Heidegger — takes experience as a complex imbrication of past, present, and future happening at once in any instant. In a metaphysical sense, the past is permanently *in actu*, and the happening of the past is the future. This is the temporal structure of memory. Given this starting point, the natural question becomes why this or that shard of the past should be happening right now. Why should a particular likeness "emerge into the light of consciousness" (p. 164)? Associationists, of which Wittgenstein could be considered an eccentric example, have two strikes against them. They truck in atomistic entities, and they have no way of justifying the content of any particular association among them. They have not asked the pivotal question. "For why should an image which is, by hypothesis, self-sufficient, seek to accrue to itself others either similar or given in contiguity with it?" (p. 165). This question comes very close to the original question by the editors of *Fliegende Blätter* — What beings are most alike? This version is: What ideas are most alike? On the way to an answer, Bergson discovers in his critique of empiricism more than one kind of resemblance.

One kind of resemblance predates resemblances between individuals. In reality, "we perceive the resemblance before we perceive the individuals which resemble each other." This principle goes along with a corollary: "in an aggregate of contiguous parts, we perceive the whole before the parts" (p. 165). Taken together, the two principles of prior resemblance and prior whole break down Wittgenstein's wall. Resemblance comes first, along with the whole, an originary, individualless, auratic resemblance in a partless synthesis. This other kind of resemblance is integral to the undivided whole, from which a single image is a falsifying excerpt. In this context, Bergson introduces his own account of aspect change, or the why of the association of images, in markedly different terms. "What we have to explain, then, is no longer the cohesion of internal states, but the double movement of contraction and expansion by which consciousness narrows or enlarges the development of its content" (p. 166). Put in an oversimplified way, the why of aspect change is given in terms of a larger movement. Doubtless, if you look at images or objects independently and then try to reconstruct their relations, there will always be an element of arbitrariness in your account. Bergson presents the whole under whose sway contents shift and present further aspects, revealing the shifts to be not at all arbitrary, though also not fully necessary or predictable with any certainty.

5.2.   *There is no homeotics without a cosmology.*

Memory, for Bergson, is a cosmos unto itself.[62] It is the entirety of what can happen in a specific distribution. It does not so much include an outside, and it certainly does not exclude one, so much as enfold into proximities. Memory is gelatin holding events, shakily, in their singularity, at a position in time, and at the same time it is a flow in which the relations among events shift continually. Perception calls up a radical contraction of memory to serve the needs of a present action. At the same time and with the same gesture, perceptions amass in memory and grow it. Each contraction places another pebble on memory's altar, which, enriched once again with material, is ready to contract and add itself back into itself once more, shifted and adorned with a new face. Among expansive spasms, patterns form. If you worry that this process is too subjective, Bergson does not. If you worry that the process is too arbitrary, Bergson shows its logic, whose first tenet is the repeated spasm of the whole. Its second tenet is the doctrine of dominant points. "There are always some dominant memories, shining points round which the others form a vague nebulosity. These shining points are multiplied in the degree to which our memory expands" (p. 171). With these two thoughts, the contraction / expansion of the reservoir and the mildly ordering memory points, Bergson accounts for both the haecceity of likenesses and their infusion in a medium.

How does *Aspektwechsel* happen in Bergson's memory cosmos? Absolute memory accrues perceptions, swelling up with each detail of every experience, including the inner relations between experiences, in a multidimensional continuum that preserves precise placements in sequences and is thus a strange continuum of continua, shifting without ever losing track of earlier relations. Earlier relations do however come into different relationships with the whole and thus with each other. In addition, the reservoir rotates, turned by perceptual events. In order to say why a likeness between two images lights up at some instant, you need to refer to the movement of the whole reservoir in its encounter with a perception. A decisive passage reveals that:

> Memory, laden with the whole of the past, responds to the appeal of the present state by two simultaneous movements, one of translation [*l'un de translation*], by which it moves in its entirety to meet experience, thus contracting more or less, though without dividing, with a view to action; and the other of rotation upon itself [*l'autre de rotation sur elle-même*], by which it turns toward the situation of the moment, presenting to it that side of itself which may prove to be the most useful. To these varying degrees of contraction correspond the various forms of association by similarity. (English, pp. 168–69; French, p. 184)

Which way memory turns, which side it shows in any perceptual event, what hue of light it sheds on a perception, how much it contracts, how deep its echoes go, all this has to be described in order to account for a single likeness.

5.2.1. *To explain a likeness, you need to describe the reservoir in its entirety and in its multiple exokinetic and endokinetic movements, including its rotation with respect to itself.*

For a likeness to light up, the bulk of memory contracts, and as it contracts, it rotates "upon itself," and then it translates an aspect of itself toward a perception it takes as Bergson's memory cosmos alike. Bergson does not say directly, but the doctrine of dominant memories or memory points explains why a particular memory image gets called up.

5.2.2. **In a memory field, there is something like gravity.**

Amid the turning, expanding / contracting memory mass, a minimal order reigns, loose, though powerful, by which memory materials accrete into disks around slightly denser points — "shining points round which others form a vague nebulosity." Dominant memories warp the field and attract other memories into orbit around them.

What makes one memory heavier than others? You don't reach into your memory as though into a grab bag to come up with whatever you touch first, nor is it a simple process of matching same with same. What replaces a random field or a taxonomically ordered cabinet is a viscous liquid dotted with densities. As the memory gel expands, images that have not yet been associated with others become isolated from the mass. Perhaps these are the most shocking perceptions or the most foreign, the most unhabituated, the most unassimilable. Be that as it may, unallied images stand out from the atmosphere and, individuated *per accidens*, act as attracting points for other memories and for perceptions (p. 171). Abandoned images are available as gravitational centers for experience nebulae.

Once these few eccentric shining points begin to accrete memories, each time memory expands, the points multiply. Why is this? For all the freedom of absolute memory, for all its fluidity, there is still a fact or a physics. Gravity begets gravity. One dominant memory accrues a corona of vaguely associated memories, and the dominant memory, by standing out even the slightest bit from others, produces a memory of itself, a memory of gravity, which in this way propagates itself throughout the field, deforming relations as it goes. Memory gets and keeps singular experiences, and the experience of singularity that is memory takes itself into itself, singularizes its own operation, and without any higher law, warps the field, leaving memory lumpy. Experience tends to settle into patterns, even if they are not rigid or unchanging.

Bergson's break in Wittgenstein's wall opens onto a homeotic field, containing every likeness in actuality, drawing itself in to reflect on itself and letting itself out to approach the present, making a mere impression — this empirical moment is preserved — into an experience by filling it out with relevant memory aspects — through likenesses to experience. Homeosis makes a mere point of sense into a full apprehension and a living through, enlivening mere sensation with kindred details out of the plenum.

5.3.   *The homeoplex is as malleable as Descartes's wax. It expands and reorients, contracts, and the contractions accrete to it. It projects multiple "sides" that can be called into proximity in an instant.*

What sides of memory are available to make up any new experience are not determined by a law. They are conditioned by other contractions and rotations, other experience pearls that have accreted, other clouds orbiting dense stars of memory, forming up into systems and subsystems. Fusion of a likeness out of an atmosphere depends on this sort of staccato concentric-eccentric movement.

5.3.1.   *Likenesses light up when the past reconfigures.*

This means that a likeness comes about among a set of established likenesses, some near, some farther, and through this any not yet established likeness is part of the entire reservoir in its present configuration and a coming moment of its past. Despite its relation to the entirety, any likeness derives, more proximally, from a shining point, a dominant likeness you can call a "prototype." On one hand, prototypes pile up, awaiting a spark to shine. On the other, when that happens, a likeness evokes a canon within which it feels comfortable. It invents its models. To be like is to circle in the penumbra of a gravity spot and to be arrested in the vicinity of a pattern.[63] What pulls a likeness to a halt is something like the way it is like; thus, a memory attracts perceptions just as a phenotype attracts organisms. And nevertheless, since the attraction has to be mutual, a perception has to reach for the memory, as well, the organism has to call out to the phenotype. This is why a simple original-copy schema does not describe homeotic experience. Likeness looks both ways. In truth, likeness looks more ways — a pair looks both to its poles and to its predecessors. In addition, corresponding to any likeness there is also, in the world distribution, an anticipation of likeness. To every pattern an anticipation of pattern. Anticipations of likeness do not precede the fusing out of a likeness in the way a transcendental condition logically precedes experience; rather, a likeness brushes up against a prototype and rubs off as colored chalk rubs off on a shirt.

5.3.2.   **To be like is to rub against a prototype, which in that instant becomes its anticipation.**

A universal vultus, a snapshot of the happening pattern, results from an arrest of the general drift. A likeness is anticipated when a pattern arrests it, a unique, radiating arrest in which a focus or multiple foci lag and drag and their lags ripple outward.

Why does the concept becoming not describe the movement

of aspect change? Homeosis is becoming's contrary — it is driven by impetuous stagnations, gravity, in *Matter and Memory's* parlance. In the Bergsonian *esprit*, every event, every fusing of a likeness out of an atmosphere, every memory image that comes to meet a perception, is double in another way. *"Esprit"* names the happening of a likeness and, in one and the same gesture, the preparation for future likeness regimes that might take it as a prototype. Each new likeness is a potential gravity point, every likeness is a new opportunity for an arrest of the specific motion and the general drift. Rather than "becoming like," you could call this "corruption," in its morphological sense: "co-ruption," "halting with."

5.4. *Likeness corrupts a development, retards a drift between poles, shortens a trajectory, contradicting preventing slowing lessening.*

Halting is no friend to becoming and is not itself a species of change — you could also call it, in memory of evolution's beloved concept "variation," "devariation." I called it elsewhere "the yield,"[64] and in order to have a vocabulary to talk about it, a further word is wanted: "archaic."

5.4.1. *Archaic is the time of the yield.*

Distinct from "the past," the archaic is not historical. It never gave birth to a present or called forth a future. It stagnated — stagnates, will stagnate — holding phenomena in its swampy embrace. Homeosis is the archaic phenomenon par excellence. Relations, states, points, qualities, events slow to a halt in its concentrate; force gets declined; homeosis remains from this yielding motion, an archaic mode not subject to the physical metaphors that describe time and history, such as "motion," "course," "passing," "flow." In yielding, a phenomenon abandons the invitation to become something; it remains, declining movement; it can't escape the amber of the archaic, not because it is a special kind of thing or action, not because it belongs to a special temporal category, either, but only insofar as it declines, for a time, to drift away. You can understand the movement of Bergson's memory reservoir like this: as a halt.

If before, a Snell's law for homeotic phenomena was needed to say how the two poles of a pair refract one another,[65] a Mach's principle is in order now to say how a likeness emerges from a halt. Bergson's contracting, rotating, gravity-pocked memory cosmos calls for a supplement, a principle that explains the halt and also says how local phenomena are connected to the most distant and the most synthetic, large-scale disposition of the All. Wittgenstein's wall needed Bergson's break; Bergson's break needs Mach's cosmos and its most special and most counterintuitive principle.

Don't be afraid of cosmology! Good humanists don't say such things out loud. Yet to find a principle for likeness happening, there may be no other option but to start from the largest order and proceed from there. Another step, even wilder, perhaps, is to ask help from another discourse that moves more easily about at a cosmic scale and turn from metaphysics to physics. We wouldn't be the first to do this — certainly, Aristotle did it, and Hume and even Kant have a picture of the physical world in the background of their theories of mind.

Physics seems like the last thing likeness would need, since likeness doesn't apply to bodies, derives from a species of nonmotion, and sidesteps space. For this reason, where Aristotle, Hume, and Kant, among others, deduce philosophies of spatiotemporal objects from physical theories of space, time, and motion, the same isn't possible here. Instead, a theory of likeness can be worked out from the other side of this same coin by paying attention to a peculiar remainder in modern physics that explains why things are not fully individuated and don't always move with respect to one another.

This will be both an analogy, between physics and nonphysics, and what you could call a "counteranalogy," a return of that analogy to the heart of physics. That is, a physical principle can be structurally compared to a likeness principle and additionally illuminate something about the latter. Once this happens, moreover, the physical principle will turn out to have a likeness element within it, such that it analogizes the analogy.

Paul Kammerer, when searching for the causes of series, already found an analogy between the happening of likeness and physical inertia.[66] While elaborating his law of series, Kammerer recognized that likeness among events is akin to persistence among bodies, and so he posited a "Beharrungsvermögen" for events on analogy with physical objects—a general faculty for persisting involved in likeness production. Material points show inertia, and complexes of material points show inertia with respect to one another; likewise, bodies and parts of bodies and bodies with respect to one another are inertial. When I move, none of my molecules moves faster than I do—this is a key piece of evidence for Kammerer. My elements are inertial with respect to one another, just as my body is inertial with respect to the planet at the moment. Other kinds of things, such as forces, are inertial, as are complexes of forces, and force-body complexes—all these tend to persist in their initial intentions (*Das Gesetz der Serie*, pp. 115–16). In addition to his madness for recording serial occurrences, Kammerer also made the crucial inference that inertia is a prerequisite for them. "Events that repeat themselves obey a power of inertia [*Trägheitsvermögen*] of bodies and forces, through which they come about. The law of series is an expression of the law of the persisting [*des Beharrungsgesetzes*] of objects" (p. 117). Objects produce a series ultimately through inertial powers that extend beyond the mechanics of bodies into all other realms, biological, ethical, psychological, aesthetic, social. Kammerer discovered how inertia explains likeness, but he did not in turn discover that likeness also explains inertia. To do this, he would have needed a non-Newtonian understanding of inertia.

First, the analogy with physics. With regard to inertia, the short version of Mach's principle is the following: rather than a characteristic of independent entities in absolute space, the inertia of a thing depends on the distribution of all matter in the universe. Let me give the homeotic analog right away and then explain the analogy with the physical principle afterward.

The homeoverse consists in the distribution of all likenesses at a given instant. The distribution is not static, it is reactive, though in an unexpected way. Rather than "reactive," you might call it "repassive." "Repassive distribution" means two things: all existing likenesses affect any single likeness, and any single likeness affects all existing likenesses. The reciprocal life of a likeness with likenesses and likenesses with a likeness is direct and, surprisingly, also directionless. A single likeness is held in place by the overall distribution and remains passive with respect to it, and the overall distribution is held in place relative to a single likeness and is "repassive" with respect to it.

5.5. *The homeoverse consists in the pattern of distribution and the effect that all existing likenesses have on any single likeness, and vice versa.*

Another way to say this is that likenesses are relative. A likeness lights up in and through a pair, and the poles of that pair are certainly "alike" relative to one another. Following Mach, I am also interested in a further relativity of the how of this likeness: the way the poles of a pair are alike to one another is relative to a moment extrinsic to them alone and by themselves.

Mach's principle says something analogous about inertia. It is relative — everything in physics is relative, in fact. Even in Newtonian physics, any motion is relative to the matter in the universe.[67] If this is true for motion in Newtonian physics, why isn't it also true, Mach asks, for inertia? The tendency of a thing to remain at the same velocity — Mach keeps the name "inertia" for this, but in his treatment, inertia becomes the relationship of a thing and its velocity to all the matter in the universe such that the thing's velocity and position at one instant refrains from becoming unlike its velocity and position at another instant. It is not such a leap to associate inertia and likeness. Indeed, in the physical universe, inertia produces likeness — likeness of position, state, motion, and so on. What would it take to see the order of happenings reversed, such that position, state, and motion were produced by likeness? What are position, state, motion except modes of likeness, constitutive of inertia? This is the homeotic ghost internal to physics, and the path is short from here to the homeoverse.

5.5.1. *Likeness results from inertia, if inertia is constituted by likeness.*

Likeness occurs when traits remain in the vicinity of one another and don't drift apart. There is thus inertia in genetics, just as there is inertia in culture. Where genes and memes lag and lay, they tend to persist, as Kammerer put it, in the absence of a disturbance. By this way of looking at things, nonmotion is native to the universe and motion is an interruption, an arrest of the general tendency to arrest.

For the tendency of a thing to remain at the same velocity, Mach keeps the name "inertia," but inertia becomes, in his thinking, the relativity of a thing to the matter in the universe in its current pattern of distribution such that the thing's velocity and position at any instant refrains, due to this relationship, from becoming unlike its velocity and position at another instant.[68]

5.5.2. *The similar is relative.*

True, I am interested in homeotics, in likeness and its determinations in the broadest frame. I am starting with the physical universe and its modes in order to develop an analogy. And yet before the analogy between physics and likeness can be constructed, the physical cosmos divulges a secret: it is already articulated by a moment of likeness. Inertia produces likeness, you could say, but inertia means the obtaining of a likeness — in position, velocity, a likeness of pattern in the distribution of matter. A homeotic motor may just be what is animating the physical cosmos.

Or, I want to say it this way: the analogy is counteranalogized in the fact. Who can imagine a natural science that is not also and even fundamentally the experience of resemblances? At the start of one tradition of zoological reflection, Aristotle relies on homeosis to ground the selecting, generalizing act of genus construction, to derive order in the zone of the living immanently, from within its relations. At another starting point, Darwin does something similar, with other reference points. This is true of physics, as well, in this one point, and likely in others, not only because particles or astronomical bodies are alike in some respects — there must be more than one quark and more than one star and some kinship of quarks and stars, so that the very small and very large belong to a general sweep of likeness — but because force and position and mass join up in configurations that mimic others. It is common to describe physical causality, for instance, as "like effects imply like causes" (Hume, *Treatise* 1.3.15, p. 117). Hume taught there is never only one causal event, but a specific complex of them. There are always at least two, the second containing a memory image of the first. A lone "cause" with its lone "effect" is an event falsely excerpted from a continuum of replicas.

"Inertia" means a velocity like a velocity, which can be expressed as velocity remaining the same, except that, for this inquiry, because inertia is not a metaphysical state, but actually happens, it has to be said like this: where the total distribution of matter in the cosmos is like itself, there, an inertial object's velocity is like itself. To say "is like," however, is redundant. In a Machian cosmos where nothing is beyond nature and nature is not a machine, but a dynamic, responsive relational economy, "is" means enlikening.

From here to the homeoverse is truly a short step. "Inertia" means velocity likeness, velocity relative to the total distribution, a speed that is consistently alike in reference to an outside, consistent and alike, or alike alike, alike to the second power, unvaryingly xeroxing itself, insistently overlapping. "Inertia" means likeness, the self-likeness of velocity in one and the co-likeness of velocity among two. "Likeness" means inertia: in a homeotic happening, traits remain in the vicinity of one another and don't drift away, velocity being one possible trait that could remain with respect to another.

Physical inertia, then, on the basis of the analogy and the counteranalogy, is a member of a larger group of inertial effects that obtain in the total cosmos that contains the physical cosmos. Physical inertia is a species of general inertia, which is another name for likeness as it slows and halts phenomena across fields and regions. What would happen if inertia were not active in a field? Imagine a noninertial family. A child of my mother might come out nothing like her at all. A human child might come out nothing like a human. And so on. In the cosmos, however, the unlikenesses exhibited are incredibly small. That a species is the basic unit of natural history makes this very point. Evolution works through kin clusters. That is to say again, there is an inertia in genetics, just as there is an inertia in culture. The traits of faces and dresses tend to fall into relative stasis unless there is a disturbance.

Up to now, I have merely proposed the overlap of inertia and likeness, presented as a bare fact. Inertia is not a bare fact for Mach, however; it itself has a complex logic that is not separable from the greater logic of the cosmos or for that matter from the method of its science. In order to approach Mach's greater logic of inertia, a return to Newton is called for.

At the beginning of the *Principia* (1687), Newton introduces the idiosyncratic phenomenon, in a universe of matter in motion, of no change.[69] He introduces and explains it by reference to force. No change, under this explanation, is a species of change, and so is a change that brings no change. The *Principia*'s Third Definition puts it like this: "Inherent force of matter [*vis insita*] is the power of resisting by which every body, so far as it is able, perseveres in its state either of resting or of moving uniformly straight forward" (*Principia*, p. 50). An important note not published at the time makes a key distinction: "I do not mean Kepler's force of inertia, by which bodies tend toward rest, but a force of remaining in the same state either of resting or of moving" (p. 50, note c).

Here is the deep intraphysical reference to likeness. Inertia is a force, but the force issues in sameness; it causes likeness between one moment of a motion and the next. Newton expected with this note to have clarified his concept. Inertia is not a tendency toward rest, as Kepler thought; it is a force forcing preservation, a motive to nonmotion, a difference to sameness. If what causes something to stay as it was is a force, it certainly is a peculiar kind of force. A *vis manendi* (Latin, vol. 1, p. 40, note 9), a force of remaining or a remaining force, would operate very differently than a *vis impressa* (Latin, vol. 1, p. 41), a force impressed from the outside.

A force that induces something to the same state has no ready image, and it may not be possible to imagine an inherent force at all. Newton gives no analogy to help. Could he be suggesting a change in the idea of force? Could there be several kinds of force, or at least two, whose forces, so to speak, are opposed to one another, not as opposed extrinsic forces, but as an opposition between an intrinsic and extrinsic force? An impressed force has a clear intuition. It corresponds to the mutual impenetrability of physical objects in absolute space. Two objects cannot copenetrate, and so one displaces the other, displacement being the evidence of the external impetus as well as of space itself. An impressed force announces itself by means of a change in velocity, from rest to motion or motion to rest, from slow to fast or vice versa. How does a force that produces no change announce itself? The *vis impressa* is expressed—its effect is registered, at a minimum—by the motion of the body. What effect is expressed in a stone at rest that remains at rest or in an arrow in flight that remains in flight? What is an unexpressed force?

Where a *vis activa* fails to account for the lack of change, there may well reign a *vis inactiva*, an artless—*iners*—manner of impelling that has no measurable effects, a tendency toward sameness or similarity or an approximating likening, which is, thus, in essence, an effect without a cause, more like a desistance than a resistance. Inertia results from a force of preserving, says Newton, who attributes a proximal cause where it would be logical to find none. Maybe this is why he then posits this force not any longer as a force, but suddenly as a cosmic law, in the first law of motion: "Every body perseveres in its state of being at rest or of moving uniformly straight forward except insofar as it is compelled to change its state by forces impressed" (*Principia*, p. 62).

At the end of the seventeenth century, this was a bold thing to decree. With a stroke, the law arrested Aristotelian theories, ancient and medieval, which argued that for an object to continue in motion a continual impulse is required consequently, deducing from that posited impulse a "medium" surrounding the object. With the first law of motion, Newton empties space out, erases the medium, and does another bold thing, as well. Notice how the question of an innate inert force drops out of this statement of inertia as a law. Where in Definition 3 there was a paradoxical inertial "force," here, there is a cosmic principle that accounts for the tendency of things to stay as they are, to exist in an unforced way, to associate freely with their past positions and velocities and associations, and even to decline to be compelled, up to a point, in an ease and a contentment unparalleled in the rest of physics — all without reference to the perplexing, forceless, expressionless force.

The double-edged force, the force against itself, the nonexpressing force, drops out in the law, and so looking back to Definition 3 helps understand the dilemma, which in fact has not gone away in the law; it has only been veiled. "Materia vis insita est potentia resistendi" (Latin, p. 40). Notice that the inherent force of matter is not resistance, but a power to resist. A power to a force, a power to a force to a nonforce, a thwarted and stored-up force.[70] Unlike other modes that could survive a period of latency, force clearly cannot. Wherever there is a force, that force is in action; when it is not in action, it is not. "Force" names the action, not anything that precedes or follows it. That it is under the spell of a "power" here shows that it is not a force alone, but also in some measure contains or allows for its own suspension. A latent force, a self-suspending force — perplexities like these stop the Newtonian concept of inertia in its tracks, even when the epithet "force" falls away in the first law. A force without force, a resting force, a passive force — how can it actively preserve a motion and suspend itself, enact a physical motive and desist from happening, propose a kind of motion that moves away from motion, all in a way that appears to contradict the laws of physics (and so you have to give it its own law).

Machian relativity makes it easier to think inertia without such perplexities, but in order to do so, it opens the door to likeness. It says how a "single" likeness or uniformity (if saying this makes any sense) shifts the homeoplex and how the entire homeoplex acts as a reference for a single likeness. Mach is not interested in homeotics per se. He simply wants to demonstrate, in his physics, that concepts such as cause are parasitic on the fact that phenomena are dependent on one another.[71] Phenomena, not matter in motion — he doesn't practice physics so much as phenomenal physiologics — act as though the cosmos were a big, perceptive ball whose attention to itself shifts around within its boundaries. Mach wants to be able to say how a single body (a complex of sensations) can revolve the universe (a complex of sensations) and how, conversely, the universe can act as a reference point for the motion of any single body.

In place of an inherent force, Mach posits an eccentric responsiveness. More than a decade before the commonly quoted formulation of Mach's "principle" in *The Science of Mechanics* (1883), a note published in 1872 to a lecture held in 1871 already pushes "our usual conception of the law of inertia" to a crisis point (in *History and Root of the Principle of the Conservation of Energy*, p. 77). It is only the idea of absolute space, neutral with respect to the matter within it, that makes Newton hypostasize an innate force in matter to explain self-maintaining motion. In Mach's "return to Newton," Newton looks past his own limitation. Newton was already a de facto relativity theorist, since in the *Principia*, virtually all motion is relative and not absolute, even though the explicit discussion of relativity is confined to the famous scholium to the definitions.

Newtonian motion is actually relative for Mach, and this is demonstrated thematically in the scholium and operatively across the whole theory. One great exception to this rule is inertia, which Newton always posits as absolute. At a bare minimum, each specific motion of a specific body is relative to space and time, except when the motion is inertial. Inertial motion is absolute even with respect to these other absolutes. Evidence for this is right before our eyes. Whereas Newtonian gravity diminishes with distance; inertia, being inherent and nonrelational, is the same everywhere. Inertia is like a new god (*Principia*, p. 442). Modern physics cannot stand such a divine spark, a shard of timeless and motionless creation that in practice affects all matter. It is ridiculous, Mach tells us, to postulate that motion is relative in some cases, while in other cases, it is independent and absolute. The relativity of a body's velocity vis-à-vis the earth is certainly not turned off or out of effect when dealing with uniform velocities. Mach begins his dialectic here: "either all motion is absolute, or our law of inertia is wrongly expressed" (*History and Root*, p. 77), and this dialectical *Auseinandersetzung* with Newtonian mechanics is the seam along which Mach turns the universe inside out.

If there can be no partial relativity, however, as Mach asserts, we can no longer say whether a comet is streaming past earth below it and the stars behind it or the stars and earth are streaming past it between them. Mach calls this "a great indefiniteness" produced by the law of motion (p. 75). Thinking purely in geometrical terms, you will struggle to determine whether the earth turns within a fixed celestial architecture or whether, in contrast, the sky turns around it. The Copernican turn needs a half turn more, from the natural conclusion that the earth turns around the sun to the unnatural one that the sun turns around the earth, given the right reference points. One could try to claim that both motions are absolute with respect to the absolute frame, space and time, but this, again, requires a beyond of nature, since the outermost frame is not a phenomenon. Mach rejects this option, and as a consequence, he reformulates the law of inertia, with great consequences for the theory of likeness.

5.6. *Local forces do not matter to the inertial object.*

Or as a later physicist quipped, "When the subway jerks, it's the fixed stars that throw you down."[72] To see how this is the case, Mach asks readers to carry out a procedure. Lay down a set of coordinates as a reference. Start with the surface of the earth, just as an example. A body is inertial relative to the earth and not, say, relative to a comet streaming by. When you are sitting in a chair, you are in just this situation—inertial relative to the earth's surface, speeding up relative to a comet. A contrary case can help further: if there is suddenly an earthquake, you will no longer be inertial, but accelerating and decelerating relative to the moon or sun.

Now lay down a different set of coordinates—Mach calls this procedure "indirect description."[73] Pick the nearest star that is not our sun. The star is inertial with respect to our solar system until the planets should change velocity or direction. You have chosen one particular star to demonstrate this effect. Why this star, as opposed to a billion trillion others? Why this relation, as opposed to others and other combinations of others? According to Mach, you ought to perform this speculative space travel star by star, complex by complex, through the whole cosmos "until the laying down of a system of coordinates has reached an end" (p. 78). At the end of all coordinate systems, Mach tells us, all that will be left is the matter in the universe, all of it, in its singular distribution of masses and relative motions at the instant of comparison: "because we can give preference to none, the influence of all must be taken into consideration" (p. 78). This is an axiom in inertia's logic. Any inertial motion is in contact with the total distribution of mass and motion at an instant.

Mach does not stop with this thought. His particular genius is to go beyond the theoretical to the critical, to the conditions of possibility and then to the limit of experience and often further. Thinking beyond the particular coordinate system leads him to the specific total distribution of mass and motion, what you could call a snapshot of the physical All or the cosmos's momentary "species." But Mach goes so far as to imagine the end of this arrangement, the breaking of all complexes. In order to demonstrate once and for all the relativity of inertia, he asks us to consider an extreme event — "a shattering of the universe." When we think this, he dares us to concede, "we learn that all bodies, each with its share, are of importance in the law of inertia" (p. 79). Especially distant ones, for the simple fact that the vast majority of matter is distant from any single body. What we learn about inertial movement as opposed to noninertial movement is that "the share of the nearest masses vanishes in comparison with that of the farthest" (p. 79). Local influence falls away, and distant bodies, which would have no effect on local changes such as acceleration, unless you conjure up a mystical *actio in distans* — distant bodies become responsible for the quiescence of local bodies.

5.6.1. *Inertia acts as if a treaty had been signed between the farthest and biggest and the smallest and nearest.*

It is as though the greatest unlikenesses — in location, in mass and force — were responsible for the most subtle likenesses.

Physics is alternately fascinated with and dismissive of this suggestion. Einstein counted it as a pivotal thought on the way to the new relativity theory and wrote to Mach to say so, although he later decided that "Mach's principle" — Einstein himself dubbed the theory — had to be rejected.[74] The mechanism by which noninteracting bodies determine each other's motion is mysterious — Einstein rejected any large-scale action at a distance — and in any case, he finally absorbed inertial motion into the pseudo-Riemannian manifold of spacetime.

A motion stays like itself not as the result of an internal force of resistance, but out of a distant, encompassing, foglike comparability, not caused by, but embedded in the momentary species of the universe, in and out of and with respect to the precise disposition of matter at this or that instant. It is plain now, as Mach writes in the *Science of Mechanics*, that "the question whether a motion is in itself uniform is senseless" (p. 224). Uniformity, relative likeness, is not alike relative to itself, but to the distant and total configuration. A Mach's principle for likeness tells us, in a vocabulary not so much stolen from physics as part of an internal homeotic critique of physics, how traits remain in proximity to one another. If there were such a principle or if you could adapt the physical one, the idea that two things on their own make a likeness would be as senseless as the idea that a motion is uniform with respect to itself and nothing else. Likenesses are not in themselves or for another, but in and through all, within an effective total figure, registering in various ways — in genes, phenotypes, homologies, geometries, memories, artworks, languages, families, cultures — throughout the homeoverse.

5.7.   *Each likeness is an abbreviated reference to the disposition of every likeness, and the homeoverse refers in its overall pattern to each likeness.*

Mach, when he says something similar about inertia, comes close to Bergson, and together they are thinkers of a responsively redistributing whole — on one hand nature, on the other hand memory — whose "principles," in the words of Mach, "not only admit of constant control by experience but actually require it" (*Science of Mechanics*, p. 238). Nature is not a machine (p. 224), but an experience.

5.7.1.   *Homeosis happens when a trait is quiescent with respect to another and declines to go beyond it, on agreement with a remote pattern.*

A trait refuses to accelerate, so to speak, into likeness with something else, in concert with a total distribution, a cosmic species. The converse also happens. A distant configuration pivots and shows a different face, reconfiguring local likenesses. These likenesses are nothing less than the cosmos experiencing itself.[75]

Perhaps no field shows its sensitivity to small shifts within it better than natural history. Whales were first classified with viviparous quadrupeds by John Ray in 1693. They no longer swam with fishes, their fins were not fins and their lungs not gills. The galaxy had shifted its attention from the probity of ancient authorities to proof by observation,[76] and whales dropped their scaly siblings for hairy siblings. Linnaeus finished the shift from inherited classifications to homological observations, rather than started it — his own system was a modification of that of his mentor, Peter Artedi — but Linnaeus did add the crucial insight in the eighteenth century that species are "bound together by reproduction."[77] Ancestral patterns could now be felt to control the similarities in the most recent organisms. Whales slowed down with dolphins in thrall to distant mammals. A "common ancestor" detained the whale among the cows, and fish were allowed to drift back into indeterminacy.

Given the right orientation of the homeoverse, anything can be like anything in some respect. This is why, only if we are given the actual distribution of kinships — the world species in its momentary plenitude, a cosmic face whose features extend as much into history as they do into spirit or physical matter or space or language, with their patterns of association and distance effects — can we say what counts as a likeness, can we give precedence, for instance, to my similarities with my mother over those with other primates or those with a fish. My hand is like to a star when we are talking about radiations of five points or when we talk about massy physical bodies or when we talk about things that hold other things, whether by grasping or by gravity. In a universe where a hand is like a star, given a similar number of points, and a poem is like a dream, insofar as each holds within it intimate, hidden patterns, when configurations in the homeoplex shift, out of nowhere a hand likens to a poem, insofar as they communicate in gestures, and a dream likens to a star on the prototype of things that break the darkness with fragmentary illuminations out of a great distance.

5.7.2.   *What has yielded goes on display.*

6.   *What has yielded goes on display.*

A phenomenon appears — and appears as something. A likeness however — a likeness . . . goes on display. Posit a ratio: display differs from appearance to the extent that homeosis differs from phenomenality. To put it in a handy formula, they differ in the way that "like" differs from "as."

Upon the little words "like" and "as" two vastly different sciences can be built. Appearing expresses itself in "as," homeosis in "like." The little words stand for linguistic operations and carry out operations that go well beyond language. First and foremost, as and like, and appearing and homeosis, overlap in significant ways. Phenomenological appearing and homeotic displaying both project a world in which nothing inheres permanently. Fungibility or revocability is the greatest affinity between phenomenology as theorized by Husserl and then Heidegger and homeotics as I am trying to theorize it here. Appearance and display both presuppose a world without essential beings or types, without actual unity, without, additionally, becoming. Each makes its object a posit of language and so at any moment revocable, with another as or like. If you want a world without essential beings, when you want to say what something is, you might choose to say, in place of "is," "as." Or from another standpoint, you might choose to say "like." The two little words are in complete sympathy about one thing: the being of any being depends on the operation carried out by the little word. The being "is" "as" or "like" something.

From here on, the operations begin to diverge. The first divergence of as and like comes in the strength of its commitment to its object. A thing as something may not actually be that thing, may be only acting as that thing. This is no doubt a lighter commitment to the being of the object than in ontology. Further, acting as under most circumstances comes about through an epistemic subject. I "take" something as something. I take a rock as a hammer, I take a neighbor as a comrade — the subjective force is on display in a particular way. Through my agency, I take this to be as good as, worthy of standing in for, as equivalent in some respects to . . . that. I act as though it were the other thing; its characteristics are solicited as if they belonged to the other thing: a rock's mass and maneuverability; a neighbor's kindness and shared interests. The characteristics that the objects share with the real thing solicit my agency. I act with respect to the stone in the same manner, with minor adjustments, as I act with respect to the hammer. Despite the decisive difference between as and is, for all its humility, as nevertheless wants to be is. As behaves by and large as though it *were* is. "As" means "as though being," tantamount to being, taking over the operations of being and standing in its place in all critical operations. When I say "X as Y," I act as though I was in fact asserting the being of that thing. Asserting being without asserting being, in truth, the phenomenological "as" is said in bad faith. "As Y" means "as though Y"; "as though Y" means "as good as Y"; "as good as Y" limits the time and purposes in which X can act as Y, to be sure; and yet, during that time and for those purposes, the separation of the comparison, this as that, collapses. Except for not actually being the thing, what presents itself "as" the thing has the very qualities that are needed in the moment.

"As" is "is as." In this way, it is completely imbricated with ontology. The values that used to be attached to being get transferred to the provisional role. To say this another way: when I substitute "as" for "is," value gets reassigned from the being of the thing to its temporary behavior in a network of purposes, the center of which is the user, or the "on behalf of whom" of the behavior.

"As" is powerful, as powerful as being, or more so — it makes the being of a thing flexible, fungible, provisional, and so, when certain conditions are met, revocable. Different situations call upon different qualities. "As" takes an entity that looks like its determinations are intrinsic and makes them seem at least partially extrinsic; it takes an entity whose determinations are essential or universal and makes those determinations dependent on its position in a nexus of transformable relations. Thus its purported power to challenge metaphysics. Being as depends on a position in a network, so that instead of a world of things, there is a world of purposes and subpurposes, full to the brim with possible positions for a manifold stuff to come forward and express some of its qualities in view of a purpose. And yet, being as isn't as flexible as all that. Even where being means "being as," which is to say, where being is determined by its situation, where it is the expression of a fungible, manifold stuff, where being can be revoked and transformed by hermeneutic activity, nevertheless the "as" in "being as" has such a strong presence that its science can still be called "ontology." Heidegger dubs this presence "the structure of 'as'" (*Sein und Zeit*, § 33, p. 154).[78] As is not; as structures, which is to say that in the reign of "as," being simply means structuring.

"As" has another meaning as well. "As" is related to "about." In interpretive understanding, something is "taken as" something else. "Etwas als Etwas" is the general formula Heidegger suggests (*Sein und Zeit*, § 32, p. 149). Something as something. You know immediately that the second "something" is the important position, which expresses the determinate purposivity "as what" the first "something" appears. The first "something" holds the position of the Kantian "thing in itself." As such, it leaves a nagging doubt. What kind of thing is this first something? What value or meaning can the first "Etwas" have, in the phrase "Etwas als Etwas," if it is merely to be determined by the second? The first "Etwas" is crucial in order to express appearance as, and yet, no matter how hard you think, you simply cannot say what the first "Etwas" is, nor of course can you think it totally away. For the purposes of this hermeneutic act, the first "Etwas" is nothing . . . and yet, it has some minimal being. It is the carrier of the qualities that are wanted for the second "Etwas." The second something is "about" the first. It refers back to it, it carries qualities over from it, it selects the qualities to be expressed. The something as what is about the something it is as. The basic element of "as" is to be "in view of" or "about" its predecessor, which is thus its truth. "Gemäß dieser Struktur wird etwas auf etwas hin verstanden," "Pursuant to this structure [the 'as' structure] a thing is understood as being in view of another thing" (*Sein und Zeit*, § 33, p. 159, my translation). In other words, the as structure is close to, if not identical with, a semiotic relationship, and this is why, in *Being and Time*, the discussion of the as structure leads directly to the discussion of language.[79]

"As" is a modification of ontology that stays within its logic, and at the same time it is a link, internal to ontology, to semiotics. It is as the being and is about the being. "Like," in contrast, does not substitute, does not bring qualities forward as representatives, does not solicit the agency of a subject, and does not deprecate itself in the face of an origin.

6.1. *A likeness is neither an appearance nor a sign.*

Appearance and sign evoke a cosmos that recognizes transcendence, one with a rank order of values for modes of being. A sign and an appearance may be thought of either as subordinate to what they are about and what appears or as superordinate to them. A sign may be thought to solicit a signified or be solicited by one. An appearance may be thought to determine, with its perspective, angle, intensity, and so on, what appears or to be determined by it. Transcendence comes in these flavors: rank order, order of solicitation, order of determination, and so on. The actual order of transcendence makes an enormous difference for those who live in that cosmos. Whether signs solicit signifieds and appearances solicit things in themselves or signifieds solicit signs and things solicit appearances will determine whether you believe you are living in a spare eternal system with multifarious, inessential, changing expressions or whether you take hold of an infinitely rich diversity of possible experiences by their infinite finite expressions. This is more than an inversion, as Nietzsche knew, because the worlds are unequal. The first inversion is theology, the second inversion is art. The bigger difference, however, lies between the ranked kind of cosmos and a cosmos with no rank order. In place of rank order, which fixes values for kinds of beings, the homeoverse has inertia, which slows the general drift of qualities.

6.2. *Slowing the drift and drive of traits puts them on display.*

Language can carry this out — "What was it like?" "It was like...." " And the display of the likeness, the unfurling of a predicate onto a subject, say, or an adjective onto a noun, is what stops the elements from drifting into other conjugations. This happens with images, as well, or in actions or social events — unfurling the display of a likeness may be the best homeotic explanation for adaptation to an environment in evolution theory. Adaptation displays a likeness — a set of likenesses, really — of the organism with its species and its behavior with the affordances of the niche, which is constructed and dwelled in reciprocally.

6.2.1. *A likeness goes on display when a diaphanous overlap unfurls onto a field.*

"It was like...." " Why likeness, again, each time you want to communicate a new experience? "It was like...." " Unfurl an overlap onto a field and at the same time distort that field. "It was like *this*"; "it was like *that*." Bring a pattern into contact with an aggregate that has its own echoes and overlaps. We say a likeness "lights up," and we understand that this depends reciprocally on the current face of the world, on the intersection of multiple clines. Likenesses happen in a where, in a region or area.

6.2.2. *Likenesses go on display in vicinities.*

Some familiar loci are in fact vicinities for likeness displays. A phenotype is a vicinity for display; so is a genotype. What is displayed is not the same, and how it is displayed is not the same, yet phenotype and genotype act as vicinities in which traits can be freed up, reorganized, and brought to sympathetic overlap by abandoning other pretensions. The distribution of matter in the universe is a vicinity for homeoses; memory, subjective or objective, is one, as well. Anticipations, subjective or objective, are vicinities, too — anticipations make the future like, likely project a series. Series are vicinities, as well, and then there is measurement, which has a special relationship to series that can act as an example.

Take measurement[80] — take a measurement, and you participate in an emphatic mode of display. An operation or activity taking place in a vicinity, measurement facilitates one thing to approach another. It is homeotic to a second degree: it compares things within the same domain, and it forms kinships across disparate domains. A ruler is like a physical object to be measured. We say they are both objects. At the same time, a ruler object is like to a standard of measure and the standard of measure, itself already almost an abstraction, functions as a standard because of its proximity to an idea — to two, in fact, space and number. Pragmatically speaking, to measure is to let a likeness emerge in accord with a prototype. The metaphor of "overlap" is vividly on exhibit in measuring with a ruler. The two objects nearly overlap one another in space. Homeotic overlap, however, is when they, together, overlap another, the transcendental standard on top of the empirical. The aim of any measuring procedure is undoubtedly to locate number in the sensible — already a paradoxical task. Yet the first phase of measuring always involves the fusing out of a homeotic pair, say, a ruler and a sheet of paper, in accord with an established practice of seeing likeness among extended things. Comparison of physical bodies must be an archaic gesture. To compare bodies, you first find / make a likeness between a span and a span. First of all, then, two things identified as spans are required, so an overlap. This span is like that span with respect to extension.

Here is a basic philosophical assumption that in fact is embedded in a prephilosophical intuition — the intuition of a continuum. It is assumed that any piece of the physical world is identical with (not similar to) any other piece in respect of extendedness, such that a span is taken naturally, unreflectively, to be interchangeable with any other span, on the assumption that space is a self-identical substrate that can be cut any way and never change in character. Homeotics does not make this assumption. Indeed, a span can be thought of as a phenomenon "in its own right" only after "span" has fused out of an atmosphere of other ways of taking space. Only when there is something like a span can you go out and find spans to compare.

Say there is a prototype of a thing called "span," and you look at a sheet of paper (a span "in the wild") and a ruler (a mimic of a standard span) next to it. With respect to "span," paper and ruler are tantamount to one and the same thing. In the scene of comparison, the overlap is tangible; lay ruler over paper. Physical overlay is but a symbol of the more important nonphysical overlap that governs the physical behavior to begin with. Homeotically, the paper overlaps the ruler in the same gesture when physically the ruler overlays the paper, the former the condition for the latter and both overlapping the standard "foot," wherever it is housed. Still, even in this intimate virtual arrangement, paper and ruler do not completely coincide. You can say either that the spans of ruler and paper are alike because both are like to "span," or you can say that paper reflects the ruler while the ruler refracts a standard. However you express it, the first step toward measuring happens when a wild thing approaches a standardized thing, the mutual approach of objects making a vicinity, so that a like trait fuses out in echo with a prototype.

The next step is more difficult to envision, yet it is crucial to say, in order to describe measurement homeotically, how it happens that we commonly find number in the sensible. Comparing spans is perfectly well a form of measurement on its own, without number — or rather, using only the number one: this paper is one ruler long. And yet lest you mistakenly think number is inherent either to nature or thought, it has to be shown that number, too, when it is part of a measuring activity, results from homeosis. A like span is evidently a precondition for a like length, and still, naively, we commonly think that counting up the length of a span must be an abstract or purely logical operation.

To say that we see number misunderstands the essence of number. We often assume, even when a multiplicity of individuated objects appears to us, that counting is different from perception. The assumption that the domain of perception and the domain of abstract thought are different needs to be revised. Number becomes sensible insofar as, when we denumerate an extent, we are making a likeness beyond the sensible likeness in spans. Numbering, we make a likeness between the sensible and the nonsensible, a nonsensible resemblance.

Say "two" about some entities. The presumption is that saying "two" means saying that those entities are consonant with the number two. Late in *The Foundations of Arithmetic*, Gottlob Frege at one point defines number as "equinumerous," "gleichzahlig," with a concept (§ 68). This word in Frege's vocabulary should raise eyebrows — *gleichzahlig*. In Frege's presentation, it becomes apparent that at a minimum, *Gleichzahligkeit* is a precondition for both the numbering activity and the number field. *Gleichzahligkeit* would have to make number and set alike. His assertion is explained slightly earlier with reference to Hume, where he picks up an argument, fairly common at the time, that even though we have no intuition of numbers, even if numbers are not sensible in themselves either by external (perception) or internal vision (intuition) (§ 62), numbering involves a nonarithmetic operation where one instance can be laid over another instance. This two-one / one-two is the birthplace of number and thus of the second stage in measuring. First, there is an object set to be numbered (such as subdivisions on a ruler); second, there is a subject set to which the object will be put in one-to-one correspondence. Numbering relies on an imagined scene of comparison, not unlike the comparison of a wild extent to a standardized extent. No matter that Frege calls this "identity." Object set and subject set cannot be ontologically or logically identical in the strongest sense unless they form part of a measureless substance, which would make it once again mysterious how they could be measured or numbered. Ruler extent and extent of paper are made like through a pattern of "extensiveness"; a set of subdivisions of the ruler is made like an ideal set that is serial.

Seriality belongs to measuring in several ways. In a simple scene of measuring, a child compares a ruler with a piece of paper and, finding at least one aspect that is alike (extent), ruler and paper become items in a series—ruler, paper, standard. One extent, another extent, another extent, so far without a specified order. Then there are decisive points that ally the internal series of the ruler to the virtual internal series of the paper: endpoint, endpoint; midpoint, midpoint; and so on. Number forms another series, a series within a series, as extents form a series, physical objects form a series, points form a series. Numbers are in the ideal, in the standard, in the object — 1, 1, 1; 2, 2, 2; 3, 3, 3 . . . .

Extent and seriality are two aspects of measurement — size is another. Size is relative, and relativity results from a homeotic procedure that likens one extent to another and then both extents to their internal series, where both the enlikened series, whether it is physically marked on the standard or not, and a single point light up. This is the endpoint. Attribution of size depends on the recognition of endpoints. In measuring length, we serialize like objects with abstract "extents." We serialize extents, and to do this, we locate endpoints that can be made proximal to one another homeotically before we even think about spatial distance. Once we do this, we can present the whole operation in reverse, in the order in which it happens. Measuring the length of something, first the endpoints of the measured thing light up, brought into juxtaposition with the series "endpoints," and then, following this, the extents of the standard light up as "not farther than" these points (wherever they arbitrarily land), while the other points in the extent do not light up. Measuring is not finding the number inherent in a thing or the length inherent in a thing, nor is it superadding number ideally to a natural set of points. And yet, the alternative is also not correct: measurement is not a rational construct that warps the originary temporal experience of the world, as Bergson argued (*Time and Free Will*, p. 107). Measuring is a quintessential homeotic operation that will have fused out over epochs, calling upon select prior associations (endpoint, span, number, series) and eclipsing others, such as a nonhomogenous magnitude, as Bergson describes *durée*. You could think that *durée* is more archaic than measure, but this is not right: both *durée* and measure emerge in homeotic vicinities. Extension, numbering, seriality, point-to-point alignment have been wound out of homeotic strands. Insofar as a physical extent, ideal abstract numbering, and aesthetic pattern emergence (endpoints and midpoints) work together to produce measurement, it is clear how a vicinity can be transregional, a synthesis of several regions, and indeed, the most interesting ones are.

6.2.3. *When an overlap unfurls and a likeness lights up, a synthesis of domains often takes place.*

Measurement is a mode of display. Affinities that have precipitated out of a history (endpoints, span, number) go on exhibit in measurement. The fact that number, span, endpoint belong to different domains of reality (ideal, spatial, aesthetic) only strengthens the exhibition. Display feeds on depraved syntheses of disparate or even apparently contradictory domains. Display loves category errors. To mention this exemplary line once more, Reverdy says an image emerges from "becoming proximal of two realities more or less distant," the "rapprochement de deux réalités plus ou moins éloignées" ("L'image," p. 1). We have not yet fully received the gift of this sentence. "Image" must not be confused with a secondary presentation of visual data. Reverdy holds image far from techniques of knowledge, reproduction, and transmission, be they mimetic processes of mind, chemical processes of photography, or algorithmic processes of facial recognition.

6.3.   *An image is not an image of, from, or for anything; an image happens when distant realities approach one another.*

Reverdy lists two threshold conditions for the approach of distant realities. First, the realities may not imitate one another. Second, the realities may not be opposed to one another. One could also say this the other way around: real approximations are never totally coincident or opposed. This is why in the homeoplex there is no real opposition, which Freud says in a similar way about dream experience and Kant says about the ontosphere. An image is thus a place for the coming about of a series, this and that. In an image, syntax happens. Whoever is convinced that, whatever their overlaps, language and picture at a minimum belong to separate categories, will be surprised to learn that Reverdy's conditions are met just here, where image and language merge in syntax, as the unlike becomes proximal for the purpose of enlikening.

One imagined rapprochement between language and image has been the by now traditional notion of the "sign-picture" in all its varieties. Ideograms, pictograms, and hieroglyphs have all been considered pictures that in some way also say what they depict and depict what they try to say. In modern semiotics, C. S. Peirce offers a well-known description of a sign that is also a picture: the icon. In "Logic as Semiotic: A Theory of Signs," according to his triangular definition of a sign — "A sign, or representamen, is something which stands to somebody for something in some respect or capacity" (p. 99) — the icon, for our purposes the exemplary modern sign-picture, stands to somebody for something in a particular respect, namely, in respect of being like it. There are no restrictions on *what* can be an iconic sign or to whom it may speak — only the how of its respect is restricted. "Anything whatever, be it quality, existent individual, or law, is an Icon of anything, in so far as it is like that thing and used as a sign of it" (p. 102). Thus, the icon operates in the two modes that a picture-sign needs in order to function, being like and being the sign of, or: enlikening and being about, which two fundamental motives I previously presented as at odds with one another. In the icon, aboutness and likeness coexist, albeit uneasily.[81]

There is a logic to their coexistence, however. The sensible world is made up not of things, but of qualities, for Peirce, and for this reason, icons, whose job it is to partake of the world's sensible qualities, exist in the closest proximity of all sign types to the world. Their aboutness consists in likeness, you could say. Thus, icons possess what he calls "firstness," and so in this theory, likeness is *prima semiotica*, the first and most elemental semiotic function and so not fully belonging to semiotics, either, insofar as a likeness is not a stand-in, does not truly exhibit aboutness; it is an ontological twin. A likeness possesses the same qualities as the object, and so in place of aboutness, it exhibits similarity of qualities.[82] Peirce sometimes calls this primal semiotic or truthfully presemiotic function an "idea." Among sign types, likeness betrays its object the least, and it does so because in it the first two moments in signification — sign and signified — are qualitatively proximal. Each possesses the qualities of the other. Peirce's test for this is simple and powerful. If the object disappeared altogether, the sign would still signify to the same degree as the object itself, an intensive criterion that makes it an "idea."

For this to be true, however, the special "power" of icons has to be distinguished from and not dependent on either aboutness or on the power of nature itself to produce qualities. A natural object is its qualities, possesses them as possessions, is nothing without them. So what differentiates an icon, whose likeness is about the object, from the object, whose being is in its qualities?

6.4.   *An object possesses its qualities, an icon exhibits the natural object.*

You could ask, then, what the icon offers over the thing. Iconicity adds exhibition. Without the icon, the thing would not have this critical quality of exhibition, for one simple reason: exhibition makes qualities that otherwise merely reside in an object, as the object, purposive. From purposeless, inactive, unilluminated "being," the qualities, when repeated in an iconic sign, exist "in order to show" something ("Logic as Semiotic," p. 107). Peirce tells us, in this analysis, how Reverdy's "image" operates — when a categorial distance is bridged, when two unlike media come together. Their collision puts a likeness on display. In Peirce's analysis, the distance is internal to the icon and obtains between object and sign, otherwise incompatible categories that here join forces. This can also be put in terms of inertia, yielding. An icon inhibits a thing in some respect by resonating with it and thus inhibits the thing from exhibiting other qualities, at the same time as it inhibits mind from thinking other qualities. Mind thinks what the sign inhibits in the thing, a gesture, some features, or a "like this." To inhibit a thing toward a group of traits is to exhibit those traits.

This thought is so innovative, Peirce can hardly just drop it and move to the other sign types. Instead, he extends the concept of icon into areas we would not otherwise have envisioned.

6.4.1. *Whereas it is evident that an icon pictures a thing, it is also true that a picture is an icon of the thing it pictures.*

This is the case if the picture is used to exhibit qualities, and it always is. A painting of a rabbit such as Dürer's famous *Young Hare* of 1502 is also an iconic sign of a rabbit. It is not that iconic signs make use of the representational powers of painting, but rather that painting depends for its ability to represent on iconicity's exhibiting power. No representations without iconicity — this rule is drawn from Peirce.

Beyond these two iconic modes, iconic sign and picture, there are others, as well. A diagram is an icon of the scene it sketches out to the extent that the relations among the parts of the diagram are similar to the relations among the parts of the scene. What is iconic in diagrams are not the traits of a being, but the relations among parts in a functional whole. At this moment, Peirce is bold and does not shy away from suggesting the existence of nonpictorial icons. For example, a predicate is an icon of a subject, according to Peirce.

6.4.2. *Elements of language iconize other elements of language.*

Following the logic of exhibition, a predicate "exhibits" its subject in a certain way, since an iconic operation is at work within the sentence. "This is that" means "This is like that" or "This unfolds an overlap." Or "Here is a vicinity." An image operation of language stands in here for classic forms of judgment.

There is also, Peirce says, an iconic element in a rule, which can be seen for example in an algebraic formula. A formula with variables is not simply a stand-in for the numerals it represents; it also gives the rule for their combination. More than this, the formula exhibits for the first time the relations among the numbers in the most precise and explicit terms, and it is the presentation of the rule that must apply for the formula to be true.

6.4.3. *Iconicity obtains for objects other than objects of perception, and in some of these modes, it exhibits truth.*

In "Logic as Semiotic," Peirce shows the scope and importance of the iconic relation throughout semiotics, aesthetics, mathematics, and philosophy. Beyond whatever meaning relation might also obtain, a sign can be like an object, a picture is like its subject, a sentence is like a picture, a formula is like a diagram. These are specific iconic operations that take place in specific instances. A subtle, internal, but no less important iconic moment affects all these instances, as well, in their reproducibility, in their applicability to more than a single anomalous case. The formula $a^2 + b^2 = c^2$ speaks about more than one possible equation, since, self-evidently, a set of numbers, even if you were to put them in the very same order, for instance $3^2 + 4^2 = 5^2$, does not express what the formula expresses. Expressed in the formula is also the general and necessary character of the statement, or to put it homeotically, its copyability. Beyond the exhibition of general copyability, by which you can use the formula as a template for other equations, one further general aspect goes on display in any iconic experience. "For a great distinguishing property of the icon is that by the direct observation of it other truths concerning its object can be discovered than those which suffice to determine its construction" (p. 106). The icon exhibits truths not already known and is the only sign type that can do this.

6.4.4. *An icon displays a truth not exhibited in the thing itself.*

Peirce insists on the fact: for a nonobvious truth to appear in a logic of signs (and truth is always nonobvious), only an icon suffices.[83] Truth is equivalent to the exhibition of qualities, where exhibition emphasizes those qualities, illuminates them, positions them as eminent in and because of the iconic relation, without which an object has no truth. More than one likeness does not fundamentally change the truth action of the icon, as for example when "by means of two photographs a map can be drawn, etc." (p. 106).

6.4.5. *A likeness steals a truth from a thing it did not know it had and puts that truth on display.*

Take what Peirce says and reverse it. Two photographs do not so much make a map; a map sees traits in the photographs that the photos qua photos do not see. A map pulls itself together out of its prototypes, the photos — no doubt about this. More importantly, the photographs see themselves as if for the first time in the map. This refractability is already operating in the photographs themselves. Two photographs break the spell of mimesis — one establishes the landscape, the other shows features from a skewed angle, loosening them from geometry and forging the place out of them. A map draws out the likeness among mimetic photographs and the landscape and becomes the icon that displays new truths none of them possesses alone.

Do not immediately discount the obvious, for this is where the icon is at home. Index and symbol, the other sign types analyzed in Pierce's article, work differently, and yet in important respects, they, too, are iconic. It is obvious, and yet the truth of this fact has not yet been sufficiently examined. I mean the iconicity between one symbol and another symbol and between one index and another index. Any time a sign repeats, this effect operates. A second symbol or index exhibits a first symbol or index, as when I use the word "smoke" and then mention that I have used the word "smoke." The difference between use and mention is display. Anything may become an icon. Why would this not include a symbol as an icon of — a symbol? An index can be an icon of another index, but for some reason, this effect, close as it is to the origins of language, Peirce calls trivial for the science of signs. He does not want to dwell on the fact that letters and words, which are indexical, form up into clines and derive their significative powers from the iconicity of their twinning inner communications and the seriality of their happening. He sidesteps the historicity of speech. A spoken word has to be like another spoken word, so that you may know you are speaking, so that you may be speaking. Discussing the index, Peirce recognizes the inner iconicity of index to index, but subordinates it absolutely to the relation of "standing for": "It is not merely that one occurrence of an A is like a previous occurrence that is the important circumstance, but that there is an understanding that like letters shall stand for the same thing, and this acts as a force carrying the attention from one occurrence of A to the previous one" (p. 110). "Carrying the attention" from one letter to another of the same kind, he insists, is not essentially a homeotic happening, but essentially a semiotic one.

Likeness among letters — the cline of scriptural experience, A then A then A — today's A shining through yesterday's and tomorrow's — Peirce puts aside this primal experience of speech. The series of letters, words, or utterances is, rather, held in a unity by the understanding, which is described as a force that, although it appears quite mysterious, unifies the stream of language. The force of understanding directs attention to the transcendental "sign" in which all instances of "A" are supposed to have a share. Peirce contradicts his own insight here. As he himself would say, firstness precedes secondness. He can claim a "same" sign underlying all copies of that sign and a force that directs the attention to unify all the copies, only after the firstness of iconicity has already done its work.[84]

6.5.   *Signs fuse out of a process of making similar.*

Each sign type has this crucial iconic moment. When you attend to this, you recognize that no sign, no use of a sign, is ever single. Both a single sign and a single manner of use are for multiple uses in multiple situations by multiple users, and the clinic multiplicity is the precondition for any single use. Further, beyond the ontological status of the sign, signs in use by a group follow habits of use, and those habits have to be kept up by the group. Daily, hourly, minute by minute, the group makes itself like what it was, enlikens itself—avoids departing from itself too radically, a conservative tendency that seems to mark all human groups and perhaps anything we call a group.

Where an icon enlikens an object, a sign enlikens another instance of the sign and at the same time mimics the habit of signification, again exhibiting semiosis forward and backward. Peirce wants to include iconicity in semiotics, but he does not want to admit that iconicity burns its way through all of semiotics. Throughout "Logic as Semiotic," Peirce returns to iconicity as a touchstone and defends semiotics from iconicity, often by admitting its existence in order to restrict its scope.[85] Were it given a general scope, logic, even language itself, would not be fundamentally semiotic, but homeotic. In human signifying practices, iconicity intervenes between subjects and predicates, things and qualities, icons and things, and signs and signs. The ubiquitous icon has a foothold in Peirce's phenomenology, as well. A thing, he says, is its qualities (p. 104), and thus in this regard, a thing is already an icon of its qualities, broken in two and refracting.

6.5.1. *Pictures and language exhibit realities refractingly.*

This is not to say that language is picture language and pictures are language pictures. In order for the likeness among language and image to light up, they cannot be collapsed into one another; they cannot even be brought too near. I can suggest a general parameter here for our logic, to be tested further. A likeness has to cross at a minimum the linguistic and the pictorial. Thus, signs are icons of things and icons of themselves; logic, as semiotic, is iconic. Moreover, semio-iconic logic extends right into the sentence.

6.5.2. *To state something is to put a likeness on display.*

Stating gets its power from homeosis — the likeness of a predicate to a subject can be thought of as prior to a logical relation. When it is thought of in this way, a predicate takes a photograph of its subject and lets a few traits shine through. The interpretation of a statement is then a further image, a caricature of the predicate photograph, magnifying some traits, reshuffling, reselecting, reprinting others, and making them available for future iconic processes. There may be no simpler and more encompassing theory of writing than this, a continual refraction and possibility of further refraction. Logic, in this regard, is a mode of display in which the relations of elements in a subject, as Peirce says, can be received as what they are not in the subject itself.

6.5.3. *Truth emerges in transit between a subject and its likenesses.*

When an index or symbol has been substituted for a thing, no further truth about the being can be found or made, unless, that is, you convert the sign into an icon (p. 106). Already revealed objects, long-fixed relations, and inherited truths can be accessed through indices and symbols, which are instruments for their manipulation and communication of knowledge. Display, in the sense Peirce gives to exhibition, takes a step back from settled knowledge in a revelatory activity of the icon that does not operate by substitution, no longer blocks out the "first," returns to the thing itself, returns to the thing as yet unknown, and orients itself solely by echo, selectively illuminating today's dullness with yesterday's borrowed light.

To say that language is historically the preeminent mode of homeotic display, other aspects of language should be taken into account, as well. Although the icon catches hold of and spreads out across Peirce's entire semiotic program, the effect is still confined to those parts of language covered in Peirce's semiotic program. Left out altogether are the history of language and its transit through actually existing events, linguistic and otherwise, not to mention the sensual existence of language itself, that is, its nonsignificative aspects, of which there are many. When Walter Benjamin attempts to think out a homeotic theory of language in 1933, he is not concerned with explaining semiotic aspects in homeotic terms, although a revision of semiotics may be an important aftereffect of his theory. Rather, when you take language as a historical accumulation of events, rather than as a system or as a paradigm for human meaning, as Peirce does, homeosis occupies a very different place.

Part of the time, Benjamin's procedure takes the form of a joke, a joke on the theory of evolution. When it claims to have eradicated archaisms in its method, evolution theory nonetheless retains one in the maxim ontogeny recapitulates phylogeny. Throughout the short sketch or protocol "Lehre vom Ähnlichen," "Doctrine of the Like" (usually translated as "Doctrine of the Similar"),[86] Benjamin alludes obliquely to Ernst Haeckel's infamous conclusion, in Haeckel's own words: "Ontogeny is no more than a brief recapitulation of phylogeny" (*Generelle Morphologie der Organismen*, vol. 2, p. 7).[87] Recapitulation is a form of homeotic display. With this proposal, Haeckel was rescripting an older, eighteenth-century observation in the evolutionary terms of the nineteenth century and at the same time rescripting Darwinism according to a yet later impulse, the attempt to preserve the hierarchy of animals with humans on the

top through a theory of development against the leveling tendencies of Darwinian evolution. Be that as it may, Benjamin alludes to
Haeckel's principle neither to support nor to refute it, neither to
preserve nor to topple human beings from the throne, but instead to
bring to mind the way in which more than rescripting an older truth,
a truly archaic remnant survives in the most advanced evolutionary
method. Biology imagines that incommensurate realms of existence
can resemble one another, although there is no causal link, or no
direct one. Development of a being resembles development of a species and, more vaguely perhaps, but nonetheless just as significantly,
embryonic development resembles the development of all species.
Zoogeny shines through phylogeny, phylogeny shines through ontogeny, the various developmental levels are folded over one another.
When Benjamin argues that the ability to find resemblances between
the macrocosm and the microcosm has largely disappeared, it is a
comedy, perhaps a comedy of errors, since the archaic habit remains
in the most modern theory of evolution, largely unmodified. The
most modern theory is also a theory of the persistence of the archaic,
in its content and also in its method.

The joke is on biology, and on us — evolution science has not
evolved much — and yet the analogy between the most modern and
the prehistorical is a serious premise for a theory that wants to discover where likeness went and how it disappeared from view. A new
theory of human being based in a mimetic force or faculty can be
thought on analogy with evolution, if the archaisms of the method
can be brought out. The archaic never left; it changed locales, moved
methods. We no longer see the cosmos in our palms; we see a lizard
in a human embryo. The embryo arrests history, repeating its arrest
in each pregnancy, in the vacation from development repeated in
each teleology, each an echo of the primal chaos, the primal soup of
nondevelopmental resemblances.

And just as the phylogenetic came to refract through the ontogenetic, in Benjamin's own moment, the cultural was refracting
through the psychological. More than Darwin or Haeckel, although

he is thinking of them in passing, Benjamin may in fact be thinking of Freud, who already in *The Interpretation of Dreams* puts the sensual experience so intense in childhood in the driver seat of the adult psyche. In the adulthood of individuals and of history, what Benjamin called "the mimetic power," "die mimetische Kraft," which later became a "power of comprehension," "die Auffassungsgabe," moves to a different domain and shifts to the background ("Lehre von Ähnlichen," *Gesammelte Schriften*, vol. 2, part 1, p. 205).

6.6. *Language is the adulthood of likeness.*

This is the simple proposition that Benjamin weighs here. Being an adult means that the intense, primal experience of likenesses essential to ontogenetic and phylogenetic childhood are now incorporated into adulthood and late history as what they are not, according to the law of the archaic, which says it may never develop and never go away, though it can enter into the most various relations. As he does elsewhere, Benjamin explores a Kantian vocabulary in the *Ähnlichkeit* experiments. A *Vermögen* — faculty, capacity, reserve, store of riches — is the place for mimesis in the latest stage.

A note on the term "mimesis" as Benjamin uses it: he makes a leap out of Aristotle's idea, where mimesis appears as a threat to reality and as a portal to reality. Benjamin lands on a generalized likeness that can obtain even among things not correlated in reality, not adequated to one another, not used as portals or referred to as beings. Why, then, does Benjamin insist on that humanist picture for the place of mimesis in the latest stage — a being with a soul that is a collective of faculties, *Vermögen*?

Benjamin is thinking of "faculty" in a peculiar sense. Of facultative souls, he admits: "Indeed, there may be no single one of their higher functions that is not codetermined by the mimetic faculty," "Ja, vielleicht gibt es keine seiner höheren Funktionen, die nicht entscheidend durch mimetisches Vermögen mitbestimmt ist" (*Gesammelte Schriften*, vol. 2, part 1, p. 204). In this way, mimesis, which is but a formalized process of finding / making *Ähnlichkeiten*, is something like a faculty of faculties, the mysterious mode or power that determines the soul "in its higher functions" — or rather codetermines it. The codicil to the text points out that "becoming like" is the landmark trait of *homo homeos*, a reversion to an archaic humanism based in behavior and imagination. In essence, then, the facultative mind as it is construed since Kant, or even since Descartes, appears, when you ask the question of the conditions for it, as a remnant of social activities of mimicry and becoming like. Enlikening, however, is not a capacity. It does not bring a stored-up resource to bear on a situation; it does not actualize a potential; it does not condition an outcome. Likeness is strictly speaking impotent. The mimetic faculty is not a faculty — to call it that is part of Benjamin's joke, which now extends from evolution theory to faculty psychology. Likeness in the human soul is a remnant of archaic practices that were protosocial and prepsychological.

"It is no great error," Benjamin writes in a note shortly before he began drafting the *Ähnlichkeit* texts, "to want to construct experience in the sense of life experience according to the schema of that experience at the foundation of the natural sciences. Not the causal nexes discovered over the course of time; rather the likenesses that are lived are decisive here." The experience at the basis of natural science is lived likenesses. Undoubtedly, such an experience can be found at key moments in the practice of any science, in the laboratory and at the accelerator, in the observatory and the underbrush. Benjamin extrapolates from this commonality among the sciences a more general principle, "experience is lived likenesses" ("Zur Erfahrung," *Gesammelte Schriften*, vol. 6, pp. 88–89). The basic act of natural science — observation ("Beobachtung," p. 89) — looks very much like the basic act of nonscientific experience: living likenesses. First, before anything is perceived or apperceived, observation transits the homeotic field. In ignoring nonscientific experience completely, it seems, natural science has preserved the most nonscientific as its core — not that scientific experiment is the basis of all experience,

but rather that experiment relies on the constant return of an irre-
ducibly archaic mode. Where you least suspect it, where it is most
covered over by the veils of observation, enumeration, comparison,
measure, and prediction, perhaps also because the belief in calcula-
tion, measurement, prediction, and the regularity of natural laws and
processes is so widely accepted, indeed, because it is not questioned,
there where natural science is fully convinced of itself, just there,
the homeotic exhibits its primacy without shame right in the open.
Where homeosis is obviously secondary, in natural science practice,
it is most at home and clearly primary.

In social relations, in culture, in capitalist behaviors — in short,
where objects are for use and exchange — homeotic relations bur-
row deeper and are harder to recognize. Observation, *Beobachtung*,
for Benjamin has to mean what it meant in his dissertation on German Romantic art critique, namely, *Versenken*, which it is good to
translate as "immersion" (*Gesammelte Schriften*, vol. 1, part 1, p. 69).
Immersive observation is the mode Benjamin proposes we take up
in order to return early twentieth-century experience to its birthplace. "Immersion" implies a lack of distance between the observer
and the observed, a state described in another text being written
in the 1930s, "Berliner Kindheit um 1900." "Die Farben, die ich dann
mischte, färbten mich," "The colors I mixed then would color me."
(*Gesammelte Schriften*, vol. 4, p. 262, p. 392). Experience is a cardinal
vicinity for the display of likenesses insofar as one cannot remain
aloof from it; one must be immersed in it to "have" experience, making experience more like being stained, like a child with tempera
paints on hands and clothes and face. Where observation is immersive, one becomes like.

Language is not the scientist, but the underbrush and the birds.
Benjamin wagers a hypothesis that the "mimetic endowment [here
he uses a subtly different term than *Vermögen*, this is *Begabung*, which
is less an ability than a gift or a talent for a particular behavior] that
earlier was the foundation of clear-sightedness, has over the course
of thousands of years of development gradually wandered into speech

and writing and has made the most complete archive of nonsensible likeness [*unsinnlicher Ähnlichkeit*] in them" ("Lehre vom Ähnlichen," *Gesammelte Schriften*, vol. 2, part 1, p. 209).[88] Benjamin is not interested in the semiotic aspect of language, as Peirce was, even if Peirce took semiosis far from its medieval roots and found in the icon an overlap with natural qualities, that is, in a sensibilist version of being. Benjamin is interested in three historically irreconcilable domains that together — homeotically, he will argue — produce what we call "language." Those domains are speaking, writing, and meaning.[89]

For those wondering how spoken speech, meant meaning and written writing come together as language, how they function as a single phenomenon, for communication or for information storage, for storytelling or for lamenting or complaining, for critique or speculation, it is not, as semiotics maintains, due to conventional substitutions — sign for thing, inscription for vocalization, sensible presentation for supersensible meaning. Recall the Hebrew letter *beth* — a glyph depicting a house, later a logogram of the word "house," and after that a phonogram for the sounds b/v. Active, though concealed, the archaic house dwells in the alphabet. This is one way speech and writing constitute archaic funds. Although history may have vacated the sensual component of likenesses, the place for sensual likenesses has been kept by language, bones without flesh, branches without leaves. Language, according to Benjamin's "second" theory of language, is not a differential system, as semiotic systems are; it will also no longer be, as he proposed in his "first" theory of language, a continuum of translation among languages leading to god's language.

6.6.1. *Language looks like a differential system, a semiotic system, because the homeotic affinities among its parts have been carved away by history.*

On its cutting edge, language still operates by resemblance, by onomatopoeia, mimicry, through approximations of structural, functional, imagistic, sonic, multisensory and nonsensory *Ähnlichkeiten*, which, as they settle, lose their homeotic character. In order to hear the mimetic character of language in formation, you could, as Rudolf Leonhard, a now little-known poet, novelist, and lawyer whom Benjamin exalts in "Lehre vom Ähnlichen," advises, act as though the history of your language didn't exist (*Das Wort*, p. 4). Of his method, Leonhard says: "Sie ist ganz bewußt unhistorisch," "It is quite consciously unhistorical" (p. 4). Leonhard becomes Benjamin's prime example of a method for reviving likeness practices out of the archive of language. "Quite consciously unhistorical," Leonhard's method retards developments such as semiosis and brings progress in the study of language to a halt. Benjamin quotes only one line from Leonhard's treatise cum lexicon, *Das Wort*, "Jedes Wort ist — und die ganze Sprache ist — onomatopoetisch," "Each word — and all of language — is onomatopoetic" ("Lehre vom Ähnlichen," p. 207; *Das Wort*, p. 6), a statement that is grossly untrue until you catch the sound, as Benjamin apparently did, of the revisions to the idea of language that are underway in Leonhard's text.

Onomatopoetic speech doesn't operate the way we were taught it does: a word phonetically reproducing a nonlinguistic sound (instead of mimetizing a thing), a sonomimesis of a nonhuman voice — cock-a-doodle-do, chicken; buzz, bee. And it does not carry out a linguistic mimicry of a nonlinguistic noise — sizzle, splash. Leonhard's book develops a generalized onomatopoeia, which, because it claims that onomatopoeia is characteristic of all language, reveals "the eternal secret that a series of sounds [*Lautfolge*] are assigned to a determinate mental representation [*Vorstellung*] and with this to a determinate reality [*Realität*], that the sound series produces this mental representation with the force of compulsion of a higher reality" (*Das Wort*, p. 3).

In short, Leonhard's onomatopoeia tells how sound, sense, and reference are integrated. They integrate with the force of a higher reality without any higher reality. Remaining from a higher reality is its just force, that force whose motive brings together a series of sounds, a mental presence, and a reality in likeness of one another. The main axis of spoken speech is a threefold unity — *Lautfolge*,

Vorstellung, Realität — Sound series, image, reality — that comes together without coming into contact with anything higher and yet has the same intensity of force as though it had. Sound series, idea, and reality overlap in what Leonhard calls "die 'Eignung' des Wortes," "the becoming fitting of the word" (p. 5). A word *eignet sich*, becomes onomatopoetically proper, adapted, through its sound, to a sense and a reference, according to two canons, the canon of "Sinn" and the canon of "Bedeutung," terms Leonhard fits out with new senses. Both *Sinn*, or sense, and *Bedeutung*, or signification, function according to a "Klanglogik," a sound logic, that begins from a single principle. Sound, image, and meaning always form an absolute unity (p. 9). They are in fact so little separable that not only is there nothing that can explain their interrelation, but each and every linguistic phenomenon always has to be explained in terms of all three. Language supports the coming together of the world. Leonhard's arguments are not systematic, but his evidences are intriguing. Why, for example, have "all civilized and rich enough languages" equally divided their vowels among the main color words? White, black, red, green, blue, yellow, orange, purple. The distribution of the limited number of vowels equally among color terms suggests that vowels have become sound images of colors, and vice versa. Once you admit this, colors start to bleed through words, and you hear "orange" easily on encountering the fruit or see the typed word "yellow" yellowly. A dabbler and eccentric, not to mention dyed-in-the-wool socialist, Leonhard imagined a sociality of the sensible and the spiritual side of language coming together in a "Wortbild," since language is "a phenomenon of sense [*ein sinnliches Phänomen*] that is spiritual [*geistig*] to the extent that the senses have spirit [*Geist*]" (*Das* Wort, p. 5).

6.6.2. *Likeness is the* Geist *of the senses, and language is the productive imagination of likenesses.*

Once Leonhard divides language into *Sinn* (*Wortbild*) and *Bedeutung*, the primary locale for the display of transregional mimeses (in

Benjamin's sense of the word) becomes sound. Something less than metaphysical, but more than material, and not at all semiotic, sound echoes in the mental field, drawing the mental and the physical into a vicinity. Upon seeing an orange, before we are blessed with a representation of orange, we are blessed with an echo of the word, the *Wortbild*, as if spoken once again, "orange." The word image resounds immediately for the hearer, homologue of the spoken word, already with elements of sense vibrating within it. The sense is within the sound, as the word metes out its phonemes — oh-ran-juh. The speaker does not make the gesture toward sense — the word does (p. 9). An experimental lexicon that attempts to make the unconscious connection between sensuousness and sense within words perceptible, *Das Wort* has you hear-read-see, for instance, the German word *beweglich* (pp. 15–16). When the consonant "g" gets in the "way" (*Weg*) of the vowel "eh," so that tongue and mouth need to move more vigorously to overcome the obstacle, this organic configuration symbolizes the meaning, *beweglich*, "motile." The relative retarding of the first syllable and the consonant that follows, "be-wuh," mimics a small movement — *beweglich* — giving way suddenly to a big movement. One must be agile, *beweglich*, to say this word; the word sounds *beweglich*, and this is an example of the way a *Wortbild* mimics the ideal reference (*Bedeutung*) over the course of speaking and hearing and seeing and moving body parts.

Or take another example: *Hülle* (pp. 28–29) expresses an encompassing act, an embracing enclosure, and the word in both written and spoken modes, in marks and in sounds, refracts this sense (*Sinn*). Although by all means the "H" is loose and the "-ülle" echoes *Wolle* (wool), evoking a soft, fuzzy containment, another word, *Fülle* (full), comes right up near to it and indicates that although not hard and closed like *geschlossen*, nevertheless, *Hülle* — "casing," "shell," or "husk" — implies that (enlikens) under its looseness, within its warm embrace, nestles something full to the top with contents. *Sinn* enlikens to *Sinnlichkeit*, sense is contained in sensuousness.

Leonhard cautions not to take signification (sense and reference) as the primary gift of speech. Evidence for this comes in an apparent pleonasm, where the signification does not reside in the words qua signs or the syntagm as a semantic unit. "Whoever says 'Hülle und Fülle' does not state a tautology, but rather reaches an extraordinary richness of expression and its totality through the addition of two complements. The expression adds not mathematically, but organically; and it is certainly also no accident that the two words rhyme" (pp. 28–29).

Leonhard proposes, in place of syntax and semantics, a sensual reinforcement, when words are put together, that makes each more than its individual *Wortsinn*, word meaning, engendering a new complex, a totality complete in itself and other than the sum of its parts. These words refer to one another, if reference means refraction. Conventionally, we imagine the spectrum of language running from nonsense to meaningful speech, from foreign to domestic sounds, from idiolect to standard dialect, from falsity to truth. These are criteria, internal to language, for judgment on good or bad speech, useful or useless communications, intelligible or unintelligible messages, and so on. But what happens if we drop these conventions and see language instead as a field for the imbrications of sound, image, and meaning?

6.6.3. *Language enlikens, in visible marks no less than audible sounds — an extending tonal poem — as alive to homeoses as the variable techniques of evolution are.*

Feathery imbrications, cumbrous overlaps, clots or bulges in the cosmos go on display in and as language, which analysis misconstrues as structures or beings or regions of being, these linguistic bizarre-privileged items in the universe need to be cataloged and studied. They hold the patterns of likeness routines past and currently running.

This brings up an urgent question. What does it mean to make these peculiar nonobjects, overlaps, dense spots, bulges, BPIU, into subjects for investigation? In other words, is a science of likeness possible? Roger Caillois spent his working life living this question and answered it several times "yes," though his yeses were also deeply qualified.[90] His formulations are all tentative and span forty years of writing around the early cofounding of the Collège de Sociologie and around the lifelong collecting of stones whose patterns mimic culture and nature, a collection that landed at the Muséum nationale d'Histoire naturelle after his death. These are the limit lines of his lifework — stones and the social, and also butterflies and ancient myth, plants and religious rituals, psychoanalysis and zoology, and always language, since, as much as he took leave of surrealism, Caillois continuously rehearsed the art of juxtaposition and in doing so offered the richest lexicon for homeotic knowledge, which could be called, in his words, the "natural fantastic," an obvious translation of "surreal" out of the idioms of psyche and art and into the wildest zones.

Caillois separates this science from all other sciences, even though homeotics remains — how shall I say it? — primordial in those sciences. Natural sciences need homeotics, yet its purpose is never to aid natural science. In its idea, natural science is for making distinctions, not for celebrating confusions. Entity from entity, trait from trait, behavior from behavior, geography, history, structure, function, mass, charge, spin, and so on, modern secular natural sciences echo Aristotle's dream to distinguish each and every thing in the cosmos by genus. Especially important in ontological sciences is the separation between an object and its surroundings, and the complement to this, the delicate separation of an object from its parts, whether we talk about an organism and its organs or a particle and its subparticles. Caillois discovers or invents a disturbance in the distinguishing faculty, a malaise of the mind that lets parts flow together and objects merge with their environments. He calls this facultative decline or failure, in an eponymous text from 1935, "legendary psychasthenia," a malaise in which the capacity to make distinctions weakens.

6.7. *Homeotics is the science of the "step backward" that life takes when it assimilates to its surroundings or melts together with another being.*

Stepping back ("Mimicry and Legendary Psychasthenia," p. 30) into confusion will be the chief purpose of this parascience, if it ever gets founded, championing again and again retarding processes, slowdowns, remaining and tracing out again what remains so as to encourage it to remain, acting in the mode of an aid to nature, an artificial inertia superadded to natural physics, turning processes into sentences, catching movement and fusing out details that in turn freeze their objects in a moment of drift.

If you can find them, homeoticians will be those connecting facts from distinct realms, burying old enmities, and with the same stroke letting overharvested fields go to seed. This is not peculiar to homeotics, or it is, but it affects other sciences, as well, at moments of incipience and decay. Caillois points out that Newton made the wild connection between an apple falling to the ground and planets hesitating to fly away in all directions ("A New Plea for Diagonal Science," in *The Edge of Surrealism*, p. 346). Homeotics is the science of the instauration of new sciences. Freud connected adult dreams with infantile desires. Plato connected sensible appearances here with insensible patterns there. Mendel connected genotype and phenotype (though he didn't name them that). One task of a trans-science like this is to catalog scientific births, sonogram the embryos of emerging branches of study. A transscience maps the overlaps and names the prototypes of overlaps among the systems of nature and culture, as Caillois himself began to do, as evolutionary theory sometimes does. The difference between surrealism and evolutionary theory is small, but significant. One makes overlaps and invents categories for them; the other observes overlaps and fits them to metaphysical categories that have not been fully subjected to homeotic synthesis. A perpetual challenge to this science and to this bizarre kind of science is to distinguish it from art making — but this is to want to separate what can never be fully separated. Where art and science overlap . . . .

6.7.1. *Homeotics registers transregional growth.*

A seed grows through the plant's leaves and through the butterfly whose wings when closed are like a leaf and through the bird that doesn't eat the butterfly and through the natural historian's illustration of butterfly on plant and through the taxonomist's classes and the geneticist's sequences. There is no limit to homeotic growth if you conceive of the butterfly as a leaf of the same plant and the same plant as a wing of the same butterfly and science not as stem or root but as itself a wing or leaf of the bizarre growth chain. Objects with wings and leaves outstretched into multiple regions that by old lights would be considered distinct — a general theory of their collaboration and covariance has remained elusive.

Caution: this is not a theory of natural mimicry. Throughout the early essay "Mimicry and Legendary Psychasthenia," Caillois argues every way he can against the causal logic underlying evolutionary theories of mimicry among animals and plants. To his antieconomic ear, nature's reasoning has to be luxurious, excessive, decorative, and desiring; the reason of nature is not only or not even primarily about defense, efficiency, and fitness; it is not, in other words, a parsimonious logic, not an economy, but an ecology. He calls the correct principle "dangerous luxury" and through this juxtaposition of remote words postulates another mode, a becoming like for its own sake, or better, becoming like for the sake of nothing other than generosity among the furthest outposts of being.

Why opt for a principle of parsimony in the first place? What is a cause, after all, but an excuse for a further effect? Parsimonious science that reduces effects to causes betrays the nature of cause, which is to be lavish and not to hold back. As it is, natural and social sciences, each according to its particular rules, both take a snapshot of an organism or a phenomenon in its least productive phase, where it is akin to itself. They take another snapshot of the mechanism or the structure on which it supposedly depends, though it may be hidden behind or within the apparent phenomenon. The task of a science is always to justify the bringing together of two unlike snapshots. Set this table beside the atoms that make it up. Set an atom beside the forces that make it up. Under what warrant do you assert that they belong together? You allow their similarity to shine through your account of them. That the diagonal science of the natural fantastic would do just what its objects already do — bring images together, allow overlap — gives it the sheen of consistency. Caillois calls the universal possibility of overlap among images the "teleplasty" of everything, and he calls the overlaps, when they happen or are brought to happening, "actual photography" ("Mimicry and Legendary Psychasthenia," p. 23). A Cailloisan cosmos takes snapshots of itself from all angles at all times and precesses this way, teleplastically expanding and shifting its contents without formal continuity. This is "a photography on the level of the object" (p. 23) or a generalized enlikening.

6.7.2. *The one who experiences the cosmos in this way, the homeotician, is a rational schizophrenic.*

The homeotician's aim is to lessen distinctions and allow the surroundings to bleed into them. The darkness of the occult is an emblem for the strategic loss of distinction. It is fair and right to call this an "occulting" science, heading for the end of vision as distinction making. And yet, you can still see in the dark. You see homeotically.

One page in Caillois's famous essay is a phenomenology of the homeotician's overcast experience. I quote it in full below. The Cimmerian homeotic experience of this scientist is akin to "the invariable response of schizophrenics to the question: where are you?"

> I know where I am, but I do not feel as though I'm at the spot where I find myself. To these dispossessed souls, space seems to be a devouring force. Space pursues them, encircles them, digests them in a gigantic phagocytosis.

It ends by replacing them. Then the body separates itself from thought, the individual breaks the boundary of his skin and occupies the other side of his senses. He tries to look at himself from any point whatever in space. He feels himself becoming space, dark space where things cannot be put. He is similar, not similar to something, but just similar. And he invents spaces of which he is "the convulsive possession."

To possess homeotic truth is to possess it convulsively, such that the impulse to occupy the space of truth drives scientists to turn themselves inside out.

> All these expressions shed light on a single process: depersonalization by assimilation to space, i.e., what mimicry achieves morphologically in certain animal species [what I have been calling "overlap" — P.N.]. The magical hold (one can truly call it so without doing violence to the language) of night and obscurity, the fear of the dark, probably also has its roots in the peril in which it puts the opposition between the organism and the milieu. Minkowski's analyses are invaluable here: darkness is not the mere absence of light; there is something positive about it. While light space is eliminated by the materiality of objects, darkness is "filled," it touches the individual directly, envelops him, penetrates him, and even passes through him: hence "the ego is permeable for darkness while it is not so for light"; the feeling of mystery that one experiences at night would not come from anything else. ("Mimicry and Legendary Psychasthenia," p. 30)

A homeotician is objective only in the dark, where, as for Baudelaire's hashish smoker, objects cross over into the observer and push out consciousness.

6.7.3.   *At the bitter end of their struggle to possess their objects completely, scientists are possessed by them and driven out into their milieu.*

Caillois's statement "The mantidae were probably the first insects on earth" ("The Praying Mantis," in *The Edge of Surrealism*, p. 70) is hyperbole, but as such, it points toward a danger of homeotic procedure. Do not confuse this with a genesis story or even a genealogy, a trap Caillois sometimes falls into. (See the mythography he gathers for the "empusa," the technical name for the mantis.) Even Caillois, primitive architect of homeotics, tries to winnow out the essential connections from the loose or analogical ones. A homeotician refuses to do this, staying with Caillois's schizophrenic intuition even where their own faculties are put at risk or dissolved. Caillois sometimes uses resemblance to indicate something deeper, which he calls a "mystery." The homeotician ought to refuse mysteries. "The mantidae were probably the first insects on earth" serves to say not that they are first in time or that they are the origin of a species, but that they have remained in a swamplike stupor of unchange and carry its ambiguity to us.

6.7.4. *Archaic items such as the mantis are continuously available to receive and hold, store up and express, disseminate and evoke resemblances.*

Survivors — not unscathed, but remaining because almost fully antiprogressive — of countless atmospheres, Mantidae are the most opaque parts of overlaps, among the densest points in the world.

Caillois calls these items "bizarre-privileged," as I have noted, in a footnote to a late essay "The Natural Fantastic." Other names exist for them, as well. Peirce called them revealers of "new truths," Bergson called them "shining points" in memory, you can call them "astral owl eyes," which allow others to borrow their light. Caillois sometimes uses more conceptual terms, such as "imaginative syntheses" ("The Praying Mantis,", p. 69). Across his lifework a chain of near synonyms links up — "lyrical objectivities" (p. 80), "objective ideograms" (p. 80), "anticipatory replications" ("The Natural Fantastic," p. 353), "mysterious relays" (p. 355).

In a strong sense, these terms must needs remain provisional, since no one, not Peirce, Benjamin, Caillois — not even Plotinus — claims that homeosis is the only constituting or synthesizing process in operation, and yet, even when other principles such as causality are admitted, Caillois's point on this matter is important to keep in mind: "it is utterly unthinkable that causal series could be totally distinct. This also contradicts experience, which constantly demonstrates their numerous intersections and sometimes supplies overwhelming, crushing expressions of their unfathomable solidarity" ("The Praying Mantis," p. 80). The mantis is among the most bizarre and most privileged items. Unfathomable solidarity among elements of causal series is especially luminous in the mantis, in whom the name ("mantis," "empusa"), the bug's sloth, the flower some species look like, the homanthropy of face and body, the religious attitude, the bug's enactment of unfettered human desire — desire for copulation, for decapitating, for killing and devouring — all this makes up an intensive eye of the universe, all these eyes within an eye, a potato's eye, a tiger's eye stone, the eye of god, yours, mine, through which human practice, fears and the recognition of fears, a plant's plaintive desire, a bug's violent theater, and god's creation and disappearance are displayed.

6.7.5. *The purpose of a homeotic science could not be to winnow out what is "merely like" from what is "really and truly like"; it finds / makes items that collect and refract likenesses in particularly intensive ways.*

"Convergence" is a term Caillois prefers. Although he postulates that the world is a unity ("The Natural Fantastic," p. 356), he does not mean that it is uniform; he means that sets of overlaps and echoes extend and can be extended across human practices, such as writing, diagramming, photography, memory, dreams that themselves have analogs in natural history, and so forth. "In a finite, teeming world, things are repeated and respond to each other. There are discernible cycles and symmetries, homologies and recurrences. Everything fits into one or several series" (p. 356). World is an assembly of teeming items, among which some moments photograph others, and scientists can participate in and allow a portfolio to gather up, a series to come to a temporary stop through techniques of yielding they develop, and as they stop the images, they in turn are:

> stopped by an image that disturbs [them], an image reminding [them] of another or else holding out the promise of different ones. The return of the simulacrum lets [them] glimpse the tattered shreds of a concealed order [they] can barely reach, and never with certainty. Dazzled or enlightened, [they try] to understand and, at times, to expand the rules of a game [they] never asked to take part in, and that [they are] not allowed to renounce. (p. 357)

No words ring truer for a homeotic science than these, which I have quoted here while adding a light shift in emphasis in order to allow one feature of Caillois's nontragic view of human intelligence to carry over into other patterns. The feature is "expansion." Neither Occam's razor nor any other act of reduction (skeptical, phenomenological, mathematical) can apply here; expansion, carrying over, preparing for another echo in a different clime — all are anticipated and welcomed. All reductions expand the homeoverse by exactly that much.

6.8. *Likenesses tend to multiply.*

For example, one series that Caillois describes contains so many perspectives, is so dense with conduits to incompatible regions, that you can take hold of a whole vicinity by means of it. The eyes on the wings of a particular moth are not the most efficient way for it to escape being eaten by birds ("Mimicry and Legendary Psychasthenia," pp. 23–24). The eye spots produce a direct confrontation with the predator's sense apparatus, when physical evasion of the predator would be much simpler and better secure the moth's escape. The eye spots exist within a different logic. The *Caligo* moth's wing eyes imitate owl eyes, and, Caillois reports, the moth-wing eyes are what in fact get painted on the sides of barns in Brazil (p. 19), not the eyes of the owl itself, to invoke the evil eye of legend that at the same time protects the bearer and infects the spectator. The mimic is the magic. The implication is that the power to ward off invaders is higher in the mimic than in the original. A great part of the power comes from the mimicry itself, not from the reality behind it. An owl's eyes have the power to hunt down, the moth-eye likeness has the power to display and transplant this power as a symbol.

6.8.1. *Bizarre-privileged items in the universe can also be called "eyes." Along their corrugations radiates a protective and infectious power.*

Watching over the transregion, eyes of the universe ward off motion and change and infect the precincts under their watch with rays of prototypical likenesses drawn out of their folds. No one discipline alone, at least in the way the current diaspora of disciplines has accumulated, can handle or even see all the layers.

6.9. *The world builds up.*

Any science, and this includes literary criticism, philosophy — any knowledge production with a claim to capture the whole from a perspective — each projects a future total science that encompasses the whole toward which it is progressing. Here Caillois's special genius manifests itself. Homeotic science is not the total science of a specific region, and it is neither the general science of all regions (a grand unified science) nor a science of sciences (philosophy). You do not need a "general physiognomy" of the world in order to take in homeotic relations ("A New Plea for Diagonal Science," p. 344).

6.9.1. *This science compares disciplines, sciences, regions of being, objects, histories, to discover and display their significant overlaps.*

This means that a homeotician could emerge in any discipline, really in any occupation whatsoever. The mark of a true homeotician is to refuse one particular assumption, the assumption made by "method." The idea of method presupposes that the segments of the world are

continuous, so that when two physicists touch two elementary particles or energies, or when physicists touch matter and chemists simul-
taneously touch a certain compound with emergent properties, all the
scientists are ultimately touching the identical body of nature. The
science that does not make the assumption that nature has a single
body is called "diagonal." There can be a science of sciences that is not
the sociology or the history of science, not the study of science's own
structures and evolution, but a movement that traverses them as vicinities in which patterns have come to rest. There are techniques for
gathering the "residual characteristics" of other paradigms, for exhibiting unusual interplays between competing paradigms and among
incongruent fields or fields that stand in presumed hierarchies, such as
physics and chemistry. "The universe is radiant. It supports any secant,
median, chord, or bisectrix" ("A New Plea for Diagonal Science," p.
345). Which diagonal you take in the universe determines the field you
will describe. The aim of the diagonal science is not to explain nature
according to human measure; it is much more to describe human
things as internal to noncausal nature by pointing out where human
traits are objectively mimicked in the universe's eyes. This process
happens, no doubt, outside "the framework predicated on the struggle
for survival and natural selection" (p. 346), although as we've seen, a
universe in which selection can take place, a universe where individual
organisms have the need to survive, is itself predicated on multiple
homeotic processes, such that there can be matter, places, configurations of environments, organisms in enough profusion to compete,
resources in enough profusion to support organisms at all, and so on,
not to mention the very homeotic processes that keep species alike in
some respects and allow them to vary in others, where species are the
maintenance routines for likenesses, exploiting the "not quite" of likeness at the expense of the "nearly so," without which there could not
exist a single individual, let alone a group.

6.9.2.   *There is a likeness theory of the social, in which likenesses serve
enlikening.*

256

7. *Likenesses serve enlikening.*

I imitate you, I become like you; you educate me, I become like you; we are intimate, I become like you and you become like me. This is sometimes called "rubbing off." Our behavior, thought, and speech, habits, expressions rub off. A newborn rubs off on a toddler, teens rub off on their friends, the roles they are supposed to enact rub off on adults. To every stage and age, for each entity and group, there is a rubbing off or a becoming like that accompanies and enables.

7.1. *Becoming like should not be confused with becoming.*

What do we call it when one thing cozies up to another and expresses traits in sympathy? How does one thing express its likeness to another? If likeness calls a halt to becoming, what is it that happens when an apprentice takes on the skills of a guru, when a student becomes like a teacher. It is not becoming, but becoming like. Recall the context in which the concept of becoming makes sense and the important differences will emerge. "Now everything that comes to be [*panta ta gignomena*] comes to be [*gignetai*] by the agency of something and from something and comes to be something" (*Aristotle's Metaphysics,* Book Zeta, 1032a13–14; *Complete Works*, p. 1629). Take Aristotle's definition of becoming in the *Metaphysics*, which sums up a major strand of earlier Hellenic thinking on the meaning of *gignomai*, to come into being or to come into a certain state of being, and most importantly to come to be a "something." Look how deeply enmeshed "becoming" is in a theory of entities acting causally within a metaphysical superstructure. Every becoming thing becomes by means of something (efficient cause), and becomes from something (first cause), and becomes something (final cause). This metaphysical scaffolding is the content of becoming; becoming has no intentionality of its own, but borrows direction and will from the causes, which are its constraints and goads. It consists in a plastic interval, a temporal material on which the causes let loose their impulses. It is transient; becoming gets plied and discarded.

Even where the concept "becoming" has been revised and renewed, even where it does not hold to the Aristotelian limitation, but is a process on its own terms, it clings to several Aristotelian requirements. For instance, "becoming is never imitating," Deleuze and Guattari say in *A Thousand Plateaus*.[91] While it is easy to agree with this—and even easier if it is put in reverse: imitating is not becoming—here, too, becoming is being's shill, double, alternative; becoming is the doorway to being. Meaning an unfulfilled, incomplete being, on the way to a substance, becoming gets defined against finished, fulfilled, completed being. In Aristotle and for the millennia of the *scala naturae*, becoming per se meant incomplete and imperfect. In Deleuze, writing on his own and with Guattari, and over the last century or two of alternative ontologies, it meant remaining constitutively unfulfilled, in passage out of the home territory, open to further determinations, in and as its native plasticity, flying away from substance. Yet even where a becoming doesn't become anything, it is still highly regulated, a process, a habitual practice of habitual activities.

7.2.   *Strictly speaking, homeosis is neither a process nor a practice.*

Process and practice share a pattern with "becoming," the pattern of a gradual change toward a result or a series of actions in motion toward an end. In contrast, likeness is a halting that happens, and if you can understand the modality of this happening, you can come to understand why saying "enlikening" is more correct than saying once again the old ontological "becoming."[92]

7.2.1. *Enlikening sometimes looks like a process.*

To call the happening of likeness a "process" is problematic, because it assumes an internal, necessary, directional movement through recognizable stages toward an obligatory result. A process whose stages do not constrain the outcome to a degree higher than chance is not a process, but a proceeding. Whether you emphasize the result or the process itself, whether it is a functional process that starts in a will and ends in an object of the will or a self-organizing process modeled on a concept of organic nature that, once triggered, proceeds on its own, in all versions, process progresses through noncontingent transitions. In its logical form, it is the eventual correlative of causality: when X is happening, Y will happen. The most common synonym for "process" is "growth" — or rather, growth is the organic intuition on which the functional metaphor of process feeds itself. Alfred North Whitehead: "Process is the growth and attainment of a final end" (*Process and Reality*, p. 150). What is "growth," if not a name for a process? What is "process," if not a technical name for growth? There is nothing wrong with this double borrowing, growth from process, process from growth. The tautological origins of process metaphysics are of interest, but origins aside, in this metaphysical schema, process follows a particular pattern. A force moves automatically through noncontingent transitions that progressively constrain the outcome.[93] Process is the effecting and effective motivation of constraints on free happenings so that they eventually conform to laws. Process is law's executor, the police of happening. As such, it is a conservative figure, a bulwark against excessive freedom. What makes a process seem "natural," even if it is humanly planned and executed, is the way one stage "grows" out of another without external inputs and the way the end is formally contained in the order of stages, not in the origin, as in a standard teleological movement. The order of stages makes the end inevitable. This is the only difference between process metaphysics and dialectical metaphysics. In dialectical metaphysics, the end is in the beginning; in process metaphysics, the end is in the law of the transitions. Process can be described, then, as the obligatory succession of realization upon an order. In a process, will seems to converge with the natural order of things. Process implies a natural will.

7.2.2.   *Enlikening sometimes looks like a practice.*

And as with "process," "practice" implies a dynamic substrate, a will to an activity whose shape emerges in its transitions, and not out of its beginning or its end. Practice dwells farther from necessity than process, and farther from metaphysics, and yet it is equally productive and equally deceptive about its assumptions. To call the happening of likeness a "practice" suggests that it can be put into practice by an agent and made habitual without the collusion of the larger cosmos. Practice implies a technique that proceeds out of trial and error, that depends on habit formation, in situations where predictability cannot be expected, but has to be made. Thus practice implies also a willed building up of regularity, predictability, a way of making an unreliable situation reliable. Practice assumes a contingent situation, much like process, but practice steps in where process has not yet become established. Process is supposed to produce a result each time by organizing happenings into a sequence of necessary steps. Practice works within variable situations, testing, trying, repeating gestures in order to regularize the world. Practice implies an empirical will.

Lacking any motive or other relation to a will, homeosis cannot be confused with process or practice. What is the relationship between it and process or practice-oriented behaviors? To answer this, it is best to step into the social zone, a zone far from the cosmos or artworks or evolution history. Homeosis holds a special place in social ensembles. It restlessly knits together the most disparate phenomena. It transits the classroom, the workplace, the cinema, soccer matches, bar scenes, dating circuits; it cultivates those cultural mirrors into which you and I gaze expectantly, looking for

ourselves and finding instead facsimiles — apery of all sorts, fash-
ionistas, impersonators, appropriators, parodists, celebrities, fakes,
falses, and frauds, all that reflects and refracts because our customs
and habits and, in truth, our economy depend upon it. To see the true
authority of likeness in the social zone, however, look further, into
occurrences that at first glance appear to follow different principles.

Even in a social structure in which "process" is the primary
element, you can find homeosis at work quietly in the subsubbase-
ment.[94] Marx's critique of political economy is such a social structure. Although likeness looks tangential to the analysis of capitalism, it nonetheless happens inside of and beneath capital's routines,
marking out a subordinate noneconomy within the strict relations
of exchange. Volume 1 of *Capital* is dedicated to describing strict
capital relations.[95] Now, it was no small adjustment to social thought
when Marx identified society as an amalgam of processes instead of
as a collection of things, institutions, people, wills, or laws. The real,
in Marx's mature political economy, is a process, while the product
aligns with the ideal; that is, a product is a falsification — strategic and
necessary, yes, but covering the real moment — of a process. Process
and product — two poles in Marx's theory. Products are ideals that
emerge from reification — the process they deny in order to become
carriers of value. In Marx's systematic, there is in fact no product
without a process, and the real novelty of capitalism is that it depre-
ciates products almost to the point of valuelessness and appreciates
processes (the process of valorization, say, or exchange, or labor)
almost until they become absolutes. Products serve processes; they
are pauses in repeatable courses of events that stop at nothing to go
on and keep going on. A product interrupts two main processes, or
really three — labor, this is where Marx focuses attention in volume
1, reification, and don't forget circulation, treated in detail in volume 2. Through labor, a product gets produced, through reification, a
product becomes independent, stepping away from and denying the
process, once the laboring activity has done with it. At this point, the
reified labor process is incorporated into the exchange process. From

Marx's perspective, reification is the chief danger of capitalist society, which turns endlessly from real (processes) to ideal (things) by means of reification's special powers. More than valorization or reification, however, the true process of capital is this exchange of the real for the ideal, and that is just where Marx inserts his knife. To the three main processes, however—production, reification, circulation, all of which participate in the process of idealization of the real—a fourth should be added, a relatively hidden process, or rather a nonprocess and nonproduct that crosses the rest and that is as unreal as it is nonideal and nevertheless constitutive of the social sphere.

Consider the social process that is production—and especially its natural aspect, labor. Consider a tool-and-die maker fabricating a mold. The mold is for the purpose of reproducing a thing to make many of it, while the production process itself consists in following a prototype—a prototype mold, a prototype process, a prototype arrangement of equipment on the factory floor. A stockpile of the same product, the horizontal dimension, goes hand in hand with the descent from prototype to process, the vertical dimension. A machinist works in both dimensions of homeosis at once, horizontal and vertical, in any single job of work. Techniques are employed, along with molds and tools, and just as importantly, there participate remembered stances, habituated gestures, assimilated ticks, mimicked qualities in which the worker is mime and the predecessors are prototypes. Happenings of likenesses—the labor process needs a myriad of them. Further, within labor, whether consumed or produced, likenesses serve further enlikening. The reproduction of a coat apes a thousand prior reproductions and offers itself up to be aped in turn. Along with the production of a coat, there comes the enlikening of coat sellers, coat wearers, and eventually also coat disposers. Enlikening happens within and beneath the processes. "Within" and "beneath" mean that it does not congeal in the product; it is not reified, commodified, valorized. That is because it is neither real nor ideal; instead, it happens clandestinely, traversing the products, cutting through the labor, production, valorization, circulation, exchange, and consumption to enliken another day.

7.3.   *An economic process nourishes itself on likenesses, and in order to be economic, it has to produce at the very least a likeness of itself, that is, it has to happen at least twice.*

If you now turn from a single example, tool-and-die making, to the productive economy as a whole, you can see that whatever else it is explicitly, a modern economy is also implicitly a system for exploiting and managing enlikening. The rule of all processes and all products under this kind of economy — under any economy, since it is the medium of production and exchange — can be expressed like this: no process and no product is ever one alone. If a commodity is a hapax, one alone with no echo, it hardly belongs to an economy, let alone a society. If a process is one of a kind, with no echoes, no successors, and no competitors, it is doomed to remain asocial and paraeconomical.[96] In our current historical configuration of production and exchange, the fact of more than just one has become the law. This law can be stated in the negative: never one laborer, never one commodity, never one single need — that would be truly ridiculous — never a single invention without copies, and most often vast quantities of copies and whole industries dedicated to engendering them. Indeed, economies arise when like needs and like processes supply like qualities, a cycle that — according to the reproduction of capital — makes capital appear as "an eternal natural law of human production" (Marx, "Results of the Direct Production Process," p. 406).

Fascinated by the way capital presents itself as a natural law, as eternal and unchangeable, Marx nevertheless does not take an interest in enlikening, although he read Darwin, and to be candid no part of the capital system can function without homeotic magic that multiplies products and their qualities. Marx's reticence, one could guess, stems from the fact that enlikening is neither a material process that he can uncover nor an ideal process that he can undermine. Likeness is the aesthetic substance of the social, and as such, it cannot be critiqued at least insofar as critique still means changing society. Still, despite Marx's silence on the issue, the capitalist economy is a good laboratory for a theory of likeness, because the sociality identified with it is especially permeated by enlikening. Labor, exchange, capitalization, as well as time and space under this system — all aim at homogeneity, variety, continuation.

Volume 1 of *Capital* starts with an analysis of the commodity, which Marx calls society's "elemental form" (p. 125). As the elemental form, it must, beyond being elemental, reproduce itself and thus be permeated by likeness — there is not just one and not just one kind; it multiplies and varies. The homeotic character of the commodity is more than this, however. He goes on: "the commodity is, first of all, an external object, a thing which through its qualities satisfies human needs of whatever kind" (p. 125). Despite the talk of commodities, he is in the domain of processes right away — philologically, he lingers among processual deverbals here at the start and throughout the analysis: production, circulation, capitalization, which entail reification, appearance, substitution, inversion, conversion, circulation. Processes are not homeotic, since homeosis is not a process. All these processes, all these little teleological machines, seem to avoid homeosis altogether and move from and to differences. And yet along with the processes and their verbal representatives, there is also a conventional ontology of things as "carriers" of other things known as qualities, qualities that Marx calls the "bearers" of value. In part, at least, he remains in a medieval ontology under whose rules qualities carry the burden of being; that old ontological truism persists through the whirlwind of dialectical processes; the premodern remainder, in "quality," likeness exercises its rights.

A peasant mills wheat; a tailor cuts wool cloth; a clerk writes on paper — all by means of the purposes, contexts, tools, materials, and wills that the market provided them, no question about that. The ontological armature is there, too: Marx insists what is made in production are not commodities, but qualities. A product may result from a process, and the product in which the process congeals may become a commodity, and when taken to market and put up against the world of commodities, the commodity may thereby be

an equivalent. However, what bears the value that makes equivalence possible is not the commodity as a congealed process, but the
qualities that, across every process, are borne bravely forward, in the
purchase of raw materials through the workshop to market across
multiple exchanges and into the consumer's factory, home, or mouth.
You could say, qualities carry the commodity to market, offer it for
sale, and finally fulfill the buyer's need.

Marx further insists that beyond the abstract "use," what is used
in use are not things themselves, but their qualities, which derive
directly from the qualities of the labor put into them (*Capital*, vol.
1, pp. 126 and 136). Despite his investment in processes, qualities are
indispensable and act like things for Marx. They are atoms of substance that persist. Though not traded directly, qualities are what
are ultimately taken and given — and the fuel in the machine, the
true stuff of production and consumption, is qualities' likeness.
Labor is an exchange of qualities from human being to thing. Market is an exchange of qualities from thing to thing. Consumption is
an exchange of qualities from thing to human being. Likenesses are
the true goods exchanged in any commodity transaction. A bolt of
fabric sells, "becoming like a bolt of fabric," with all the qualities
that go along with this enlikening, to the buyer, who may need it
for "becoming like a coat." Shaving and shaping labor gives a round
quality to a millstone similar to other roundnesses; heating and hammering labor gives a favored tempered quality to steel in a tailor's
sheers; monitoring and adjusting labor gives a paper mill the suitable
settings to screen out a roll of paper. Labor qualities such as these
are attachment points for need qualities, such as the tailor's need for
hard sheers and the schoolteacher's need to print on flat paper. The
qualities all transmit through likeness. Labor output transits to needs
through qualities, qualities perform their magic through likeness
(akin to what was made before, akin to what was needed). It is possible to see capitalism, more perhaps than any other world system,
as primarily about the production, exchange, and consumption of
homeoses, for qualities, for output and needs, for — of course — the

growth of capital and the growth of that growth. Capital shrivels and dies without enlikening. The qualities that make up products are only partially determined by nature, which undergoes its own continual homeoses in any case. Iron comes out of the ground with a certain hardness. More qualities are put into the iron through the labor process — flexibility, color, density, shape, and so on — which depend on a specific, regulated mimicry, a mimicry that continually enlikens to itself in order to continue on in that way, to be a technique.

Qualities come in many varieties. On the production of variety, Marx gives a good example of how it comes about: "In Birmingham alone 500 varieties of hammer are produced, and not only is each one adapted to a particular process, but several varieties often serve exclusively for the different operations in the same process. The manufacturing period simplifies, improves and multiplies the implements of labour by adapting them to the exclusive and special functions of each kind of worker" (*Capital*, vol. 1, pp. 460–61). Traits of tools vary, become established, and disseminate; production thus approximates a gene system for disseminating, establishing, and varying characteristics that derive from — mimic — archaic patterns, no matter how far they progress or drift from their origins. No one would argue that the 500 species of hammer don't share a common ancestor in the pounding stone. New products are novel arrangements of qualities, which may ultimately, after several derivations, come to diverge greatly, as do the needs to which they will correspond, various hammers to various workers.

Kinds of labor and kinds of commodities vary; on this the growth of capital depends and depends absolutely. Varying, they shift qualities along one series or another, take in this or that other series, branch, return, circle, layer up, this beside and throughout production and consumption. Qualities enliken in the production of multiples, and qualities also enliken along chains of variation. Variations are for variation. Needs vary in relation to newly produced qualities, and produced qualities vary in relation to newly minted needs. A vast array of enlikenings occur in production, when stockpiling a supply,

when drafting designs, in the history of commodities as well as tech-
nologies, in labor practices, workshop arrangements, and so on. Any
particular quality may be short-lived — one quality often comes to
serve, through its very success, as the stage on which a new variation
steps forth, while enlikening is virtually permanent.

Why, given the centrality of enlikening to production, exchange,
and consumption, does the main argument of the first sections of
Capital push thought so quickly away from the like, toward equivalence? Something else is wanted, for dialectics, for critique. Equivalence begins its meteoric rise in the exchange process as soon as
the enlikened homeotic qualities become bearers of the alien spirit,
value.

7.4. *The social process of capital turns enlikening as the basis for production of qualities into equivalence as the basis for exchange of value.*

At the moment in the system when a commodity enters the market,
when it is up for trade, the quality that matters is quantity, a special
quality, by some magic different in kind from all the others, that
emerges when the myriad qualities in a labor output get expressed
in terms of a single quality of a single commodity, money. The single
quality of money is amount. Money seems as far from enlikening,
varying, clining, twinning as anything can be. Another homeosis
occurs, however, at the heart of the market, just where everything
is comfortably equivalent. A remnant of the merely similar lodges
in value's throat. For a bolt of fabric is a bolt of fabric. There is no
way around that. This simple fact underpins market logic and its
dialectical exposition, even if Marx passes over it. To reiterate: without at least two coats, there is no market for coats, no exchange,
no circulation, no production, and so on. Human being is species
being, and commodity being is also species being. Coat is a species that varies and deviates, returns and crosses with itself, only to
lurch outward at times toward another species. A variety of needs

for coats and a variety of coats make the production of a coat species and the exchange of individual coats into reasonable undertakings. For Marx's critique to succeed, exchange value needs to arise as though by magic, in a conversion of the purely heterogeneous into the equivalent. By the time a commodity gets to market, the variability of types and the replicability of qualities should no longer matter. Instead of a variety of qualities, there is one mystical quality in which all qualities become equivalent. Value exists when "a common element of identical magnitude exists between two different things" (*Capital*, vol. 1, p. 127). Marx cries, how twisted capitalism is when it makes what is by nature different equivalent! This is capitalism's basic perversion and the source for many of its other perversions. Here at one source of capitalism and a source also of its critique, Marx relies on a philosophical cliché, that what is different is essentially different. The transformation of difference into equivalence Marx calls a "reduction" (p. 127), an operation on a thing "in which all its sensuous characteristics are extinguished" (p. 128). Equalization murders difference. That is the ontological wage of capital.

Yet there is a good indifference, isn't there? Or at least a neutral one, operating all the while along human as well as natural clines. Something other than the forced equalization of differents, something less than leveling, perversion, reduction, murder allows a bolt of cloth to be made and traded and used as what it is, a bolt of cloth, and not as a nest of yarn or a clod of cotton. It can be called "cloth" and used as cloth because it enlikens cloth, because it has been made indistinguishable from cloth, has been allowed to slow up and arrest with itself. This arrest allows a coat to be a coat, its use to be its use — almost the same as another coat, not drifting into pure heterogeneity at any point. Indistinctness of "coat" qua coat allows the need for it — cold weather — to be that need, again, as it happened the last time, insofar as this cold is like that cold, this need like that need, this use like that use, this coat like the other coats, in reciprocity, need, and output, like necessities calling for like sufficiencies, in a happening not so different from the circulations of a market, namely, as a circuit of enlikening, coat enlikening to coat, varying in thicknesses, fit, and appropriateness to climate, which is not just geographical or seasonal, but temporal—lest you forget, the same coat doesn't suit the climate by the afternoon at least half the time when you set out on a fall morning with a coat on. The dream of pure heterogeneity is the dream, you can say, of the ideal agreement of a product to its ideal use, once and for all. This is a theological view, an extension of creation into mere homeotic life. In that view, there is a hammer for every nail. Our experience with uses, however, shows that there is no nail so unique that it would require its own absolutely distinct hammer.

7.4.1. *Use is not a process of applying ideality to ideality; use is approximating.*

To this or that nail you approximate this or that hammering, these nails approximating nails, these qualities emphasizing what they can enliken in the encounter. Are clawing, levering, pulling derivatives of hammering? Approximately. Is the tool world an evolution of likenesses seen one way in a negative, as almost and not quite—not quite a hammer (then what is it?)—seen another way, in a positive, as almost and most of all, almost a hammer? (How much would you pay for an "almost hammer"?)

Capital is permeated by uniformities that are assumed to be real, but are actually idealizations of preexisting kin relations.[97] The most trenchant formulation of this unspoken assumption is: "coats cannot be exchanged for coats" (*Capital*, vol. 1, p. 132). No value is traded there, where the similar reigns. Today, a more subtle version of this statement is needed that takes into account planned obsolescence and fast fashion. Nonetheless, exchange still thrives on the idealizations equivalence and difference. Coats cannot be exchanged for coats in the exchange process, since they are not different. Exchange is the exchange of false equivalents whose truth is their real differences, or so goes Marx's conviction. And yet it is obvious that coats cannot be exchanged at all unless there are multiple coats to cover multiple bodies and multiple climates and varying accidents of weather.[98] As with the labor process, there is a requirement for multiplicity. Value could not become a quantity, that mysterious transformation represented by money, if commodities did not become multiplicities, that is, serial varieties of themselves. No exchange would occur if there existed only one coat. The one in possession of it would likely not want to part with it. Wares such as coats are so alike unto one another as to seem uniform, and this perceived uniformity in the commodity world is the vehicle for an exploitative work situation, as well as a subsistence home situation. Note, too, that Marx talks about the ware "coat" and not the wearing of the coat or the coat as it wears and wears out, and yet these eventualities hint at the inevitable decay of a coat into what used to be a coat, the decline of use into usedness and ultimately uselessness, which can also be described as becoming only or merely like the former coat — slipping from mostly all into almost and not quite, as some qualities become unlike the standards they formerly lived up to. Enlikening happens this way, too. A commodity comes to be through the happening of homeosis, fairly like, whereupon it becomes valorized and exchanged, and subsequently it decays back into homeosis, barely like.

7.5. *In general, becoming transits through becoming like.*

This holds in all social milieus, not just the milieu of capital. Once I become like my parents, I can become a student; once I become like a student, I can become a math teacher; once my writing becomes like writing, I can become a writer and so on.

7.5.1. *In the most quotidian sense, learning involves enlikening. Becoming what you are means becoming like another.*

The specter haunting education is not enlikening per se, but its vilified cousin, imitation. You don't have to turn to Plato once more to read about this; Rousseau is closer to us and makes the point just as clearly. To be educated, a child should be guided "by the laws of the possible and the impossible alone" (*Emile*, p. 92). Experience of what can and cannot be done is the only safe teacher, and since experience follows the laws of reason — for instance, the law of non-contradiction — when you put yourself in experience's hands, amour spropre, innate reason, guides and educates you from the inside out, without trespassing on the impossible. From this principle Rousseau derives the dictum: a child must do nothing in relation to others, but "respond only to what nature asks of him [*sic*]" (pp. 92–93), which means a child should learn "without emulation" (p. 130).

Emulation Rousseau pushes out of the picture. Yet mere responsiveness to nature's demands can easily fail. To see this, look into a warped mirror, a dark image of Rousseau's natural education — Jean Itard's account of the education of a wild child in his book on the savage of Aveyron. When the boy at the center of the account, later called Victor, appeared in the woods of Caune in the new revolutionary district of Aveyron around 1800, Rousseau's dictum could finally be tested on a subject untouched by society. For the rest, there was no chance, Itard laments, for true education by nature in a century, the eighteenth, where an individual was from birth infected with the habits, ideas, and prerogatives of society (*An Historical Account*, p. 6). In the nineteenth century, this instinctive and automatic "emulation" did not go away; it only increased in frequency. The nineteenth-century continental individual has the "capacity of developing his understanding by the power of imitation, and the influence of society" (pp. 4–5). Itard meets Victor the "savage" as the perfect Rousseauvian subject, a total anomaly among social beings, one "who owes nothing to his equals" (p. 5) and thus really the first creature who could prove or disprove the supremacy of natural learning, by reason and the senses, over social learning, by emulation.

The main focus of Itard's attention is Victor's senses. A nature boy like this will have developed his senses completely, without imitation, and thus they should be the most pure, the most reasonable. One thing is for sure, his sensibility is not of this world. Hot baths don't tire him, a pistol fired next to his ear barely raises a reaction, he can sit in the wind and rain for hours half clothed without the complaints that would surely issue from Itard's sedentary class. Even though the boy's senses have in fact been educated by nature, Itard's attempts to "stimulate" the nervous sensibility of his patient look for all the world like he is habituating him to the goods of civilization — baths, clothes, pistols, darkening curtains on the windows, warm comforters, milk — in short, accustoming him to the comforts of the bourgeois interior. "Some modern psychologists have presumed that sensibility is in exact proportion to the degree of civilization," he says (p. 43). The obstacle to this education is precisely the natural development of the boy's senses. Nothing is more anathema to civilization than indifference to its sensations, excessively soft and excessively harsh, and Itard takes Victor's unreactivity to result from a lack of habits. The most natural of abilities, which should be formed straight from experience, in truth requires a conforming, habituating education — "to lead the mind to a habit of attention" (p. 47). A pleasure offered Victor several times turns into a "want" (p. 68). Overcoming Victor's dullness requires Itard to train him in the pleasures of recapitulation.

One of the stimulants Itard employs to habituate the natural boy to social sensing is more like torture. He shocks Victor with electricity from a Leyden jar, but to read the Leyden jar and the shock as a tool for disciplining the savage is to misread it. Itard puts Victor's hand on the jar and sends a high-voltage charge through him. By the third time, Victor develops a strategy. He takes his teacher's hand, Itard's own, and puts it on the jar, so that voltage courses through his teacher's body instead of his own (pp. 53–54). A more perfect allegory for the acquisition of sociality would be hard to find. A torture repeated becomes second nature, and one learns, along with how to tolerate it, how to force the experience onto someone else.

7.6. Homeosis is bound up with power.

This, too, Victor learns. Recapitulation teaches him about homeosis. Rather than a sovereign wielder of power, homeosis plays the role of an intriguer at court. At the right moment, it can cause the ruination of a sovereign system. Victor the wild boy does not learn in the Rousseauvian sense, but he does get the point: to emulate, to participate in enlikening is to steal some power from the master, even to use it against him. This is also one of the lessons, a side lesson, but a strong lesson nonetheless, of Gabriel Tarde's book on the centrality of likeness to the social, *Les lois de l'imitation*, written in an absolutely anti-Rousseauvian vein at the end of the nineteenth century. Itard and Marx, though vastly different in almost every respect, were both leery of imitation — mere reproduction, uniformity, and conformity for their own sakes, of little value in the bigger systems. Tarde, in his turn, was quite partisan toward the warm middle of a homoform society, toward experiences with diminishing value.

Like Paul Kammerer after him, Tarde went from a complete amateur to a scientific star, then fell far, fast. He was: a French provincial judge for twenty-seven years who started writing on criminology; a criminologist who leapt into debates in the formative years of sociology; a great sociologist who lost an epochal debate on method with Émile Durkheim; a lauded father figure who, in the eyes of a new generation of sociologists, looked hopelessly out of touch and incoherent. To some, his incoherence has seemed to be a starting point for other modes of social thought — to Gilles Deleuze and more recently to Bruno Latour, among others.[99] Those who want to recover Tarde want to recover what he said and what he meant. They want to salvage his primal plurality of social elements, so good for pitting against Durkheim's free individuals constrained within institutions. They want to emancipate a speculative approach to social processes from a scientific approach. But listen for a minute to what Tarde did not say and to one unsaid thing in particular: imitation is power. Imitation fledges in a hierarchy, and then it poisons the nest; it steals power from aristocrats and restructures their possibilities — precisely what, judging by his actions, the wild boy of Aveyron began to do when he imitated his educator.

Now, there is a superficial power politics in Tarde's book on imitation. Subjects want to become rulers, and so they imitate them. "For the father is and always will be his son's first master, priest, model. Every society, even at present, begins this way" (*The Laws of Imitation*, p. 78). From master to model — here is a power theory and a theory of envy and a usurper's desire that looks something like that of his almost exact contemporary, Nietzsche: "in the beginning of every old society, there must have been, a fortiori, a great display of authority exercised by certain supremely imperious and positive individuals." This quote is actually from Tarde (p. 78).

Perhaps by now I believe too much in causeless likenesses. Still, the year of Nietzsche's madness, 1890, was also the year of Tarde's madness for imitation. And although Tarde might have supported a return to "supremely imperious and positive individuals" in some new form, he in fact made a negative image of the will to power and hypothesized another mode of power altogether that was nevertheless also, like Nietzsche's, antithetical to the slave morality, albeit by another route. Power in any society is a positive force that belongs not to the first imposer, the imperious authority, the master, but rather to those who imitate them. This is the deep politics in Tarde's account of likeness, which, incidentally, is anything but ontological. His is one of the few nonontological imagoes of likeness, insofar as acts are the basic unit of social likeness, rather than beings or facts. And acts are not the outgrowths of beings who can act; acts do not spring from a potential for action. Acts involve a nonaction or an inertial act parasitic on authority.

7.6.1. *A real act is imitative.*

You might not conclude that any real act is imitative immediately from what Tarde says — what he says overtly is: "Socially, everything is either invention or imitation" (*The Laws of Imitation*, p. 3). This is the first big announcement of the major problematic in his study. There are two forces, two powers that move social dynamics: invention and imitation. He elaborates with a comparison — "And invention bears the same relation to imitation as a mountain to a river" (p. 3). To investigate this metaphor or simile, this likeness at center stage in a now out-of-date social theater, a picture of Tarde's sociology as a science is needed.

When you imagine social science on the model of natural science, you consider sociology the study of cause and effect. And yet, Tarde warns, there would be no science, natural or social, if there weren't also, to the side, in the middle, all around and fully on its own account, a zone of likenesses that follows a different pattern (p. 5). We know effects by their cause and causes by their effects, but if effects, and causes, for that matter, did not also have likenesses, then every cause and every effect would be absolutely singular, and to know one would be to know nothing. This explains why sociology as a science has to be, by and large, the study of likenesses. The singular cannot be the object of sociology.

Sociology as a science up to that time had operated on a misconception. It always concentrated on the novel case and the unusual instance, rather than on the regular and humdrum rhythm of the warm middle. "The historian and sociologist . . . veil the regular and monotonous face of social facts, — that part in which they are alike and repeat themselves [en tant qu'ils se ressemblent et se répètent], — and show only their accidental and interesting, their infinitely novel and diversified aspect" (English, pp. 8–9; French, p. 9). You could say that science qua science wishes to take note only of revolutionary and transformative instances — out of care for history and norms, and sometimes out of a spirit of social change, to be sure — and yet, for Tarde, the real care for the social expresses itself in the study of imitations. Real care, care for the middle, the average, the repetitive, the majority, "the monotonous face of social facts," has to be tracked, recorded, conceptualized, and communicated in a science open to homeotic phenomena and their hidden power dynamics.

That "invention bears the same relation to imitation as a mountain to a river" has significant consequences later in the text. What is the implicit basis for the comparison? How does a river relate to a mountain? Ask this another way: What favor does a mountain do for a river?

A bit further on in the argument, Tarde changes course. "To sum up," Tarde says, "everything which is social and non-vital or non-physical in the phenomena of societies is caused by imitation [*a l'imitation pour cause*] (English, p. 50; French, p.55). Now the other pillar of social being, invention, has vanished, and the social per se is identified with imitation alone. Has he forgotten the power of invention, which should be the only true power, or has something in his argument changed?

You might worry at this point that what Tarde is describing is a classic liberal economy, where innovators and those who own innovations rule while the sprawling rest labor and consume. Labor and consumption, as I established in the reading of Marx's *Capital*, are at least in part homeotic activities anyway. Still, some of the statements in *The Laws of Imitation* could conform to the classist interpretation of society as made up of innovators and the rest. "Inventions become great historic figures and the real agents of human progress," Tarde does say (p. 102). Note that he talks here of inventions, and not inventors. Still, the unhistoric, noninventive rest, the warm middle that he claimed was the object of true sociology, is given the somewhat unappreciative label "somnambulists."

7.6.2. *"Society is imitation and imitation is a kind of somnambulism."*

Immediately following this motto, which is printed in italics in Tarde's text (p. 87), there is a theory of deepening assimilation whereby societies become ever more homogeneous as history advances, such that you might think you have here also an anticipation of neoliberal social theory and perhaps a foreboding of fascism.

And yet... and yet, despite what he says about inventions, the

276

invention drops out of the equation altogether when the social per se is invoked. What are imitations without inventions? The factual answer to this is "society," but what does imitation have to mean in order to arrive at this answer? His point is the rather self-evident and more political insight that inventions are nothing without imitations. This is why inventors are not social actors in any true sense. They are in fact asocial. Moreover, what Tarde calls "the one-sided, passive imitation of the somnambulist," a being who is "deprived of this power of resistance" (p. 79), while certainly less innovative than the inventor, is at the same time more powerful socially. The warm middle sleepwalks and on its perambulations wields what I will call "reflective power." It is not power as usually thought, a power to cause, a force that meets and challenges counterforces, coercive force or ergative force, or even the complex interactive forces of chemistry and biology.

7.6.3. *The social depends on reflective power and would not happen without it.*

Reflective power cannot be confused with force. What's more, ergative force, power qua efficient cause, would not happen without reflective power to amplify and propagate it. The point I want to emphasize is that reflective power, true social power for Tarde, is homeotic.

Reflective power has a few of its own axioms.

7.7. *The imitation is higher than the invention.*

On one hand, in a strong sense, the imitation gives birth to the invention by preferring it and taking it above all others into its generous embrace. It also means, on the other hand, that the imitation is free, in the sense of not being beholden to any higher instance, because it is independent of a claim to be the source or the originary instance. The first imitation is also free in that it is not tied to a single objective, to bring something into being; thus, it is neither possessive nor defensive.

7.7.1. *Through reflective power, the thing imitated opens to many possible dispositions.*

This is true of the first imitation of an invention, and only the first imitation. In comparison, the invention itself is deeply conservative. It has to determine and establish itself as itself in opposition to anything that might claim to be like it. I am developing Tardean imitation theory here somewhat beyond its concerns — hearing what he did not exactly say — and yet it is not a leap to say, as well, that the first imitation of an invention has its own conservatism, too. Looking longingly toward the invention, the first imitation admires it, emulates it, wishes to become it, and practices protective fidelity toward it. You, it says, are my mother. Yet in actuality, it is not invention that gives birth to imitation, but, according to this revolutionary reading, imitation that allows invention to count as invention, just as the world of an infant into which it is born and which it disturbs is what gives the infant its natal quality, and not the parents or the exclusive relationship between infant and parents.

7.7.2. *Imitation is the mother of invention.*

Tarde inverts the relation and flow of power, raising the imitation above the original like a river over its mountain. Yet this is not Tarde's full tactic. What remains most unsaid in the treatise, and at the same time most strikingly hearable, is the distinction between the first imitation and the second imitation (and all subsequent imitations), which, to make a similar analogy or metaphor, has the same relation to a river as a river has to a lake. The mountain makes itself clear. An invention is a high platform down from which an imitation falls, gaining in the movement away the momentum and limited freedom of a river. With no real power for itself, the mountain, the invention, can express its power only as resistance to any movement away, rising higher and higher until it looms so high over sociality it becomes like a god, more and more isolated and de facto less powerful, and in this way allowing the river all the more reflective power as it courses off the top. It is the river that converts the mountain's isolated and useless height into energy and experience. This, the socialism of the imitation, is where these premises have been heading.

In adding the relation of river to lake, we are not on thin ice, I think, to develop further this water analogy. Rivers cross Tarde's text, and lakes spring up in strategic places, especially in analogies or ratios. "Legislation is to justice, a constitution is to politics, what the Lake of Geneva is to the Rhone" (*The Laws of Imitation*, p. 310). This later analogy is interesting in its own right, because the lake in question is not the source of the river, which lies in the Alps. In Lake Geneva, the Rhone temporarily pools up and gives the opportunity for a city before it drains down through France and out into the Mediterranean. The change in the idea of power is symbolized in the flattening of the mountain and the broadening of river into lake or sea. The difference in the second imitation is that it has no care at all for the invention. Its desire is for the flat and broad plain and the communities of life that can be sustained there.

7.7.3. *A second imitation freely donates the reflective power invested in the first copy.*

There is a cost for the free disposition and unfettered distribution of power in practices, living arrangements, and shared projects, and that is the diminishment of force or will into a general and diffuse activity that Tarde calls "social life."

In a most emphatic way, Tarde lays the final strokes on a canvas started by Rousseau, who banned imitation as a social good, painted over by Jean Marc Gaspard Itard, who contravened Rousseauvianism experimentally, outlined by Marx, who pointed through his silence about it to likeness as a primary motive in sociality. As a motive force in sociality, it is not so much likenesses as products but enlikening as an ongoing happening that is primary. As a form of power, enlikening brings the invention toward the copy and the copy toward a perilampsis of homeoses — like–*comme—como—wie* — water flows off a mountain, courses down a river, and diffuses into the lake whose shores and islands are perhaps thereby made habitable. Enlikening thus has stages, whether for capitalist sociality, pedagogical sociality, or "social life" as Tarde names it. These stages are the following, this time in conceptual, not metaphoric terms:

a. Enlikening begins with a desire to have what the superior has, so with a kind of ressentiment. What Nietzsche failed to intuit is that the social desire to have what the master has is not reactive, but mimetic.

b. In imitation, servants take possession of a master's things. Perhaps they hope to become masters themselves. Be that as it may, the truth is that because of the enlikening mode of power, the servant instead enters into society with the master as an equal. This is not far from Hegel.

c. The social is a vicinity for circumradiation.

d. Social authority shifts its meaning. No longer does authority mean higher, better, stronger, richer, freer. Authority is a tiny spark whose life is realized only in a material that is willing to burn it up.

e. Successful imitation cancels the model's authority and redefines modelhood as a site for a loss of power, failed prestige, empty priority, obscurity, ignominy. This kind of diminishing power I call "reflective." Its character is inertial; it wheels into the vicinity of an invention and holds there, holding the invention in one of its meanings. From this it follows also that when the model loses its status (because the imitation shows it to be imitable, and thus to have little or no force within itself), the imitation is no longer an imitation in the same way. With the invention dethroned, the first imitation becomes an object free of "originality," a free object, though not yet as the product of a free act.

f. Primary imitation changes the nature of power, from force with its resistances, from jealous possessiveness with its counterstruggles, to a reflective act with its inertial happening. Secondary imitation, in response, a reflection of a reflection, becomes a free act of construction and distribution that may well look, from the perspective of the inventor, like no real action at all.

g. Released in secondary imitation is the reflective, inertial power of enlikening, the first real social activity — first, although replicated multitudinously and monotonously.

Under the sway of this Tardean systematic of enlikening, human sociality, with its tendency toward replication and rereplication, in its meandering, dissipating, and yet relatively constant, asymmetrical, but always downward and outward distribution of likenesses, perhaps the most vital condition for sustaining a world-wide group in diaspora among itself — sociality itself, as a whole, comes to look like a bizarre-privileged item in the universe, a BPIU in its own right, and as such a good object for a homeotic science, after the fashion of butterfly wings, praying mantises, language, and anything.

7.8.   *Anything can be a BPIU.*

Teachers

To teachers — in the sense Michal Ben-Naftali gives that impossible occupation — without whom nothing resembling a book could have come about — thanks are due. Kenny Schwarz would have read the book, as he did unbidden every book and article I ever wrote, with that generous admiration for things that were alien to him. It probably would have reminded him of something in his own thinking or experience with patients, and he would have lent me a book on psychoanalysis, like he lent me his spirit since I first opened my eyes, taught me to tie a hook and to catch a thought. To colleagues and former teachers who make university life what I thought it would be when I was in graduate school, a place to try out serious sentences in playful conversation: Carol Jacobs, Henry Sussman, Kirk Wetters, Katrin Trüstedt, Rüdiger Campe, Peter Fenves, Joshua Wilner, Martin Doll, Benjamin Pollock, Eli Friedlander, Isaac Nakhimovsky, Gary Tomlinson, Paul Kockelman, Marta Kuzma, Christopher Wood, Paul Franks, Emily Greenwood, Francesco Casetti, Kathryn Lofton, Caleb Smith. These cothinkers make up an ideal university, together with — Willy Thayer, who walked New Haven with me and his thoughts grew over mine like moss. Matt Shafer did the free disposition of one's own (Hölderlin) and emboldened me through his writing. Laura Phillips awakened the inner association of images (Menzel) and assisted with art-historical research. Carolyn Walker Bynum showed me how similitude precedes parousia in medieval art and read and critiqued an early draft of Premise 1. In the tympanum of his ample theoretical ear, Eyal Peretz registered and recast the first tentative thoughts on likeness. Anthony Adler criticized the idea mercilessly and brilliantly in a letter and perforated the project with his ferocious philosophical imagination. Andrew Libby continues to occupy the position of guru. Everyone should have this kind of friend. Audiences at Yale, Oxford, the Goethe-Universität Frankfurt, the Ruhr-Universität Bochum, the University of Western Ontario, and the University at Buffalo were, against good sense, willing to consider kinships among elephants and atom bombs, moths and tables, fruit and emperors. Hindy Najman, Nikolaus Müller-Scholl, Jörn Etzold, Maud Meyzaud, Friedrich Balke, Jan Plug, Allan Pero, and Rodolphe Gasché kindly invited me to lecture about likeness. For this I am deeply grateful. Ramona Naddaff is a true editor and paradigmatic philosophical reader; without her guidance, the book would be a poor facsimile of a book. Peter Szendy generously read and commented on the final draft. Bud Bynack is a textual spirit who, like the "Editor" in Carlyle's *Sartor Resartus* is at home in the seams.

Carolina Baffi, *docta* of my *ignorantia*, continues to teach me *incomprehensibilia incomphensibiliter amplecterer.*

Notes

1. Roger Caillois takes the butterfly *Kallima* as a prime example for his redefinition of natural mimicry in "Mimicry and Legendary Psychasthenia," trans. John Shepley, *October* 31 (Winter 1984), pp. 16–32.

2. *The Book of Resemblances*, a multivolume, Talmud-style polylogue by Edmond Jabès is a repository of likeness thinking the likes of which has not been seen. Edmond Jabès, *The Book of Resemblances*, 3 vols., trans. Rosmarie Waldrop (Middletown, CT: Wesleyan University Press, 1990). "There is no rest in the kingdom of resemblances," Jabès laments (vol. 1, p. 56), and his book is as restless as the kingdom it charts. If you look hard, you can see right through my book to Jabès's *Book*. He can conjure in an aperçu what it takes me pages to build up out of major and minor premises, historical evidences, and critical images. Perhaps it is not so bad that things happened this way; perhaps the late 1970s was the time to evoke the magic of likeness and now is the time to unfold its petals, to make it available to more people, the time to feel and say, resolutely and bravely, what Jabès's evocation of resemblance is good for. This is no doubt the rule for certain kinds of intellectual work — after the evocation comes the vocation. After the inspiration comes the work. If, when looking through this book, you perceive Jabès's *Book* behind it, it is as one of the characters in his book laments: "'Our story will never be anything but the story of a book seen through a glass of dead days where likeness sheds its leaves'" (vol. 1, p. 6).

3. One exception to this rule is D. J. Connor's "On Resemblance," *Proceedings of the Aristotelian Society*, n.s., 46 (1945–46), pp. 47–76.

4. In the Darwin section of *Les airs de famille*, François Noudelman analyzes the "rupture" Darwin brings about in the thought of analogy. Darwin bases a whole regime of truth on resemblances, making it imperative to distinguish resemblances that signal real

affinities from those that do not. François Noudelman, *Les airs de famille: Une philosophie des affinités* (Paris: Éditions Gallimard, 2012). pp. 79–80.

5. See David Quammen, *The Tangled Tree: A Radical New History of Life* (New York: Simon and Schuster, 2018).

6. A recent, clear statement of this position can be found in Elliot Sober, *Evidence and Evolution: The Logic behind the Science* (Cambridge: Cambridge University Press, 2008), especially p. 297, "Comparing Kinds of Similarity." See also Elliot Sober and Mike Steel, "Similarities as Evidence for Common Ancestry: A Likelihood Epistemology," *British Journal for the Philosophy of Science* 68. 3 (2015), pp. 1–22.

7. The "species problem" is still unsettled, though it has changed form several times since Darwin. See Carl T. Bergstrom and Lee Alan Dugatkin's textbook *Evolution* (New York: W. W. Norton, 2012), ch. 14, "Species and Speciation," pp. 454–97.

8. W. S. MacLeay, *Illustrations of the Annulosa of South Africa*; see Notebook D, note 50-1m p. 347, in Paul H. Barrett, et al. (eds.), *Charles Darwin's Notebooks, 1836 – 1844: Geology, Transmutation of Species, Metaphysical Enquiries* (Cambridge: Cambridge University Press, 2008).

9. A biography of likeness would have to include the invention of homeopathy, which takes the likeness milieu of nature as its starting point. See Alice A. Kuzniar. *The Birth of Homeopathy out of the Spirit of Romanticism* (Toronto: University of Toronto Press, 2017).

10. That likeness knows no degrees and there cannot be more or less of it contradicts Kant's account of the schematization of quality in the "Anticipations of Perception" section of the *Critique of Pure Reason*, though in no way is the objectless experience of similarities to be confused with mere sensation of the manifold. If "all objects of perception, insofar as they contain sensation, must be ascribed an intensive magnitude, i.e., a degree of influence on sense, i.e., a degree of influence on sense" (B 208), then homeotic experience has to be thought outside an "influence" theory of empirical consciousness. Unlike a sensation, a similarity is not "capable of a diminution, so that it can decrease and thus gradually disappear" (A 168, B 210). In Kantian perception, a color, say red, always has a degree $\neq$ 0, is infinitely (continuously) variable (A 174, B 216), and thus "reality in the appearance" (A 168, B 210) consists in intensities filling space that emanate or radiate, exciting more or less sensation in the subject or insofar as the objects are more and less "illuminated" (depending if you take this to be in the subject or in the object) (A 176, B 217). In homeotics, color is infinitely interesting, but not infinitely graded in degrees or intensities. Let color stand as the emblem of all experience. For homeotics, experience is certainly not of objects with

qualities dialed up or down in degrees; experience is simply not graded. In place of intensive magnitude, homeotics posits a discontinuity between a likeness that has fused out of an atmosphere and the confused vapor out of which it emerged. This means that time is no longer the guarantee of experience, but if there is time as succession, it is the result of certain patterns of likeness fusing out in one atmosphere or another.

11. In what he calls a "preliminary remark" to an extensively short and intensively long note from 1919, Walter Benjamin acknowledged this received fact. "Only substances can be similar in a real (nonmetaphorical) sense. The similarity of two triangles, for example, would have to show the similarity of some 'substance' within them whose manifestation would then be the identity [*Gleichheit*] (not similarity!) of certain relations they had in common" ("Analogy and Relationship," *Selected Writings, Volume 1*, p. 207). As his exclamation in the middle of the remark indicates, similarity conceived in this way is self-canceling. Two things that are similar are thought to share a substance, and if they share a substance, they are not similar, but identical, or instances of a universal.

12. Letting is involved in the happening of a likeness, as one of Edmund Jabès speakers notes: "To resemble . . . does not mean to become the other, but to let the other be you, to some extent" (vol. 2, p, 14).

13. Translations of Aristotle are mine, unless otherwise indicated.

14. A philological study of likeness terms in Plato and pre-Platonic Greek philosophy is Jenny Bryan's *Likeness and Likelihood in the Presocratics and Plato* (Cambridge: Cambridge University Press, 2012).

15. Semiotic theories of mind were prominent in philosophy from the late Middle Ages until the Cartesian variations overturned them and the likeness mind came back to the center of concern. By "Cartesian variations," I mean progressively expanding idealist and empiricist schemata, which took their departure from Descartes, who himself proves to be an interesting case. On one hand, Descartes denies likeness, and on the other hand, he continually reiterates it. The *Meditations* says repeatedly that the truth of a perception does not and cannot lie in its resemblance to things. The wording of the denial is interesting. "And the chief and most common mistake which is to be found here consists in my judging that the ideas which are in me resemble, or conform to, things located outside me" (*Meditations on First Philosophy*, p. 26; *Meditations de Prima Philosophia*, p. 37). This turns out to be not a critique of resemblance so much as a rejection of one source for experience; if experience proceeds from without ("extra me prositis"), it is prone to error. Note that "resemble" is made equivalent to "conform" — "similes . . . sive conformes" (*Meditations*

de Prima Philosophia, p. 37); in the French translation: "sont semblables, ou conformes" (*Meditations, Objections et Réponses*, p. 29). Note also that the French translation by Duc de Luynes (1647) renders "similes" as "semblables," which is to be sure a standard equivalent in seventeenth-century dictionaries, where it is not specified whether *semblable* should be associated with "being of the same nature," "sharing a quality," "equal," or "merely resembling."

To be able to reject entirely resemblance between things and ideas, Descartes introduces a causal theory of perception in the Sixth Meditation: "although I feel heat when I go near a fire and feel pain when I go too near, there is no convincing argument for supposing that there is something in the fire which resembles the heat, any more than for supposing that there is something which resembles the pain" (*Meditations on First Philosophy*, p. 57). A causal explanation for sensation is not liable to error in the same way, since with regard to pain and heat and the like, you no longer need to compare effect with cause; they are qualitatively distinct and incomparable. In contrast to the immediate experience of consciousness, resemblance provides only obscure data, "nihil nisi valde obscure & confuse" (*Meditations, Objections et Réponses*, p. 83). As far back as "The Treatise on Light," Descartes rejected the resemblance theory of sensation (p. 4), and yet, he never rejects resemblance altogether. After he rules out similitude between mental contents and bodies in the Third Meditation, he goes on to steal likeness from perception theory and use it to legitimize ideas: "although one idea may perhaps originate from another, there cannot be an infinite regress here; eventually one must reach a primary idea, the cause of which will be like [an 'image' or 'likeness,' Latin *instar*] an archetype which contains formally <and in fact> all the reality <or perfection> which is present only objectively <or representatively> in the idea" (*Meditations on First Philosophy*, p. 29; *Meditations de Prima Philosophia*, p. 42). To the rather sparse Latin original, the French translator saw fit to add the words "par representation" (p. 33): the primary idea will be "like in the manner of a representation." Perhaps this was added in order to clarify the phrase "comme un patron," like an exemplum or archetype. "Like an archetype"—the simile sets up a chain of likenesses that becomes a go-to figure in philosophical prose. Import the likeness power of art or language or technology, and you can describe mental things; at the same time, you can keep your distance from art or language or technology. The idea *is not* an archetype—it *is like* an archetype. And what is likeness? The soul is given an impossible command: to access the power of patterning without succumbing to its "obscurities," and for this reason, primary ideas must be merely "like" likenesses and not actually likenesses.

Is a second degree of likeness, then, closer to the truth? What is it like to be like a likeness? Would we want to make the fairly precarious argument that because truth is only like likeness, therefore it can keep its distance from it? Despite a strong critique on one side and a distancing gesture on the other, in his theory of ideas, Descartes makes a decided turn toward the homeotic mind, and this turn has a legacy.

Cartesian variation A: John Locke. Ideas begin their life at the senses, which "convey into the mind several distinct perceptions of things" (*An Essay Concerning Human Understanding*, pp. 109–10). So says Locke in book 2. Though a metaphor of locomotion takes over here, what is "conveyed" through the senses, the essential attributes of things (Locke calls things "bodies"), which famously get the name "primary qualities," are in fact "resemblances" of bodies (§ 15, p. 136). The motion metaphor and the likeness nonmetaphor cannot be reconciled. Physical bodies move; resemblances — resemble. Despite the crossed metaphors, whereas Descartes tries to limit the scope of likeness — ideas are like their sources in one way — for Locke, ideas are, in addition, like to bodies. "Conveyance" plays on the physicalist semantics of the "per" in perception, but in fact opens a multivectoral resemblance, body to percept, percept to idea. A line is drawn, a chain of transparent mirrors lines up.

And although it might seem counterintuitive, given the pains Locke takes to distinguish secondary from primary qualities, secondary qualities also belong to resemblance. At first glance, secondary qualities cannot be like anything. The most common example is color — color is secondary because it resembles nothing in bodies; that is, it is purely mental, or so Locke argued, and in this way, color lacks one of the vectors of likeness: no body is actually like it, only mind is. Although we are talking about a negative, the missing vector of likeness, this lack nevertheless inaugurates a positive and very stubborn habit in European philosophy, in the Cartesian variants as much as in Descartes himself, a habit of judging the truth of cognition by the strength of the resemblance present. When Locke denies resemblance to color, he instaurates resemblance as a sine qua non of truth. Secondary qualities are not a matter of truth because nothing can be picked out that they resemble, or at least nothing external to mind.

Cartesian variation B: Bishop Berkeley. Philonous's famous rhetorical question in Berkeley's *Three Dialogues* sums up the repositioning: "Can anything be like a sensation or idea, but another sensation or idea?" Subjective idealism continues the habit of balancing truth on resemblance, although the habit is complicated in the new framework insofar as resemblance is now internal to the ideal. This homeotic wave reaches a crest in Hume, who to all intents and purposes avoids the question of bodies and concentrates wholeheartedly on the inner dynamics among likenesses. Perhaps he does believe, as some interpreters think, that bodies are ultimately the source for mental resemblances; his tendency is still by and large not to say anything on the matter.

16. "Resemblance, then, is perhaps the most crucial concept upon which Humean associationism rests." Don Ross writes this in a summary of the mechanisms of mind and the philosophical innovations that make them thinkable in book 1 of the *Treatise*. Don Ross, "Hume, Resemblance and the Foundations of Psychology," *History of Philosophy Quarterly* 8. 4 (October 1991), pp. 343–56.

17. A detailed survey of Hume's theory of mind can be found in Oliver A. Johnson, *The Mind of David Hume: A Companion to Book I of A Treatise of Human Nature* (Urbana: University of Illinois Press, 1995).

18. A thorough study of causality in Hume, taking up both the traditional interpretation of him as a version of a realist and the more radical skeptical interpretations while returning to Hume to reconstruct his arguments, is Helen Beebee's *Hume on Causation* (London: Routledge, 2006). On the role of resemblance in causality as Beebee sees it, see especially section 3.5, "The Uniformity Principle" (pp. 50–56).

19. What about surnature, what of the first and the highest things? The real game begins here. On *eikasia* and other likeness words and effects, Plato has a lot to say, as do Plotinus, Proclus, and Ficino, as well. One might well think that with the fortunes of likeness go the fortunes of "Platonism." The fortunes of justice swing with *eikasia* and *mimesis* in *The Republic*; Plato's ontology swings with "the likeness regress" in the *Parmenides*; the possibility of philosophy swings with the philosopher's shadowy double in *The Sophist*. Diotima builds a ladder through *eidola* of virtue to the original of virtue (212a) in her speech in *The Symposium*. Socrates, she says, has the most images, *agalmata*, of virtue in his speeches (222a). Organizing this multiplicity of Attic words and effects — *eikasia, mimesis, eidolon, agalma* — is the question of being, to be sure, as Heidegger proposed, though the concern that shimmers in them is not with being per se, but rather with the "being of the beautiful, as Seth Benardete liked to call it, or you could call it "the good" — or "likeness." Plato is often caught up in the task of distinguishing among likeness effects and searching for a center from which to manage them.

Which effects have to do with "picturing" higher things, offering a "route" to being, and which have to do with degraded processes of copying that lead spectators astray? Which among these words and effects stretches the bond between ideas and phenomena to its breaking point, and which allow ideas to shine brightly through phenomena? Among the words and effects, *mimesis, eikasia, eidola, homeosis,* one stands out as troublesome, infectious, and perhaps also somewhat unsafe.

A few remarks on likeness effects in Plato. Among the effects named with a variety of Attic words, which can be rendered, generally and nontechnically, across these dialogues, using English words such as "image," "appearance," "semblance," "imitation," "phantom," "portrait," "copy," and others (the subtle varieties of word and sense deserve careful philological treatment in their original scenes), the word *homoios* hovers in the background. *Homoios* is often used to explain the other effects, and it is just as often itself left unexplained or left out altogether, though it is often implied. *Mimesis* and morphically related words carry many senses in the *Republic*; the lexical field of *mime-* bears witness to different processes and relations in a multiplicity of scenes in the dialogues. Mimesis words gesture toward—copying a model (tracing out? sculpting?) . . . stamping a plate (inversion of an image, flattening) . . . imitating a good action (think of the desire and Eros involved in this) . . . dumbly mimicking (think of the mindlessness involved in this; derision follows) . . . representing in the sense of letting a truth shine through a medium (acknowledgement that you see the truth and can't touch it, and you may not see where it comes from) . . . representing in the sense of standing in for an absent thing and deriving power to act in its place . . . copycatting in the sense of incorporating a foreign thing into you . . . being similar such that two things derive their qualities from a third, common, higher thing . . . being "like" in an as yet mysterious sense, having to do with a nonessential sharing . . . looking like, indicating an essential difference, but nonetheless at the same time a coming together or bringing near of far things . . . being like—a way for something to be anything—it can be *X* possibly because it is so very close to *X* in certain respects.

20. A memory of this is printed in our copies of Genesis, where two famous likeness effects assist in the creation of Adam: *kidmutenu besalmenu* (Genesis 1:26). *Demuth,* the first word and effect, seems to signify similitude of external appearance without a discernible ontological hierarchy, something like a double or twin. *Tselem,* the second word and effect, may imply a secondary, derivative mode of being, something like an idol (see Numbers 33:52, among other passages). Adam's being, we learn, is to be like, and he is like in two distinct ways. On one hand, he is a mirror of the external appearance of god, a twin to the divine; on the other hand, he is a vacant shell, a surface resemblance with no follow through, an idol under a monotheistic regime. One thing is clear, for the first human being and all who follow: they will not only be like themselves, but they will carry

on the troublesome double likenesses, one empty, the other full, one direct, the other indirect — if we can read them that way — to god.

21. That a thing is a plenum of likenesses contradicts Kant's highest requirement for human experience in the "Axioms of Intuition" section of the *Critique of Pure Reason*, that "the conditions of the possibility of experience in general are at the same time conditions of the possibility of the objects of experience" (A 158, B 197), where "the objects of experience" are supposed to be spatiotemporal things, that is, extensive magnitudes, wholes of parts, and ultimately autohomogenous units, each of which is quantitatively one and open to measurement and whose pure forms are geometric figures (though only bounded ones).

22. Keep in mind Wittgenstein's distinction in *Philosophical Investigations*, § 66, between having something "in common" and the "whole series" of "similarities, affinities" that "crop up and disappear." On family resemblances, see *Philosophical Investigations*, §§ 65, 66, 72, 78, 79.

23. Hear Wittgenstein yawp: "don't think, but look!" "denk nicht, sondern schau!" (*Philosophical Investigations*, § 66). In these fragments, he attempts a reduction to resemblance, and does so, first of all, by bracketing the understanding. "Look, for example, at board-games, with their various affinities [*Verwandtschaften*]. Now pass to card-games; here you find many correspondences [*Entsprechungen*] with the first group, but many common features [*gemeinsame Züge*] drop out, and others appear . . . . And we can go through the many, many other groups of games in the same way, can see how similarities [*Ähnlichkeiten*] crop up and disappear" (§ 66). What is first a pair becomes a group, then a chain; family relations, *Verwandtschaften*, become *Ähnlichkeiten*. Games, *Spiele*, express themselves in *Charakterzüge*, character traits.

24. On the challenge to "the thing," Edmond Jabès got there before us and left us a note: "Everything is out of phase where likeness emerges. Being is not being, things are not things." *The Book of Resemblances*, vol. 1, p. 78.

25. Franz Brentano's late ontology explores the fundamental self-likeness of things. See *Philosophical Investigations on Space, Time, and the Continuum*, trans. Barry Smith (London: Croom Helm, 1988), ch. 1, "On What is Continuous," pp. 1–30.

26. Cohen is doubtless thinking of Kant, who does not mince words: "Alle Anschauungen sind extensive Grössen" (*Kritik der reinen Vernunft*, B 202). "All intuitions are extensive magnitudes" (*The Critique of Pure Reason*, B 202). This proposition about experienceable things, the principle underlying the Axioms of Intuition, makes experience depend on the internal *Gleichartigkeit* of objects, their homogeneity with themselves that makes up their

"extension." No experience without space, no appearance in space without magnitude, no magnitude without inner *Gleichartigkeit*, autohomogeneity. In the list of types of conjunction (*Verbindung, conjunctio*) that follows the statement of this principle, Kant distinguishes between the more and less homogeneous ones. He lights on the Latin word "nexus," rendered in German by "Verknüpfung." A nexus holds its parts together by more than mere contingency. In order to visualize this, Kant gives an example of two triangles—the triangles formed by drawing a diagonal across a square. The two triangles do not belong to one another by necessity, unlike the zones of the square divided by the diagonal, which do belong to the square by necessity. These triangles are *ungleichartig*, whereas the square underlying them is *gleichartig*.

To explain this, Kant falls back on a type of attraction among the regions within the square to one another that allows the thing to be itself, to be more than a loose affiliation of regions, to be one, that is, homogeneous. In order to construct an individual thing, Kant goes far in claiming that, on analogy with quantity, the fabric of extension made up of infinitely many *Gleichnisse* adds up to an individual thing—not parts making up a whole. Sectors of extended things are a priori *verbunden* (B 148), and to explain this type of interconnection, he introduces a homeotic relation—homogeneity, which distinguishes itself from identity. What's more, the homeotic relation underlying magnitude goes beyond individual things to any extent of space and time and beyond that to the form of space and time themselves (B 149). Space and time, following Newton, exhibit homogeneity in every respect, which is to say that they exhibit perfect likeness among all sectors.

27 . Space is considered to be, quoting Eckart Förster in *The Twenty-Five Years of Philosophy: A Systematic Reconstruction*, trans. Brady Bowman (Cambridge, MA: Harvard University Press, 2012) "the possible orderings of the material received by sensibility" (p. 11). This is Förster's concise summary of the meaning of space in Kant's *Inaugural Dissertation*, a crucial step on the path to space as a form of intuition that it becomes in the *Critique of Pure Reason*.

28. Klaus Taschwer gives persuasive evidence that the results of the midwife toad experiments were in fact manipulated, but not by Kammerer himself, in the only thorough study of Kammerer's life and quirks, *Der Fall Paul Kammerer: Das abenteurliche Leben des umstrittensten Biologen seiner Zeit* (Munich: Hanser, 2016). Building on Taschwer's account with his own careful reading of Kammerer's *Das Gesetz der Serie*, Kirk Wetters compares Kammerer to Thomas Kuhn and ascribes them both to a genus he calls "systematizers of anomalies," which itself is a paradigm-shifting description of the modern scientist. Kirk

Wetters, "The Law of the Series and the Crux of Causation: Paul Kammerer's Anomalies," *MLN*, 134. 3 (April 2019), pp. 643–60.

29. "The Aristotelian teaching of causes lasted in the official Western culture until the Renaissance. When modern science was born, formal and final causes were left aside as standing beyond the reach of experiment; and material causes were taken for granted in connection with all natural happenings though with a definitely non-Aristotelian meaning, since in the modern world view matter is essentially the subject of change, not 'that out of which a thing comes to be and which persists.' Hence, of the four Aristotelian causes only the efficient cause was regarded as worthy of scientific research." Mario Bunge, *Causality and Modern Science*, 4th rev. ed. (New Brunswick: Transaction Books, 2009), p. 32.

30. Before there was art, as Hans Belting put it, there were icons, which were images in the sense that they acted as "surrogates for what they represent." For this view of the image, see Belting, *Likeness and Presence: A History of the Image before the Era of Art* (Chicago: University of Chicago Press, 1994). Likeness takes a back seat to surrogacy, with all its theological powers and dangers.

31. What happens to likeness as a force to contend with in Plato's writings? For Plato at certain moments, mimesis is an effect of likeness, or rather, likeness contributes to mimesis's force — or likeness is really an act of mimetizing. "'But making yourself like someone else [*to homoioun heauton allo*] — either in the way you speak or in the way you look — isn't that imitating [*mimesthai*] the person you make yourself like?'" (*The Republic*, 3.393c, translation modified). This passage ups the ante on a phrase in common Attic speech, "to homoioun heauton allo," "making yourself like another," by making it into a technical procedure, mimetizing, *mimesthai*. Instead of let's say, joining up with the other in likeness, it becomes, with this important sentence, being in imitation of the other and so at a distance ontologically. Socrates sets the two words against one another here, "mimesis" against "likeness," in a way that echoes through political theory as well as art theory, not to mention metaphysics. When we talk about likenesses among *anthropoi*, we are really talking about imitating a being, Plato tells us, an act that implies not only that we are like them, but that we may *be* them, although this is deception. *Mimesthai* claims victory over *homoioun* at this juncture by swallowing it whole. This makes sense, since because likeness is not a gateway to being, and yet it comes up again and again in ontological discourse, it must be modified, removed, superseded, incorporated, digested, included in a higher, more organized, more ontological figure. Likeness making gets renamed "imitating" — that is to say, made philosophical, made more than its own mere self. Or else how would dreamers tell they were dreaming?

"Think about it," Socrates admonishes Glaucon in *The Republic*, book 5. "Isn't dreaming like this? Suppose one thing, A, resembles another thing, B. Isn't dreaming the state, whether in sleep or waking, of thinking not that A resembles B, but that A is B?" (5.476c). Let us think this later statement through with Socrates—"Think about it," he says. Socrates tells us that they are dreaming who take a likeness for a being. How we can know that a likeness is not a being, however, is an ongoing problem in the so-called late dialogues. This problem aside, before even dividing good from bad mimeses, Socrates feels, for whatever reason, that he can critique the poets and control the moral ideals of the polis only after substituting *mimesthai* for *homoioun*. That likeness does not allow these kinds of distinctions, for Plato, is one conclusion to be drawn.

No doubt this intuition, not about the dangers of mimesis, but about the ungovernability of homeosis, precedes Plato, and Socrates's rejoinder in the *Parmenides* is also a response to an ambiguous inheritance. Plato's dialogue *Parmenides* inherits and reformulates aspects of the problematic laid out in Parmenides's philosophical poem. Doesn't Parmenides's poem say there cannot be nonbeing, and, further, being is different from difference? Plato takes up this problematic again and again. How is the paradox of negating negation and differing from difference solved, or at least set aside in Parmenides's poem? Look again: likeness does it. The poem argues: "there is no difference, since all is alike [*pan estin homoion*]" (fragment 8, line 20). Here is one heirloom phrase that Plato had to contend with when he put on the Parmenidean hand-me-down. Where there shall be no difference, no negativity, on the way to a uniform totality, the All is said to be like. If you want to introduce difference back into the All and techniques for working with difference back into philosophy, as Plato and subsequently Aristotle try to do, this use of likeness, to homogenize and exclude negation without paradox, needs to be superseded. The need to supersede likeness is at work in the *Parmenides*.

If we summarize, Plato's three concerns about mimesis are its potential multiplicity, the low degree of reality it unleashes into the polis, and its political effects. Mimetic effects are so central to Plato's theoretical project that his student could not help pose the question sometime after his death: Is mimesis primary or secondary, original or derivative? Aristotle's answer: mimesis is ontologically derivative and epistemically primary. Unlike homeosis, mimetic techniques are primary for access to what is. In the *Poetics*, mimesis takes the place of thought. If thought is being's access point in theoretical metaphysics, tragic mimesis is the access point in literary theory. How does this work? "Through contemplating [images] it comes about that [people] infer and understand what each element means," for instance, and most importantly, that "this is that" (*Poetics* 1448b14–15).

32. The treatise that deals with the oneness of the One most directly is 6.9 (*Enneads*, MacKenna trans., pp. 614–25). A good explanation of the reasoning in this section is given by Eyjólfur K. Emilsson in *Plotinus* (London: Routledge, 2017), ch. 3, "The One and the Genesis of the Intellect." See especially pp. 71–75.

33. Do not imagine that transparency is anything like identity, and yet it is also not difference. Edmond Jabès again is at the crest of the wave. One of his voices enunciates: "'No two transparent works will ever be alike,' he also said. 'And yet, what is a drop of water like if not another drop?'" *The Book of Resemblances*, vol. 3, p. 80.

34. No doubt our world is networky, or at the very least we believe strongly in the metaphor of the net and its work, permeating as it does our technical language and scientific fantasies. We are quick to accept this image of the interrelatedness of things. Plotinus's cosmos is at once more fractured and more fused. One could wager that the term "network" is better than the concept of relation for recent phenomena, because it replaces the intuition of a link between individuals with the intuition of an interconnection among groups. More accurately, "network" generalizes the "link" between two individuals into a linking among all individuals. Asymmetrically distributing, reciprocal and reconfigurable, a network nonetheless maintains one aspect of relation. Its interconnections are still between individuals, and its nodes are ontologically distinct. Inspect the work of the network: its fine filigree interlaces multiple paths to and from independent nodes and still keeps those nodes separate. The work done by the "net" metaphor is to provide a place to house complexity for an ontology unwilling to give up on self-sufficient and essentially simple points.

35. Foucault's assertion in *The Order of Things* that the premodern period was categorized by a "taxonomic function" that organized phenomena into grids on the ordering principle of "adjacency" (pp. 107, 121) cannot be explained solely as the result of the belief in "visible resemblance" (p. 121), since resemblance between adjacents collapses adjacency into overlap and diaphany. Michel Foucault, *The Order of Things: An Archaeology of the Human Sciences* (London: Routledge, 1989).

36. Art theorists sometimes call this a "multistable image," although it is hard to think of any image that isn't multistable, given that at a minimum, any figure has to emerge from a ground, and any figure / ground or picture has to emerge from its material support in the very same way that this face emerges from a rock and the face / rock from the photograph. Canvas / picture, shadow / figure, sky / cloud / shape, my face / my parents' faces / my

ancestors' faces—it is difficult to think of an image that is not multistable, and variously so. This may be what it means to be an image. An image consists in its irresolvability into multiple distinct figures. The "rock-face" is evidently dual, and it doesn't take much to "see" at the same time the photograph qua photograph, giving us a "photo-rock-face," and so on, then a "page-photo-rock-face," and so on, until we recognize that the world is multistable, its local emphases and overlays transparent, so that multistability is not a special case, but a general fact of the world and its self-experience and that it is not multistable, but multiunstable, and not perceptual, but homeotic.

37. On photography as a medium for likenesses, Kaja Silverman has given us *The Miracle of Analogy; or The History of Photography, Part 1* (Stanford, CA: Stanford University Press, 2015). Silverman sees photographs as revealers of "similarities" and similarities as structuring being, thus mixing several registers—phenomenological, ontological, and homeotic—that I think are best kept separate for the sake of analysis. Photography, she tells us in the introduction, "is the world's primary way of revealing itself to us—of demonstrating that it exists, and that it will forever exceed us. Photography is also an ontological calling card: it helps us to see that each of us is a node in a vast constellation of analogies. When I say 'analogy,' I do not mean sameness, symbolic equivalence, logical adequation, or even a rhetorical relationship—like a metaphor or a simile—in which one term functions as the provisional placeholder for another. I am talking about the authorless and untranscendable similarities that structure Being, or what I will be calling 'the world,' and that give everything the same ontological weight" (pp. 10–11). The equalizing force of likeness is beautifully described here.

38. When does an atmosphere yield likenesses, and when does it absorb them back again into the general confusion? What allows or incites a fusion out of a jumble or out of an all too familiar and faded pattern—a scarred cliff face, a brace of ducks? What makes a vicinity a vicinity and a pattern a pattern? This was once a question for Gestalt theory, a specific subdiscipline of empirical psychology with strong philosophical implications. In the 1890 essay credited with inaugurating the subdiscipline, "On 'Gestalt Qualities'," what Christian von Ehrenfels calls "background" and compares with "determinate Gestalten" and also "Gestalt-qualities," which "step forward" and "stand out noticeably from their surroundings" ("On 'Gestalt Qualities'," p. 113) soon after take shape as the famous pair figure and ground. How do figure and ground differ from likeness and atmosphere? It is perfectly plausible to say that the face in the rock in Jastrow's example is a figure and that it "steps forward" from the ground, which must consist of all the nonfigures that surround

it. Ehrenfels's examples are instructive. A square "projects from its background in virtue of its distinct colouring" (p. 113). But what makes its coloring distinct? What is the content of distinctness such that a range of gray shades, let's say, are not considered distinct in the same way as the white square upon them? Ehrenfels takes this "distinctness" to be a prima facie feature of the figure that is "upon." His example is a white square against a black background, which steps forth, as he says. What makes the square step forth and the background remain in place? Because it is distinct. Yet by this criterion alone we cannot rightly say that the figure steps forward. A new confusion, which turns the celebration of a distinct Gestalt into a caution: How is a Gestalt singled out? Ehrenfels gives an equivocal answer when he says the figure steps forward. This is because the background also steps forward at the same moment, steps forward as the background. Is "backgroundness" then emphasized in the same gesture, in the same way? We can easily imagine a scenario in which the white square was not picked out, but the larger black square was, with an unfortunate square white hole in the middle.

There is another problem, which comes up in his discussion of art, specifically of painting. Someone sees a painting. Their imagination is active in construing the Gestalt painted there; in the first viewing, a process of scanning, aggregating, "figuring" takes place — "A significant exercise of our capacities is required in order to utilize in our presentation the slight distinctions in light and colour and the foreshortenings in the perspective plane as associative tokens enabling the realization of the total luminosity and three-dimensionality of the painting" (pp. 111–12). After this, however, the same "significant exercise of our capacities" is not needed again. Once we have construed or constructed the figure, it is, as it were, "given" on all subsequent viewings. And yet we have all experienced what it is like when someone with greater construing powers, a teacher or connoisseur or even the artist themselves, with a single word or gesture, makes other figures or a more unified figure step forward in a painting. Our first unification of the figure changes, even disappears, and is extended or replaced by a new one. Still, Ehrenfels would say, the second time we view the painting, we need no teacher, we simply "see" the new, more complex unified figure that was pointed out to us previously. His emphasis on the second time is a clue to the homeotic substrate with which he is tacitly working. In the second go-round, the second scan, one is able to receive the first scan bleeding through, and then there is a figure, and then there is a ground, stepping forward-backward.

39. A peculiar aspect of the duckrabbit figure is that it contains its own atmosphere. The lighting up of rabbit and duck likenesses feeds back into the figure, so that contrary

to what Wittgenstein believes, both figures are in force at once, in their overlaps, as atmospheres for one another. It is easy to read this composite as a pictorial presentation of evolution's basic intuition that the common ancestor is in all organisms as all organisms were in the common ancestor. This is not all. Neither the psychology of perception nor Wittgenstein's game theory accounts for the relation of this peculiar auto atmosphere to the explosion of likenesses — ducks, rabbits, ears, bills, eyes, fur, feathers — that inaugurated the confusion to begin with. Among the huge stock of traits in the world, natural and artistic, a rabbitduck should not be a surprise. Once you accept this, you can see world-bearing stones and humanoid asteroids, Jesus in a pancake. A rabbit itself was once an unthinkable combination of traits, from the perspective of the last nonrabbit ancestor. A rabbit was once as marvelous as a hippogriff or a gorgon. The pattern "rabbit" became established when the interferences stabilized, and the sutures vanished.

40. At one point in the mid-1920s, Walter Benjamin thought the opposite. "All form, every outline that man perceives, corresponds to something in him that enables him to reproduce it. The body imitates itself in the form of dance, the hand imitates and appropriates it through drawing. But this ability finds its limit in the world of color" ("The World of Children's Books," *Selected Writings, Volume 1*, p. 442). This passage, a repetition and extension of some thoughts Benjamin made a decade earlier on color in dreams and in children's art, supports a set of associations: between form, in the sense of outline, and mimesis, in the sense of ontological reproduction whose expression is the imagination, and between color and freedom whose expression is fantasy. Fantasy freedom is a receptive, not a productive freedom. "This ability finds its limits in the world of color. The human body cannot produce color. It relates to it not creatively but receptively: through the shimmering colors of vision" (p. 442). Free to take on the colors of the world in infinite variety, the child is not limited by outlines to producing imitations of objects.

There is a lot to agree with in this schema, especially the conclusion, a response to the "Supplement" to Goethe's *Theory of Color* in which Goethe discusses "transparent color." Benjamin responds affirmatively to Goethe: "Just think of the many games that are concerned with pure imaginative contemplation: soap bubbles, parlor games, the watery color of the magic lantern, water coloring, decals. In all of these, the color seems to hover suspended above the objects. Their magic lies not in the colored object or in the mere dead color, but in the colored glow, the colored brilliance, the ray of colored light" (p. 443). Color "suspended above the objects" no doubt does draw a limit to mimesis, which sees color in service to the presentation of objects qua objects. Yet color should not be limited by the need to liberate art and dreams from mimesis. Just as there is "opaque color" and "transparent color," in Goethe's estimation, which correspond to "coloring of objects" and "color above objects," in Benjamin's thinking, there is also the question, what color? Color is separable, in a pictorial plane, from the objects it constitutes — not contained by their outlines (though these are also a matter of color, ultimately). Color and its difference allows shapes to be outlined (through contrast), and it produces as well what Benjamin calls "glow," "brilliance," and "ray." Benjamin conjures a landscape in which "the eyes and cheeks of children poring over books are reflected in the glory of the sunset" (p. 443) or where colors make up something like a pure atmosphere in which likeness circuits of all kinds may fuse. Likeness, too, exceeds morphology and in this way leans toward color. Morphology misrecognizes likeness as a matter of outline, limits it to mimesis. Color is the limit of mimesis, Benjamin notes. And yet color is the perfect example of a field that is merely and fully like and only like, where everything is like everything else, sharing now more and now fewer aspects. What is a "scale" or a continuum of frequencies or a "palette," if not exactly this? Benjamin thought early on that color is a zone of free difference that is not the distinction between objects. It remains to say how the appearance of pure difference in the color palette can be redescribed homeotically.

41. Do not confuse the *sem* in "semiosis" with the *sem* in "resemblance." The *sem* in "resemblance" (corresponding to *sam*, *same*, *homo*, the *sem* in "as*sem*ble") should be distinguished from two morphemes that resemble it: the *sem* in "disseminate" (Latin *semen*, seed) the *sem* in "semiotic" (Greek *sema*, *semaino*: sign, token; signal, signify).

42. On the development of Arcimboldo as an artist, see Thomas Dacosta Kaufmann, *Arcimboldo: Visual Jokes, Natural History, and Still Life Painting* (Chicago: University of Chicago Press, 2009), pp. 26–36.

43. For descriptions of the overlaps among art studios and laboratories, see the Introduction by the editor, Sven Dupré, to *Laboratories of Art: Alchemy and Art Technology from Antiquity to the 18th Century* (Cham: Springer, 2014), pp. viii–xix.

44. Kaufmann, *Arcimboldo*, pp. 140–41.

45. "Arcimboldo, or Magician and Rhétoriquer," Roland Barthes's 1978 article on the artist, (in *The Responsibility of Forms: Critical Essays on Music, Art, and Representation*, trans. Richard Howard [New York: Hill and Wang, 1985]) implies that a decision on Arcimboldo's artistic métier has to be made. Either it is magic, or it is rhetoric. Barthes decides for the latter, though he can't discount the former. He divides the rhetorical effects of

Arcimboldo's "heads," at first, into metaphor and metonymy (see p. 129, or p. 132: "Everything is elaborated within the field of commonplace metonymies"). Rhetorical units give way to other "'curiosities' of language" (p. 131), such as synonymy and homonymy. Barthes points out that in the painting *Autumn*, a prune stands in for an eye, on analogy with the French fruit word "prunella," which easily recalls "prunelle," eyeball (p. 130). Barthes is convinced that Arcimboldo's "composite heads" have the structure of language, language thought of semiotically. "Arcimboldo imposes a system of substitution (an apple comes to stand for a cheek, as in a coded message; a letter or a syllable comes to mask another letter or another syllable), and in the same way, a system of transposition (the whole figure is somehow drawn back toward the detail)" (p. 137). This is a seductive and understandable conclusion. The picture can't be what it is, and the name for this nonbeing is semiosis.

What Barthes says next opens this conclusion to doubt. He identifies Arcimboldo's "peculiarity" in a semiotic field. "However, and this is Arcimboldo's peculiarity, what is remarkable about the composite heads is that the picture hesitates between coding and decoding: even when we have displaced the screen of substitution and of transposition in order to perceive the head composed as an effect, our eyes retain the tracery of the first meanings which have served to produce this effect" (p. 137). The hesitation between coding and decoding, the head's existence "as an effect," makes this art hesitate in a peculiar manner between signification and something else, that thing we experience when "our eyes retain the tracery," which indicates the limits of signification.

Whereas homeosis in syntax takes the form of the like, the *wie*, the *comme*, the ὡς, in rhetoric, it may well take the form of a synonym. In this oeuvre, "the synonyms are unremittingly flung on the canvas" (p. 140). No need to look to Arcimboldo—homeosis is at work in the semiologist's own procedure. Barthes types out a metaphor—synonyms "flung"—to bring into the closest proximity a painting act in the studio and a language act in the writing room. Needless to say, the proximity of his language and Arcimboldo's art is accomplished through making a resemblance. No doubt a kinship is forming in this essay, an affinity being spelled out among critic and painter. The extent of Barthes's hidden homeotics is expressed in this key passage on the stuff in Arcimboldo's paintings:

> these different objects have shapes in common: they are fragments of substance singled out, made equal, and arranged—pigeonholed—in the same line: the nose resembles an ear of corn by its oblong and swelling shape; the fleshy mouth looks like a split fig whose whitish interior illuminates the red notch of the pulp. Yet, even

when analogical, the Arcimboldesque metaphor is, so to speak, one-way: Arcimboldo persuades us that the nose naturally resembles an ear of corn, that the teeth naturally resemble seeds, that the flesh of fruit naturally resembles that of the lips: but no one would say the contrary naturally: the ear of corn is not a nose, the seeds are not teeth, the fig is not a mouth (unless it is mediated by another organ, this one female, as is attested by a folk metaphor which we find in many languages). (p. 138)

Barthes has an intuition: these paintings show an unprecedented expansion in the consciousness of likeness. In addition to painting, Arcimboldo designed theatrical props, sets, decorations, floats and sets and costumes for tournaments, imperial celebrations; he lived at court infused with the triune emanations of natural science, alchemy, and magic; he combined the copying of nature with the intuition of "surprising," as Barthes puts it, homeotic connections between the ontologically unrelated. Semiology's substitutive logic fails to describe the "magic" of the paintings. These are neither pictures nor signs.

46. An overview of the history of the Gestalt idea is given by Johan Wagemans in "Historical and Conceptual Background: Gestalt Theory," in *The Oxford Handbook of Perceptual Organization* (Oxford: Oxford University Press, 2015), pp. 3–20.

47. This vase figure and the discourse of "figure and ground" were invented in the doctoral dissertation of Danish psychologist Edgar Rubin. The book developed out of his thesis, *Synsoplevede Figurer: Studier i psykologisk Analyse* (København og Kristiania: Gyldendal, Nordisk forlag, 1915), proved important for early Gestalt theorists, such as Kurt Koffka.

48. Ernst Mach makes a similar point in *The Analysis of Sensations and the Relation of the Physical to the Psychical*, trans. C. M. Williams (La Salle: Open Court, 1984), p. 343.

49. On Proclus's philosophizing through commentary, see Anne Sheppard. "Proclus as Exegete," in Stephen Gersh (ed.), *Interpreting Proclus: From Antiquity to the Renaissance* (Cambridge: Cambridge University Press, 2014), pp. 57–79.

50. Harold Tarrant, "Proclus' Place in the Platonic Tradition," in Pieter D'Hoine and Marije Martijn (eds.), *All from One: A Guide to Proclus* (Oxford: Oxford University Press, 2017), pp. 35–36.

51. See the chart in "Appendix I" of D'Hoine and Marije Martijn, *All from One*, pp. 323–28.

52. Let $\eqsim$ mean "like." Following classical logic, we would say that where $B \eqsim A$ and $C \eqsim B$, $C \eqsim A$ (Call this Formula 1, a logic of equivalence). The underlying principle here is

transitivity. *A* and *C* relate to one another through *B*; the truth of one relation transits to the other. This is true only under a logic of equivalence. Can a logic with an equivalence principle be valid for likenesses? The answer is probably no, due to the inherent asymmetry of likeness. For one thing, there is no reason to believe that *C* is like *B* in the same way that *A* is like *B*. There is no requirement that the two likenesses be equivalent. We could say, in fact, that the meaning of "like" in the first relation and the meaning of "like" in the second relation are not the same. Because the meaning of "like" depends on the contents of a likeness, at best, the two instances are approximations; at worst, they are quite unlike one another.

This leads to another displacement or asymmetry that would have to operate within a likeness logic. The movement of the logic would likely produce an effect on the logical operator itself. Truth might move reliably through the equations $B \doteqdot A$, $C \doteqdot B$, $C \doteqdot A$, and yet the meaning of truth would have to shift, insofar as *C*'s being like *A* is not true outside of the proposition *B* is like *A*, and yet the truth of $B \doteqdot A$ is not the same truth of $C \doteqdot B$, even if some traits remain similar. $C \doteqdot A$ is an echo of $B \doteqdot A$, a variation, a divergence and a convergence. This rolling vergence can be noted in the order of statements. Only once *B* likens *A* can *C*, through *B*, liken *A*. In likeness logic, there is no independence, such that *B* and *C* could be accidentally or essentially alike outside of *B*'s reflection of *A*. It cannot even be asserted that *B* stands in the middle of *A* and *C*. *B* in the middle faces *A* in one way and *C* in another way. A short way to say this is that across this proposition, $\doteqdot \neq \doteqdot$, or there is transitivity among terms, but not among operators, and this is a grave problem. Transitivity requires that although the variables differ, the operations are identical each time a formula is written. We state this thus for equality statements: $\equiv \, = \, \equiv$, equivalence is exactly equal to equivalence. For likeness logic, however, $\doteqdot \neq \equiv$, likeness 1 is unlike equivalence.

Better, then, would be to write it with shifting operators: $B \doteqdot A$, $C \rightleftharpoons B$, $C \approx A$, ... (Formula 2, nonequivalent logic) — so long as the ellipsis does not imply continuation in the same way, but only in a qualitatively approximate way. Or the likeness formula could also be written like this: $[(B_1A)_2C_3B]_4C_5A]$ (Formula 3, clinic logic, intersection of clines). The latter, I believe, is closest to what Proclus intends: the cline is not linear, but subsumptive and encompassing, spiral, perhaps, or growing into a strange crystal formation. You can see in this formula that the operator, likeness, has itself become a variable, and the compound variation is what produces asymmetry on a large scale.

Something that Freud says about the logic of dreams applies here. Likeness knows negativity, but it does not know contradiction. In dreams, repressed material wants to be expressed, not held back, and so anything that appears as contradiction is really a distorted expression of a positive association. In the homeoplex, there can be no contradiction, because there is no real or logical symmetry.

53. The difficulties Hegel finds in the nature and reciprocal relationship of likeness and unlikeness don't afflict Proclus as such. In the greater *Logic*, Hegel identifies likeness and unlikeness with an "external," in his sense of the word, thus trivial and fleeting version of identity and difference, corresponding to mere diversity [*Verschiedenheit*], rather than true identity and true difference in and for themselves (*Wissenschaft der Logic*), Bd II, pp. 49–52. Partial, misleading, and of course also a necessary stage in the logic's development, likeness and unlikeness are external to a being and they also behave as external to one another, and as a result they turn into one another continually. Looked at one way, likeness actually is unlikeness. Looked at another way, unlikeness actually is likeness. Thus likeness and unlikeness meet their fate in his science, as he goes on to say, "But through this, their separation from one another, they sublate themselves" (p. 50), that is, they transmute into something higher. They are in fact "determinations of difference [*Bestimmungen des Unterschiedes*]" (50). What he means by this, I think, is twofold. First, he implies more than says that like and unlike are both ways to say "different," and interestingly not, for that matter, "same." As ways to say "different" they lack a strong enough or delimiting enough negativity to maintain their own difference. This weakness leads to his second meaning. Like and unlike are determinations of difference in the way they relate to one another. They claim to be different each from each — like, unlike — but their difference cannot maintain itself. They are not different enough to maintain the distinction. In other words, they are more like than unlike, which in his system means the logical architecture cannot be generated out of them. So much the worse for the system. In contrast, "difference" is different enough from "identity" to keep it in business. Different but not different enough. Hegel smells the affirmative perfume of likeness here, although by his own method he is forced to cast even that in negative terms. He labels the two, ultimately, indifferent, their mutual likeness amounting to a kind of inappropriate equivalence, *Gleichheit*, as concepts, as phenomena, which results in an ontological *Gleichgültigkeit*, indifference, in their being. Why resist a two-sided thing whose constitutive sides are asymmetrical? Because, in the Logic, despite its multiple varieties of negation and modes of transformation, Hegel is unable or unwilling to think a continuum of variation with a synthetic thinking, but remains, in his commitment to concepts, bound in an analytic map of thought and being, breaking the fields into separate and opposable units that then post hoc can be interpreted

to consist in "inner" relations. For this reason, he does not and probably cannot think a likeness cosmos. Proclus, in contrast, begins from the intuition that a priori nothing, no thing, is fully distinguishable, and so he does not have to build an interconnected world out of falsely separated items, but rather he has to explain how anything moves in the slightest or appears separate from any perspective.

54. See R. E. Allen's commentary in *Plato's Parmenides*, trans. R. E. Allen (New Haven, CT: Yale University Press, 1997), p. 81.

55. Yet if a pear is like the idea of a pear because like is like like, we do not exactly have a tautology, given that like is not "is" but is only "like." Asymmetry, or the quantity of likeness and unlikeness—a hair more like than not—avoids empty analyticity.

56. Contradiction, in contrast, is a fact of language. Statements that confirm or deny "the same thing of the same thing" (*Categories and De Interpretatione*, p. 47) refute themselves insofar as, if the statement is "about a universal taken universally" (p. 48), it is thus necessary, under the law of noncontradiction, that it either be true or false. Neither may Socrates be a human being and not a human being at one time, nor may his humanity go over into nonhumanity over time. The same cannot be said of contraries. Zeno mistakes a contrary for a contradiction.

57. Jabès speaks of "the resemblance of realms, of species, of nature with nature, and intelligence." *The Book of Resemblances*, vol. 1, p. 29.

58. Investigations of likeness, *Ähnlichkeit*, as a technique in many areas of culture, can be found in Anil Bhatti and Dorothee Kimmich (eds.), *Ähnlichkeit: Ein kulturtheoretisches Paradigma* (Konstanz: Konstanz University Press, 2015).

59. Despising Frazer's intolerance and deeply colonialist standpoint, Wittgenstein nonetheless sees how Frazer is the first to abstract and develop "similarity" as a single, self-standing principle for social facts. Wittgenstein, "Remarks on Frazer's *Golden Bough*," in *Philosophical Occasions, 1912–1951* (Indianapolis, IN: Hackett, 1993), p. 133.

60. A succinct X-ray of Wittgenstein's complicated discussions of seeing-as, as compared with Richard Wolheim's seeing-as, is given by Avner Baz in "Aspects of Perception," in Gary Kemp and Gabriele M. Mras (eds.), *Wollheim, Wittgenstein, Seeing-as/in, and Art* (London: Routledge, 2016), pp. 49–76. See also Stephen Mulhall, "Seeing Aspects," in Johann Glock (ed.), *Wittgenstein: A Critical Reader* (Oxford: Blackwell, 2001), pp. 246–67.

61. For a discussion of the substitution of time for space in Bergson, see Suzanne Guerlac, *Thinking in Time: An Introduction to Henri Bergson* (Ithaca: Cornell University Press, 2006), ch. 4, especially p. 106.

62. For Bergson on memory, the best philosophical treatment remains Gilles Deleuze, *Bergsonism*, trans. Hugh Tomlinson and Barbara Habberjam (New York: Zone Books, 1988). See also Leonard Lawlor, *The Challenge of Bergsonism: Phenomenology, Ontology, Ethics* (London: Continuum, 2003).

63. We can call this circling "anticipations of likeness," if we make several departures from Kant's "anticipations of perception" (*Critique of Pure Reason* A 176 / B 218–A 181 / B 224).

64. Paul North, *The Yield: Kafka's Atheological Reformation* (Stanford, CA: Stanford University Press, 2015).

65. See Premise 4.

66. See Premise 2.

67. See C. Brans, and R. H. Dicke. "Mach's Principle and a Relativistic Theory of Gravitation," *Physical Review* 124.3 (November 1, 1961), p. 925.

68. On Mach's "philosophy," including the place of physics within it, see Erich Becher's still vibrant and extremely coherent article, "The Philosophical Views of Ernst Mach," *Philosophical Review* 14.5 (September 1905), pp. 535–62.

69. To begin following a genealogy of the concept of inertia, we can turn to Allen Franklin, "Principle of Inertia in the Middle Ages," *American Journal of Physics* 44.6 (June 1976), pp. 529-45. For a run-through of the history immediately prior to Newton, see Herbert Pfister and Markus King, *Inertia and Gravitation: The Fundamental Nature and Structure of Space-Time* (Cham: Springer International, 2015), ch. 1, "The Laws of Inertia and Gravitation in Newtonian Physics," pp. 1-48.

70. Glocenius's 1613 philosophical lexicon defines *potentia* in nature as "a certain aptitude" for something, which is not yet the exercise of it. Rudolph Glocenius, *Lexicon philosophicum, quo tanquam clave philosophicae fores aperiuntur* (Frankfurt: Becker, 1613), p. 837.

71. See Becher, "The Philosophical Views of Ernst Mach," p. 560.

72. T. E. Phipps recalls Philipp Frank attributing this saying to Mach himself. Recounted in: M. B. Bell. "Mach's Principle of Inertia is Supported by Recent Astronomical Evidence," *International Journal of Astronomy and Astrophysics* 5 (2015), p. 167. Published online September 2015 in Scientific Research; http://dx.doi.org/10.4236/ijaa.2015.53021.

73. See Becher "The Philosophical Views of Ernst Mach," p. 553.

74. Pfister and King, *Inertia and Gravitation*, pp. 21–23.

75. Mach's inspiration by the psychophysics of Gustav Theodor Fechner is well known. Becher discusses the proximity of his physics and his psychology in "The Philosophical Views of Ernst Mach," p. 561.

76. Aldemaro Romero, "When Whales Became Mammals: The Scientific Jour-ney of Cetaceans from Fish to Mammals in the History of Science," IntechOpen, DOI: 10.5772/50811, p. 21.

77. Ibid., p. 25.

78. All translations from *Sein und Zeit* are mine.

79. "Language is a brew of resemblances," Jabès tells us, "their test and countertest." *The Book of Resemblances*, vol. 1, p. 19.

80. See also Premise 4.

81. When she teaches how the sacred was understood to reside in material objects, Caroline Walker Bynum reminds us of the antiquity of the likeness sign and the theologi-cal necessity for it. "Like images and relics, the Eucharistic elements," elements of these material objects, come into qualitative proximity with the divine under a demand "that the elements be like what they signified. Wine was red to look like blood. Bread was round and white not only to evoke flesh, but also to image body and community through the way it gathered pieces (grains) into one loaf." Caroline Walker Bynum, *Christian Materiality: An Essay on Religion in Late Medieval Europe* (New York: Zone Books, 2011), p. 158.

82. A good initiation into the sometimes cryptic Peircean semiotics is part 1 of Richard J. Parmentier's *Signs in Society: Studies in Semiotic Anthropology* (Bloomington: Indiana University Press, 1994), pp. 1–44. Especially illuminating is the first subsection, "Peirce Divested for Nonintimates," pp. 3–22.

83. Holding the place of truth is one of many important functions that icons and only icons play in Peircean sign theory. An important early treatment of iconicity that discusses this is the article by Paul Friedrich, "The Lexical Symbol and Its Rela-tive Non-Arbitrariness," in M. Dale Kinkade, Kenneth L. Hale, and Oswald Werner (eds.), *Linguistics and Anthropology: In honor of C. F. Voegelin* (Lisse: Peter de Ridder, 1975), pp. 199–248.

84. In another example, Peirce treats another "A" that does indeed stand for something. In a dialogue, where the speakers are marked by the letters A and B, A is the index of a proper name. Another way to say this is that "A" has a pronominal function. In the dialogue "'A' says . . . then 'B' says . . . " "A" and "B," Peirce tells us, are comparable to the relative pro-nouns "who" or "which." Without antecedents, "who" and "which" dangle, fail to signify fully; just so, an index dangles without its antecedent. Out of nowhere, then, Peirce gets concerned about a special situation. When one pronoun follows another pronoun, is the second then an index of the first?

In a sentence such as "A asked B whether he could eat dinner at eight," who is indicated by "he"? How do we know? A lawyer would want to add a parenthesis: "A asked B whether he (B) could eat at eight." The second B causes a problem for the purity of the indexical sign in this example, and Peirce knows it. The second indexical does not stand for its indexical object in the same way as "he" stands for "B" and "B" stands for a proper name. The second B is dependent on the already assigned pronominal, B, not as an index, but as an icon. Peirce asserts, though without any intuition to fulfill it, that the second B in fact stands for the same person as the first. "There is an understanding that like letter shall stand for the same thing." What Peirce is imagining is something like a tree, with the personal name at the root and equal branches reaching out to the two pronouns, the first B and the second B: "so-and-so" is both Bs; the first B and the second B are both "so-and-so."

Two thoughts mitigate against this explanation. In the order of experience, B already has to be like B in order to be used as an index in this way. Even in his own argument, Peirce does not pick the unfamiliar mark ӡ, for example, as the second stand-in. He picks a recognizable mark that has been associated with indexicality and that specific name before in his own discourse. Through the need for the second, lawyerly "B," he discovers that the "standing for" relation detours through likeness even when it does not do so not explicitly. Peirce admits as much. Receptivity to likeness carries the attention from the second B back to the first B, not directly to the person of whom it is an index.

This is the heart of a common problem in prose, the vagueness of pronoun reference. After one repetition of a pronoun, "she" ... "she," the tie to the name of the person is already weak enough that the name often has to be repeated. Likeness chains tend gradually to erase semiotic relations as they extend. On one hand, this shows the dependence of pronouns on their objects, reinforcing their indexicality. On the other hand, the weakening of the relation shows that something else is at play, as well. Clearly, there are iconic elements to indices. Some indices even indicate through likenesses. An impression left on a bed by a sleeping body is an index, and the fact that it is an index is signaled through likeness of shape and likeness of displacement, the impression standing in proportion to the body's shape, attitude, and weight under a correlated distribution into lighter limbs and heavier trunk, into almost weightless hands. A transvicinity lights up, a three-dimensional picture of weight. Indices can also be primarily icons.

85. A recent and persuasive project to place iconicity at the heart of linguistic processes is outlined in Pamela Perniss, Robin L. Thompson, and Gabriella Vigliocco, "Iconicity as a General Property of Language: Evidence from Spoken and Signed Languages," *Frontiers*

in Psychology 1 (December 2010.), pp. 1–15, DOI: 10.3389/fpsyg.2010.00227.

86. In what follows, all translations of Benjamin's works are mine.

87. See the discussion of this biologeme in Richards, Robert J. Richards, *The Tragic Sense of Life: Ernst Haeckel and the Struggle over Evolutionary Thought* (Chicago: University of Chicago Press, 2008), pp. 148–56.

88. Benjamin is not the only thinker between the World Wars to envision a nonsensuous likeness. Sergei Eisenstein, in his notes toward a cinematic version of Marx's *Das Kapital*, unveils the principle at play in his own montage work. "The 'similarity' of intellectual attractions which go into a single piece of montage is not of a sensual kind. That is to say, it's definitely not one of appearance, either. Those fragments 'resemble' each other in terms of conditioned reflexes, i.e., in terms of their meanings: baroque Christ and wooden idol do not resemble each other at all, but they do have the same meaning. A balalaika and a Menshevik 'resemble' each other not physically but abstractly." See "Notes for a Film of 'Capital,'" trans. Maciej Sliwowski, Jay Leyda, and Annette Michelson. October 2 (Summer 1976), p. 12.

89. The canonical site for a full working-through of a mimetic theory of language is Winfried Menninghaus's *Walter Benjamins Theorie der Sprachmagie* (Frankfurt am Main: Suhrkamp, 1980). Michael Taussig took Benjamin's mimesis thinking as an invitation to develop precursors and siblings in anthropological writing. See his *Mimesis and Alterity: A Particular History of the Senses* (New York: Routledge, 1993).

90. The critical literature on Caillois is unbelievably thin. One essay anthology has broken the ice and begun the task of investigating his bizarre "science": Anne von der Heiden and Sarah Kolb. *Logik des Imaginären: Diagonale Wissenschaft nach Roger Caillois* (Berlin: August, 2018).

91. Their argument is passionate, but circular. Becoming is never imitating because imitating is already becoming. Painting a bird, a painter is becoming bird, while the bird is becoming painted bird. Yet to the authors, likeness forms no part of these ontological transformations except as another name for becoming. The better to distinguish becoming from becoming like, Deleuze and Guattari give another example: "Take the case of the local folk hero, Alexis the Trotter, who ran 'like' a horse at extraordinary speed, whipped himself with a short switch, whinnied, reared, kicked, knelt, lay down on the ground in the manner of a horse, competed against them in races, and against bicycles and trains. He imitated a horse to make people laugh. But he had a deeper zone of proximity or indiscernibility. Sources tell us that he was never as much of a horse as when he played

the harmonica: precisely because he no longer needed a regulating or secondary imitation." *A Thousand Plateaus*, trans. Brian Massumi (Minneapolis: University of Minnesota Press, 1987), p. 305. Originality, in other words, is the only "true" imitation. Since a horse is already original qua horse, harmonica playing would be the proper expression of horse-ish originality in poor Alex. A horse's freedom from imitation is best represented in playing the harmonica, as a nonimitation of horse. The Platonic fear of imitation as secondary, not to mention humorous, belies the tale telling here. Becoming should be originary, serious, and in these ways equal to being.

Deleuze and Guattari say they are after a "zone of proximity or indiscernibility" between a local personage and a horse, and yet a residue of traditional ontological ranking leads to a search for real, true, substantive becoming, as opposed to superficial, transient, insubstantial variation along a cline or multiple clines. Becoming, to them, overcomes and supersedes likeness. Everything is in flux, all is in becoming, in a whole, serious, and primary way. This is a world apart from "punctual systems" that fetishize "pure qualities" (p. 306), they say. This qualification is crucial for the unique image they want to project. They want to display a metaphysical flux system whose basic motifs are flight, deterritorialization, departure, excess, and so on, which nonetheless produces convergences of all sorts. In this regard, they say about "qualities" the contrary of what we are saying. "The quality must be considered from the standpoint of the becoming that grasps it, instead of becoming being considered from the standpoint of intrinsic qualities having the value of archetypes or phylogenetic memories" (p. 306) — or almost the contrary. Deleuze/Guattari leads us to believe that becoming, just like a substance, holds the qualities and exists and persists beyond them. I am saying that the qualities in their arrangement, with their echoes, memories, archetypes, likenesses, and unlikenesses are all that are effective in the homeotic layer, despite what may happen in other modes or zones. I am also saying that, just as Deleuze/Guattari believes becoming is the milieu in which qualities inhere, I believe that becoming like is not like becoming, but more like putting the brakes on becoming, classically conceived. In order to avoid misunderstandings about the nature of becoming, call it "enlikening."

92. In the codicil to "Lehre vom Ähnlichen," Walter Benjamin notes that "becoming like" (*ähnlich werden*) has been lost to us over the course of history and has been replaced by "seeing likeness" (*Gesammelte Schriften*, vol. 2, part 1, p. p. 210). He seems to be thinking of history as the movement of likeness from social activities into perception and all along also into language.

93. A social example helps show the assumption of automaticity and noncontingency in the concept of process. An electoral process has to be initiated by a human will, as does each stage along the way—executing the constitution, choosing the candidates, campaigning, registering voters, voting, counting up, announcing and contesting results, recounting, holding a runoff, taking office. Despite the many moving parts, if the stages grow out of one another as designed, the result will be formally predictable. Some official will be elected. Human willing, in this case, subordinates itself to a noncontingent chain in order to guarantee that the outcome matches the original will. Process is the will's intermediary in social situations and an intermediary for laws or forces, "life" or "evolution," in nature. In both cases, "process" not only aids, but also partially supplants the will and the laws, as *causa sine qua non* of an outcome that confirms the initial principle.

94. In the *Grundrisse*, the largest units of study, production and consumption, on one hand, and the smaller units of the production side—production, circulation, and capitalization—on the other, are talked about as processes, as is the historical movement through which particular modes of production arise ("the process of historic development through its different phases," *Grundrisse*, p. 85) and operate ("The important thing to emphasize here is only that, whether production and consumption are viewed as the activity of one or of many individuals, they appear in any case as moments of one process, in which production is the real point of departure and hence also the predominant moment," p. 94).

95. For anyone wanting an extremely precise and succinct commentary on the whole of *Capital*, look to Michael Heinrich's *An Introduction to the Three Volumes of Marx's Capital*, trans. Alexander Locascio (New York: Monthly Review Press, 2012). An astounding book on "things" in Marx is Jacques Lezra's *On the Nature of Marx's Things: Translation as Necrophilology* (New York: Fordham University Press, 2018).

96. Peter Szendy, who read the manuscript incredibly carefully at a late stage, offered a decisive thought: homeosis may itself operate as an economy, though it is a strange one, one without equivalence, symmetry, or transitivity and perhaps also without luxury, a pure reciprocity. The strange economy, he also suggested, might go over into an ecology, precisely where homeosis slows and slackens becoming.

97. In a wider view, the overall relationship between heterogeneity and homogeneity in volume 1 of *Capital* is not stable. The turnover from quality into quantity that Marx represents as a contradiction doesn't fully explain what happens when a commodity is produced. For there even to be a quality that counts as a quality to begin with, the qualitative thing has to be made at least twice. Then the two qualitative things will be homogeneous

in relevant respects, that is, a coat keeps warm and cloth can be cut and sewn. A likeness process makes that possible. It is misrecognized, however, as the production of identity. In a true materialism, production will already be reproduction, or else you will not get quantity out of quality or turn a use into a value and a value into an exchange value. One of something will never be exchanged; it has absolute value (is priceless) or has no value at all (is worthless), both of which amount to the same thing. A singular commodity, this contradiction in terms, has no equivalent because it has no homolog. That is in essence what god was: the quintessential nonexchangeable, pure quality. That is also what world was. And it is also the classic conception of human being. God, world, soul — *metaphysica specialis* — only when this old triumvirate becomes itself commodified, that is, when the three are seen as stopping points on a cline or chain of likenesses, will a true materialism come about. After all, you don't have to be absolute and singular to be resistant to substitution. You can also be like.

98. Few could imagine in 1867 a time when those who lived at high latitudes north and south would no longer need coats. At the apex of global warming, coats, their value drained, will sink back out again into a mass of indistinction.

99. Deleuze and Guattari write on Tarde in *A Thousand Plateaus*, pp. 216–19. Bruno Latour gives his account of Tarde as a social theorist in "Gabriel Tarde and the End of the Social," *Distinktion: Scandinavian Journal of Social Theory* 9 (2004), pp. 33–47. See also David Toews, "The New Tarde: Sociology after the End of the Social," *Theory, Culture and Society* 20.5 (2003), pp. 81–98. Interest in Tarde is not restricted to philosophy or philosophical sociology. He is resurrected for communications theory in Jussi Kinnunen, "Gabriel Tarde as a Founding Father of Innovation Diffusion Research," *Acta Sociologica* 39.4, (1996), pp. 431–41, and for sociology proper in Urs Stäheli, with Christian Borch, *Nachahmung und Begehren: Materialien zu Gabriel Tarde* (Frankfurt am Main: Suhrkamp, 2009).

Works Cited

Aristotle, *Aristotle's Metaphysics*, vol. 2, ed. W. D. Ross (Greek) (Oxford: Clarendon Press of Oxford University Press, 1975).

———, *Categories and De interpretatione*, trans. J. L. Ackrill (Oxford: Clarendon Press of Oxford University Press, 1963).

———, *De anima*, trans. Christopher Shields (Oxford: Clarendon Press of Oxford University Press, 2016).

———, *De anima*, ed. W. D. Ross (Greek) (Oxford: Clarendon Press of Oxford University Press, 1956).

———, *Metaphysics*, volume 2 of *The Complete Works of Aristotle*, ed. Julian Barnes (Princeton, NJ: Princeton University Press, 1984), pp. 1552–728.

———, *Parts of Animals*, trans. A. L. Peck (Cambridge, MA: Harvard University Press Loeb Classical Library, 1961).

Barthes, Roland, *The Responsibility of Forms: Critical Essays on Music, Art, and Representation*, trans. Richard Howard (New York: Hill and Wang, 1985).

Baudelaire, Charles, *Les fleurs du mal* (Paris: Poulet-Malassis et De Broise, 1857).

Baz, Avner, "Aspects of Perception," in Gary Kemp, and Gabrielle M. Mras (eds.), *Wollheim, Wittgenstein, Seeing-as/in, and Art* (London: Routledge, 2016), pp. 49–76.

Becher, Erich, "The Philosophical Views of Ernst Mach," *Philosophical Review* 14.5 (September 1905), pp. 535–62.

Beebee, Helen, *Hume on Causation* (London: Routledge, 2006).

Belting, Hans, *Likeness and Presence: A History of the Image before the Era of Art* (Chicago: University of Chicago Press, 1994).

Benjamin, Walter, *Gesammelte Schriften*, 7 vols., eds. Rolf Tiedemann and Hermann Schweppenhäuser (Frankfurt am Main: Suhrkamp, 1985).

——, *Walter Benjamin: Selected Writings, Volume 1, 1913–1929*, eds. Marcus Bullock and Michael Jennings (Cambridge, MA: Harvard University Press, 1996).

Bergson, Henry, *Matière et mémoire: Essai sur la relation du corps à l'esprit*, 5th ed. (Paris: Félix Alcan, 1908).

——, *Matter and Memory*, trans. Nancy Margaret Paul and W. Scott Palmer (New York: Zone Books, 1988).

——, *Time and Free Will: An Essay on the Immediate Data of Consciousness*, trans. F. L. Pogson (London: G. Allen & Unwin, 1910).

Bhatti, Anil, and Dorothee Kimmich (eds.), *Ähnlichkeit: Ein kulturtheoretisches Paradigma* (Konstanz: Konstanz University Press, 2015).

Bleuler, Eugen, *Textbook of Psychiatry*, trans. A. A. Brill (New York: MacMillan, 1924).

Brans, C., and R. H. Dicke, "Mach's Principle and a Relativistic Theory of Gravitation," *Physical Review* 124.3 (November 1, 1961), pp. 925–35.

Brentano, Franz, *Philosophical Investigations on Space, Time, and the Continuum*, trans. Barry Smith (London: Croom Helm, 1988).

Bunge, Mario, *Causality and Modern Science*, 4th rev. ed. (New Brunswick: Transaction Books, 2009).

Caillois, Roger, *The Edge of Surrealism: A Roger Caillois Reader*, trans. Claudia Frank and Camille Naish (Durham, NC: Duke University Press, 2003).

——, "Le fantastique naturel," in *Cases d'un echiquier* (Paris: Gallimard, 1970), pp. 61–73.

——, "Mimicry and Legendary Psychasthenia," trans. John Shepley, *October* 31 (Winter 1984), pp. 16–32.

Chlup, Radek, *Proclus: An Introduction* (Cambridge: Cambridge University Press, 2012).

Cohen, Hermann, *Kants Theorie der Erfahrung*, 2nd ed. (Berlin: Dümmlers, 1885).

Comanini, Gregorio, *Il Figino: Overo del Fine della Pintura* (Mantua: Francesco Osanna, 1591).

——, *The Figino, or On the Purpose of Painting: Art Theory in the Late Renaissance*, trans. Ann Doyle-Anderson and Giancarlo Maiorino (Toronto: University of Toronto Press, 2001).

Connor, D. J., "On Resemblance," *Proceedings of the Aristotelian Society*, n.s., 46 (1945–46), pp. 47–76.

Darwin, Charles, *Charles Darwin's Notebooks, 1836–1844: Geology, Transmutation of Species, Metaphysical Enquiries*, ed. Paul H. Barrett, et al. (Cambridge: Cambridge University Press, 2008).

——, *On the Origin of Species*, ed. Gillian Beer (Oxford: Oxford University Press, 2008).

Davidson, Donald, "What Metaphors Mean," in *Inquiries into Truth and Interpretation* (Oxford: Oxford University Press, 1984).

Deleuze, Gilles, *Bergsonism*, trans. Hugh Tomlinson and Barbara Habberjam (New York: Zone Books, 1988).

——, and Félix Guattari, *A Thousand Plateaus: Capitalism and Schizophrenia*, trans. Brian Massumi (Minneapolis: University of Minnesota Press, 1987).

Descartes, René, *Meditations on First Philosophy*, volume 2 of *Philosophical* Writings, trans. John Cottingham (Cambridge: Cambridge University Press, 1984).

——, *Meditationes de Prima Philosophia* (Latin), volume 7 of *Oeuvres de Descartes*, ed. Charles Adam and Paul Tannery (Paris: Léopold Cerf, 1904).

——, *Meditations, Objections et Réponses*, volume 10 of *Oeuvres de Descartes*, ed. Charles Adam and Paul Tannery (Paris: Léopold Cerf, 1904).

——, "The Treatise on Light and Other Principal Objects of the Senses," in *The World and Other Writings*, ed. and trans. Stephen Gaukroger (Cambridge: Cambridge University Press, 1998), pp. 3–75.

Drury, Maurice O'Connor, *On Wittgenstein, Philosophy, Religion, and Psychiatry* (London: Bloomsbury, 2017).

Dupré, Sven (ed.), *Laboratories of Art: Alchemy and Art Technology from Antiquity to the 18th Century* (Cham: Springer, 2014).

Eisenstein, Sergei, "Notes for a Film of 'Capital,'" trans. Maciej Sliwowski, Jay Leyda, and Annette Michelson. *October* 2 (Summer 1976), pp. 3–26.

Emilsson, Eyjólfur K., *Plotinus* (London: Routledge, 2017).

Foucault, Michel, *The Order of Things: An Archaeology of the Human Sciences* (London: Routledge, 1989).

Förster, Eckart, *The Twenty-Five Years of Philosophy: A Systematic Reconstruction*, trans. Brady Bowman (Cambridge, MA: Harvard University Press, 2012).

Franklin, Allen, "Principle of Inertia in the Middle Ages," *American Journal of Physics* 44. 6 (June 1976), pp. 529–45.

Frege, Gottlob, *Grundlagen der Arithmetik: Eine logisch mathematische Untersuchung* (Breslau: Wilhelm Koebner, 1884).

——, *The Foundations of Arithmetic: A Logico-Mathematical Enquiry into the Concept of Number*, trans. J. L. Austin, 2nd ed. (New York: Harper, 1960).

Friedrich, Paul, "The Lexical Symbol and Its Relative Non-Arbitrariness," in M. Dale Kinkade, Kenneth L. Hale, and Oswald Werner (eds.), *Linguistics and Anthropology: In honor of C. F. Voegelin* (Lisse: Peter de Ridder, 1975), pp. 199–248.

Glocenius, Rudolph, *Lexicon philosophicum, quo tanquam clave philosophicae fores aperiuntur* (Frankfurt: Becker, 1613).

Guerlac, Suzanne, *Thinking in Time: An Introduction to Henri Bergson* (Ithaca, NY: Cornell University Press, 2006).

Haeckel, Ernst, *Generelle Morphologie der Organismen: Allgemeine Grundzuge der organischen Formen-Wissenschaft, mechanisch begrundet durch die von Charles Darwin reformirte Descen-denz-Theorie*, 2 vols (Berlin: Georg Reimer, 1866).

Hegel, G. W. F., *Phänomenologie des Geistes*, volume 3 of *Werke*, ed. Eva Moldenhauer and Karl Markus Michel (Frankfurt am Main: Suhrkamp, 1970).

——, *Phenomenology of Spirit*, trans. A. V. Miller (Oxford: Oxford University Press, 1977).

——, *Wissenschaft der Logic*, vol. 2 (Frankfurt am Main: Suhrkamp, 1969).

Heidegger, Martin, *Sein und Zeit* (Tübingen: Max Niemeyer, 1967).

Heinrich, Michael, *An Introduction to the Three Volumes of Marx's Capital*, trans. Alexander Locascio (New York: Monthly Review Press, 2012).

Hume, David, *A Treatise of Human Nature: A Critical Edition*, vol. 1, ed. David Fate Norton and Mary J. Norton (Oxford: Oxford University Press, 2007).

Itard, Jean Marc Gaspar, *An Historical Account of the Discovery and Education of A Savage Man, or of the First Developments, Physical and Moral, of the Young Savage, caught in the woods near Aveyron, in the year 1798* (London: Richard Phillips, 1802).

Jabès, Edmond, *The Book of Resemblances*, 3 vols., trans. Rosmarie Waldrop (Middletown, CT: Wesleyan University Press, 1990).

Jastrow, Joseph, "The Mind's Eye." *Popular Science Monthly* 54, January 1899, pp. 299–312.

Johnson, Oliver A., *The Mind of David Hume: A Companion to Book I of A Treatise of Human Nature* (Urbana: University of Illinois Press, 1995).

Kammerer, Paul, *Das Gesetz der Serie: Eine Lehre von den Wiederholungen im Lebens- und im Weltgeschehen* (Stuttgart: Deutsche Verlags-Anstalt, 1919).

——, "Dunkeltiere im Licht und Lichttiere im Dunkel," *Naturwissenschaften* 13.2 (January 1920), pp. 28–35.

Kant, Immanuel, *The Critique of Pure Reason*, trans. Paul Guyer and Allen Wood (Cambridge: Cambridge University Press, 1998).

——, *Kritik der reinen Vernunft* (Hamburg: Felix Meiner, 1956).

Kaufmann, Thomas Dacosta, *Arcimboldo: Visual Jokes, Natural History, and Still Life Painting* (Chicago: University of Chicago Press, 2009).

Kinnunen, Jussi, "Gabriel Tarde as a Founding Father of Innovation Diffusion Research," *Acta Sociologica* 39.4 (1996), pp. 431–41.

Koestler, Arthur, *The Case of the Midwife Toad* (New York: Random House, 1971).

Kuzniar, Alice A., *The Birth of Homeopathy out of the Spirit of Romanticism* (Toronto: University of Toronto Press, 2017).

Latour, Bruno, "Gabriel Tarde and the End of the Social," *Distinktion: Scandinavian Journal of Social Theory* 9 (2004), pp. 33–47.

Lawlor, Leonard, *The Challenge of Bergsonism: Phenomenology, Ontology, Ethics* (London: Continuum, 2003).

Leonhard, Rudolf, *Das Wort* (Berlin: Ida Graetz, 1932).

Lezra, Jacques, *On the Nature of Marx's Things: Translation as Necrophilology* (New York: Fordham University Press, 2018).

Linnaeus, Carolus, *Systema Naturae: Facsimile of the First Edition*, trans. M. S. J Engel-Ledeboer and H. Engel (1735; Nieuwkoop, Netherlands: B. de Graf, 1964).

Locke, John, *An Essay Concerning Human Understanding*, ed. Roger Woolhouse (London: Penguin, 1997).

Mach, Ernst, *The Analysis of Sensations and the Relation of the Physical to the Psychical*, trans. C. M. Williams (La Salle: Open Court, 1984).

———, *History and Root of the Principle of the Conservation of Energy*, trans. Philip E. B. Jourdain (Chicago: Open Court, 1911).

———, *The Science of Mechanics: A Critical and Historical Exposition of its Principles*, trans. Thomas J. McCormack (Chicago: Open Court, 1893).

Marbe, Karl, *Die Gleichförmigkeit in der Welt: Untersuchungen zur Philosophie und positiven Wissenschaft* (Munich: C. H. Beck, 1916).

Marx, Karl, *Grundrisse: Foundations of the Critique of Political Economy*, trans. Martin Nicolaus (London: Penguin, 1973).

———, *Capital, Volume One*, trans. Ben Fowkes (Middlesex: Penguin, 1976).

———, "Results of the Direct Production Process," in *Economic Works, 1861–1864*, volume 34 of *Marx-Engels Collected Works*, electronic edition (London: Lawrence and Wishart), 2010, pp. 339–466.

Menninghaus, Winfried, *Walter Benjamins Theorie der Sprachmagie* (Frankfurt am Main: Suhrkamp, 1980).

Mulhall, Stephen, "Seeing Aspects," in Johann Glock (ed.), *Wittgenstein: A Critical Reader* (Oxford: Blackwell, 2001), pp. 246–67.

Newton, Isaac, *The Principia: Mathematical Principles of Natural Philosophy.* trans. I. Bernard Cohen and Anne Whitman, with Julia Budenz (Berkeley: University of California Press, 1999).

North, Paul, *The Yield: Kafka's Atheological Reformation* (Stanford, CA: Stanford University Press, 2015).

Noudelman, François, *Les airs de famille: Une philosophie des affinités* (Paris: Éditions Gallimard, 2012).

Parmentier, Richard J., *Signs in Society: Studies in Semiotic Anthropology* (Bloomington: Indiana University Press, 1994).

Peirce, C. S. "Logic as Semiotic: The Theory of Signs," in Justus Buchler (ed.), *Philosophical Writings of Peirce* (New York: Dover, 1955).

Perniss, Pamela, Robin L. Thompson, and Gabriella Vigliocco, "Iconicity as a General Property of Language: Evidence from Spoken and Signed Languages," *Frontiers in Psychology* 1 (December 2010.), pp. 1–15, doi: 10.3389/fpsyg.2010.00227.

Pfister, Herbert, and Markus King, *Inertia and Gravitation: The Fundamental Nature and Structure of Space-Time* (Heidelberg: Springer International, 2015).

Plato, *Plato's Parmenides*, trans. with commentary by R. E. Allen (New Haven, CT: Yale University Press, 1997).

———, *Platonis Respublicam*, ed. S. R. Slings (Greek) (Oxford: Oxford University Press, 2003).

———, *The Republic*, ed. G. R. F. Ferrari, trans. Tom Griffith (Cambridge: Cambridge University Press, 2000).

Plotinus, *The Enneads*, trans. George Boys-Stones, et. al. (Cambridge: Cambridge University Press, 2018).

———, *Enneads*, trans. Stephen MacKenna, 2nd rev. ed. (London: Faber and Faber, 1959).

———, *Ennead*, trans. A. H. Armstrong, volume 5 of *Plotinus* (Cambridge, MA: Harvard University Press, Loeb Classical Library, 1984).

Proclus, *The Elements of Theology*, ed. and trans. E. R. Dodds (Oxford: Oxford University Press, 1963).

——— *Procli commentarium in Platonis Parmenidem*, ed. Victor Cousin (1864; Hildesheim: Georg Olms, 1961).

———, *Proclus' Commentary on Plato's Parmenides*, trans. Glenn R. Morrow and John M. Dillon (Princeton, NJ: Princeton University Press, 1987).

Propertius, *The Complete Elegies of Sextus Propertius*, trans. Vincent Katz (Princeton, NJ: Princeton University Press, 2004).

Putnam, Hilary, "Two Philosophical Perspectives," in *Reason, Truth, and History* (Cambridge: Cambridge University Press, 1981), pp. 150–73.

Quammen, David, *The Tangled Tree: A Radical New History of Life* (New York: Simon and Schuster, 2018).

Reverdy, Pierre, "L'image," *Nord-Sud Revue Littéraire* 13 (March 1918), pp. 1–5.

Richards, Robert J., *The Tragic Sense of Life: Ernst Haeckel and the Struggle over Evolutionary Thought* (Chicago: University of Chicago Press, 2008).

Romero, Aldemaro, "When Whales Became Mammals: The Scientific Journey of Cetaceans from Fish to Mammals in the History of Science," IntechOpen, doi: 10.5772/50811.

Rorschach, Hermann, *Psychodiagnostics: A Diagnostic Test Based on Perception*, trans. Paul Lemkau and Bernard Kronenberg, 5th ed. (New York: Grune and Stratton, 1954).

———, *Psychodiagnostik: Methodik und ergebnisse eines warhrnehmungsdiagnostischen Experiments* (Bern: E. Bircher, 1921).

Ross, Don, "Hume, Resemblance and the Foundations of Psychology," *History of Philosophy Quarterly* 8.4 (October 1991), pp. 343–56.

Rousseau, Jean-Jacques, *Emile, or On Education*, trans. Alan Bloom (New York: Basic Books, 1979).

Sheppard, Anne, "Proclus as Exegete," in Stephen Gersh (ed.), *Interpreting Proclus: From Antiquity to the Renaissance* (Cambridge: Cambridge University Press, 2014), pp. 57–79.

Silverman, Kaja, *The Miracle of Analogy; or The History of Photography, Part 1* (Stanford, CA: Stanford University Press, 2015).

Sober, Elliot, *Evidence and Evolution: The Logic behind the Science* (Cambridge: Cambridge University Press, 2008).

———, and Mike Steel, "Similarities as Evidence for Common Ancestry: A Likelihood Epistemology," *British Journal for the Philosophy of Science* 68.3 (2015), pp. 1–22.

Stäheli, Urs, with Christian Borch, *Nachahmung und Begehren: Materialien zu Gabriel Tarde* (Frankfurt am Main: Suhrkamp, 2009).

Tarde, Gabriel, *The Laws of Imitation*, trans. Elsie Clews Parsons, 2nd. ed. (New York: H. Holt, 1903).

———, *Les lois de l'imitation*, 2nd ed. (Paris: Féliz Alcan, 1895).

Tarrant, Harold, "Proclus' Place in the Platonic Tradition," in Pieter D'Hoine and Marije Martijn (eds.), *All from One: A Guide to Proclus* (Oxford: Oxford University Press, 2017).

Taschwer, Klaus, *Der Fall Paul Kammerer: Das abenteurliche Leben des umstrittensten Biologen seiner Zeit* (Munich: Hanser, 2016).

Taussig, Michael, *Mimesis and Alterity: A Particular History of the Senses* (New York: Routledge, 1993).

Toews, David, "The New Tarde: Sociology after the End of the Social," *Theory, Culture and Society* 20.5 (2003), pp. 81–98.

von der Heiden, Anne, and Sarah Kolb, *Logik des Imaginären: Diagonale Wissenschaft nach Roger Caillois* (Berlin: August, 2018).

von Ehrenfels, Christian, "On 'Gestalt Qualities," trans. Barry Smith, in Barry Smith (ed.), *Foundations of Gestalt Theory* (Munich: Philosophia Verlag, 1988), pp. 82–116.

Wagemans, Johan, "Historical and Conceptual Background: Gestalt Theory," in *The Oxford Handbook of Perceptual Organization* (Oxford: Oxford University Press, 2015), pp. 3–20.

Wetters, Kirk, "The Law of the Series and the Crux of Causation: Paul Kammerer's Anomalies," *MLN* 134.3 (April 2019), pp. 643–60.

Whitehead, Alfred North, *Process and Reality: An Essay in Cosmology*, ed. David Ray Griffin and Donald W. Sherbune (New York: Free Press, 1978).

Wittgenstein, Ludwig. *Philosophische Untersuchungen / Philosophical Investigations*, trans. G. E. M. Anscombe, P. M. S. Hacker, and Joachim Schulte, rev. 4th ed. (Chichester: Wiley-Blackwell, 2009).

———, "Remarks on Frazer's *Golden Bough*," in *Philosophical Occasions, 1912–1951* (Indianapolis, IN: Hackett, 1993), pp. 119–55.

Index

Benjamin, Walter: on becoming like, 310 n.92; on color, 299–300 n.40; immersive observation, 241; on language, 237–39, 241–43; on likeness in natural science, 240–41; mentioned, 252; on mimesis, 239–40, 241–42, 244–45, 309 n.89; on similarity, 287 n.11.

Bergson, Henri: critique of associationism, 26; *durée*, 228; *Matter and Memory*, 190, 196–201, 203, 204, 216; "shining points" in memory, 252.

Berkeley, Bishop, 289 n.15.

Bizarre-privileged items in the universe (BPIU), 103, 255, 281; Arcimboldo's paintings, *129–30*, 133, 142; Caillois on, 12, 101, 252–53; duckrabbit, 122, 128; linguistic, 246; sociality as, 281.

Blanqui, Auguste, 75.

Bleuler, Eugen, *Lehrbuch der Psychiatrie*, 154–55.

BPIU. *See* bizarre-privileged items in the universe.

Brentano, Franz, 292 n.25.

Butterflies, 49; *Kallima*, 18–19, 21, *22*, 285 n.1.

Bynum, Caroline Walker, 307 n.81.

CAILLOIS, ROGER: on bizarre-privileged items, 12, 101, 252–53; "diagonal science," 256; homeotics of, 247–56; on *Kallima*, 285 n.1; literature on, 309 n.90; "Mimicry and Legendary Psychasthenia," 247, 249–51; "objective ideograms," 146–47.

Cartesian variations, 287 n.15, 289 n.15.

Causality: action across a distance, 82–83; Aristotle on, 84, 294 n.29; Caillois on, 253; as a chain, 82–85, 87; and contiguity, 51–53, 54–55, 82–83; efficient, 85–86; in Hume, 51–54, 82–83, 84, 86, 99, 208, 290 n.18; and pairs of likenesses, 65; and process, 259; and seriality, 98–99, 253.

Chlup, Radek, 168.

Circuits, 61–62, 70, 96–97, 99–100, 111, 127; in Arcimboldo's paintings, 133–34, 141, 143; "lighting up" of, 101, 109, 120, 134, 147; of likenesses, 67–68, 70, 101, 104–105, 115, 116, 117, 120, 143, 146, 269, 300 n.40; and series, 70–71, 73, 109. *See also* Arrays; Circumradiation.

Circumradiation, 101, 105, 107, 108–111, 114, 120,

128; in Arcimboldo's paintings, 133, 142–43. *See also* Perilampsis.

Cline, 162, 164–68, 303 n.52.

Cohen, Hermann, 63, 292 n.26.

Color: as adaptive strategy, 21–24; in Arcimboldo's paintings, 133–34; Benjamin on, 299–300 n.40; Goethe's transparent color, 299–300 n.40; in Kantian perception, 286 n.10; likeness of, 21–24; as secondary quality, 41.

Commodity production, 262–70.

Congruence, 120, 122.

Contiguity, 51–53, 54–56, 82–83, 91.

Contraries and contradictories, 181–82, 305 n.56.

Convergence, 253, 310 n.91; and divergence, 78, 91, 114, 303 n.52.

Copyability, 172, 233.

"Copy principle" (Hume), 51, 52.

Correspondences, 51, 52, 57, 153, 158, 177, 292 n.23.

Cosmology, 198, 204.

Critical theory, 75.

Culture, 187, 305 n.57; Darwin's neglect of, 48–49; homeotic relations in, 121, 241; inertia in, 207, 209.

DARWIN, CHARLES: concept of heredity, 37; concept of likeness, 12, 28–29, 33–38, 40, 41–42, 285–86 n.4; construction of genuses, 37, 208; evolution theory, 39, 237; extension of Aristotle, 42, 45–46; and Hume, 57–58; "Mutual Affinities of Organic Beings," 28; on natural arrangement, 33; neglect of culture, 48–49; Notebook D from Glen Roy River, 30–31, 32–33, 46; principle of natural selection, 30; "similarity of pattern," 45; synthesizers of, 71; tree of life, 30, 39; use of traits, 39.

Davidson, Donald, 24–25.

Da Vinci, 137.

Deleuze, Gilles, 258, 273; and Félix Guattari, 258, 309–310 n.91, 312 n.99.

Democritus, 49.

Descartes: body-soul duality, 190; Cartesian space 159; "Cartesian variations," 287 n.15, 289 n.15; *Meditations*, 287–89 n.15; on resemblance, 287–89 n.15.

Diaphany, 135–36, 155, 223, 296 n.35.

Ontology (cont'd)
in Marx, 264; and the net metaphor, 296
n.34; photography and, 297 n.37; and
Plotinus's One, 105–106; and repetition,
75–76; and representation, 142–43;
similarity in, 39–40.

Overlaps, 12, 68–69, 162–63; in Caillois's
homeotics, 250, 251; case of Wittgenstein's
duckrabbit, 116–21; as circuits, 70, 101,
104, 115, 120, 127; denoted by "in and
through," 41; diaphanous, 223; and
measurement, 224–25; monstrous, 187;
and series, 104; thick points of, 69–70,
101, 148.

PAIRS, 65–68, 99, 206.

Parmenides, 25, 178; Plato's *Parmenides*, 170,
177–80, 295 n.31.

Peirce, C. S.: "new truths," 252; semiotics,
229–35, 236–37, 242, 307 nn.82–83, 307–308
n.84; worked with Jastrow, 122.

Perception: Aristotle on, 50; Descartes on,
288 n.15; interruptions of, 54–55; Locke on,
289 n.15; and memory, 198–201; psychology
of, 153–55, 156, 158; Wittgenstein's "seeing-
as" and "aspect change," 191–93, 195.

Perilampsis, 105, 107, 108–10, 112, 115, 126, 127,
169, 280. *See also* Circumradiation.

Phenomenology, 212, 219, 235, 250.

Phipps, T. E., 306 n.72.

Photography, 297 n.37.

Physics, 204–16.

Plato: interpreters of, 104, 169–70; on likeness
and mimesis, 294–95 n.31; likeness terms
and effects of, 287 n.14, 290–91 n.19;
Parmenides, 170, 177–80, 295 n.31; *Timaeus*,
49, 177. *See also* Neoplatonic thought.

Plotinus: compared with Proclus, 170–71; "distinction by state without interval," 114–16,
176; Enneads, 105–111, 133, 169, 296 n.32;
homeotics of, 12, 58, 104–105, 147, 252, 290
n.19; on hypostases, 109–110, 112, 169, 170; on
likeness, 111–12, 127–28; "One," 105–12, 113,
115, 122, 128, 169, 170, 296 n.32; transparent
sphere, 112, 113, 114–15, 116, 122, 147, 296
nn.33–34; and Wittgenstein's duckrabbit,
116–20. *See also* Perilampsis; Transparent
mirror.

Plurality, 114, 116, 173, 177–78, 180, 184, 187,
189, 273.

Poetry and poetics, 27, 66.

Porphyry, 170.

Power, 272–74, 277–79, 280.

Praying mantis, 12, 71, 252–53.

Process, 259–64, 311 n.93.

Proclus, 168–71, 290 n.19; commentaries on
Plato, 177, 179–80, 184–85; Demiurge, 182,
183, 184, 187; *Elements of Theology*, 170, 173,
175; on the One, 172–74; system of likeness,
170–78, 180–85, 305 n.53.

Propertius, Sextus, 139–40.

Prototype, 202–203, 224-25, 262.

Psychology: of perception, 153–55, 156, 158;
Wittgenstein's critique of, 191. *See also*
Gestalt theory.

Putnam, Hilary, 25.

QUINE, WILLARD VAN ORMAN, 25.

RAY, JOHN, 217.

Refraction, 68, 94, 136, 163–64, 171, 183–84, 236.

Reflective power, 277–79, 280, 281.

Relativity of motion and inertia, 212–15.

Repetition, 44, 74–76, 80, 85, 86.

Representation, 27, 66, 100, 141, 142–43, 231, 243.

Resemblance: in aesthetics, 40; Bergson on,
197–98; Berkeley on, 289 n.15; and causality, 52–54, 290 n.18; contrasted with likeness and similarity, 39–40; Darwin's
concept of, 12, 47–48, 57–58, 285–86 n.4;
Descartes on, 287–89 n.15; in evolution
theory, 28–29; as fact of mind, 47–48; family, 32, 36–37, 38, 146; Hume's view of, 12,
24, 50–58, 289–90 n.15, 290 n.16; of lambs,
30–32, 40, 41; Locke on, 24, 289 n.15; and
perilampsis, 110–11. *See also* Likeness.

Resemblance theory of sensation, 49–50,
288 n.15.

Reverdy, Pierre, 60, 228–29.

Rorschach test, 151–55, 158, 167.

Rousseau, Jean-Jacques, 270–71, 279.

Rubin, Edgar, vase figure, 152, 302 n.47.

Rudolf II, *Kunstkammer*, 137, 147. *See also*
Arcimboldo, Giuseppe: *Vertumnus*
(Emperor Rudolf II).

326

Zone Books series design by Bruce Mau

Typesetting by Meighan Gale

Image placement and production by Julie Fry

Printed and bound by Maple Press